Two appendixes exam... ...e position at
the Carlton Club Meeting of each
Conservative M.P.; and the nationwide
pattern of alliance and conflict between
Conservatives and Liberals in the
confused election of 1922.

Michael Kinnear received his B.A. from
the University of Saskatchewan, his M.A.
from the University of Oregon, and his
D.Phil. from St Antony's College,
Oxford. He is now Associate Professor of
History at the University of Manitoba.
He was Chairman of the Manitoba
Mosaic Congress, a special project
established by the Canadian and
Manitoba governments to inquire into
the future of ethnic minorities in
Manitoba. He is author of *The British
Voter: An Atlas and Survey since 1885*,
and he is at present preparing a book on
seceders from the Liberal Party between
1914 and 1935.

THE FALL OF LLOYD GEORGE

By the same author

The British Voter: An atlas and survey since 1885

THE FALL OF LLOYD GEORGE

The Political Crisis of 1922

MICHAEL KINNEAR

Macmillan

First published 1973 by
THE MACMILLAN PRESS LTD
London and Basingstoke
Associated companies in New York Dublin
Melbourne Johannesburg and Madras

SBN 333 07884 5

Printed in Great Britain by
A. WHEATON & CO.
Exeter

For Mary, David, Andrew and Sara

Contents

List of Illustrations

List of Tables

Preface

This book examines one of the most significant crises in the political restructuring of Britain after the First World War. Before the war, Liberals and Conservatives had vied for power, while after the 'red letter' election of 1924, the polarisation was effectively between Labour and Conservatives. In the intervening decade the balance of probability favoured the emergence of a three-party system, but this system failed to develop primarily because of serious tactical mistakes by the chief Conservative supporters of Lloyd George's Coalition in 1922, and also because of mistakes by the Liberal leaders over a slightly longer period.

Most of the material for this book comes from contemporary sources which were unaffected by the hindsight which afflicts historians of the period. Details well known to many people in 1922 faded from the historical record because they did not fit in with what happened later. The result has been that proposals for extended coalition which were noised about in the early 1920s have often been dismissed by historians as will-o'-the-wisps. Only an examination of public opinion can indicate whether the historians or the party leaders of 1922 assessed the situation correctly.

It is normally very difficult, if not impossible, to sample past public opinion, but fortunately the crisis of 1922 was fought in the open. Lloyd George was overthrown by a meeting attended by several hundred Conservative M.P.s, and those M.P.s outlined their views of the Government, of Lloyd George and of the general subject of coalition, to their constituents. On the Liberal side, many local associations were split over the leadership; and both Conservatives and Liberals exposed their problems in the local newspapers. In preparing this book, the author consulted more than 250 newspapers which covered political activity in virtually every constituency in Britain. In addition numerous sets of manuscripts have become available in recent years, the most significant for this study being the cabinet records and the private papers of Andrew Bonar Law, Austen Chamberlain and David Lloyd George. These manuscripts and the material from the local press made it possible to reconstruct the changing views of more than a thousand politicians during the political crisis which lasted from December 1921 to November 1922.

Historians tend to see political trends through the distorting glass of later developments. For instance it is easier fifty years later to see the reasons why Lloyd George fell in 1922 than it is to see the reasons why he might have been able to retain power. Again the Liberals never returned to office after this crisis, except as a minor fragment, and in retrospect their weaknesses are more apparent than their strengths. This book assesses the decline of both the Liberals and Lloyd George in the light of the contemporary sources. Another topic this study examines is the support for coalition immediately after the war. At that time many leading Conservative and Liberal politicians favoured coalition, either to keep themselves in office or to keep Labour out. Their hopes were dashed by the Conservative victory in 1922, which rendered coalition unnecessary. Studies of the period have generally indicated that the result of the 1922 crisis demonstrated that the Conservative leaders were out of touch with the M.P.s in trying to maintain a coalition, that the M.P.s sought total independence of the Liberals and that in effect the rejection of Lloyd George by the Conservatives at the Carlton Club Meeting of 19 October 1922 virtually doomed the Liberals to a permanent eclipse. The contemporary records show that it was not the Conservative leaders alone who favoured coalition, but backbenchers as well. The vote at the Carlton Club Meeting did not end co-operation with the Coalition Liberals, and the election campaign demonstrated that even after the meeting, most Conservative M.P.s anticipated the revival of coalition.

The book falls into four sections which deal respectively with the basic alignment of political forces in Britain after the war; with the role of the Conservatives; with the election of 1922; and finally with the significance of the 1922 crisis in the overall development of the party system. The first section, Chapters 1 and 2, looks at the role of Lloyd George as leader of the Government from 1916 to 1922, and at his frequent changes in policy. It also considers the relative strength and weakness of the Liberal and Conservative Parties, and shows how personal failings of the Liberal leaders damaged their party's chance for recovery after the war. The second section, Chapters 3, 4, 5 and 6, considers Conservative attitudes to the Coalition. Chapter 3 examines the power of the constituency parties and the extent of Conservative disunity in 1922. This chapter stresses that the main reason for the fall of the Coalition was the rebellion of the M.P.s, not the rebellion of local party groups. As Chapters 4, 5 and 6 show, the rebellion of the Conservative M.P.s resulted largely from the hesitant, confusing, and variable positions adopted during 1922 by the party's leader, Austen Chamberlain. This section indicates that most Conservative M.P.s failed to understand Chamberlain's intentions, but that they were not, in fact, in basic disagreement with him over their party's future.

The third section, Chapters 7 and 8, considers the confusion of party programmes and leaders in the election of 1922, an election which was an important crossroads for Britain. It assesses the influence of several last-minute election issues, notably the renewed Turkish crisis of November, and an election scare directed against Labour. The final section, Chapters 9 and 10, examines the influence of political and social changes in Wales on the future of Lloyd George, and the general significance of the 1922 crisis in British politics.

The Fall of Lloyd George relies to a considerable extent on an examination of electoral and economic statistics. Some of these figures have been included in this book, and additional statistics may be found in my book *The British Voter*, in my Oxford D.Phil thesis on the 1922 election, and in E. A. Rowe's thesis on the 1929 election.

Acknowledgements

I wish to thank Mr Paul Buteux and Mr Maurice Shock for their many valuable comments on the manuscript. I also thank Mr Bryan Empson, Mr Leonard Manko, and Mr Larry McNish for their help, and I thank Mrs Caroline Sharp for translating the Welsh manuscripts mentioned in Chapter 9. The Canada Council and the Faculty of Graduate Studies for the University of Manitoba assisted me, and I thank them for this. I am grateful to many librarians for letting me use manuscripts in their keeping; I thank particularly Mr A. Giles Jones of the University College of North Wales, Mr M. Macdonald of the National Library of Wales, Mr A. J. P. Taylor of the Beaverbrook Library and Mr V. M. Thornes of the Sheffield Trades Council. The staff of the British Museum were very helpful to me and I am much in their debt. I wish to thank Mr and Mrs R. O. Purcell for their hospitality, and also my parents for many kindnesses. Above all I thank my wife Mary for her constant encouragement and advice at every stage of this work.

M.K.

Winnipeg, Canada
3 December 1971

Acknowledgements

1

Lloyd George and political change, 1919-22

After the declaration of the poll on Innocents' Day, 28 December 1918, Lloyd George held a position of power almost unprecedented in recent British history. He had an overwhelming majority, had apparently eliminated his Liberal rival Asquith from politics, and the Conservatives under Andrew Bonar Law supported his Coalition. Lloyd George's international position also seemed secure. Yet within four years the Coalition fell from office, the Lloyd George Liberals lost two-thirds of their seats and the ex-premier's foreign policy was a shambles. Lloyd George himself fell from power never to return, and did not even cushion his fall in his own party, for Asquith had recovered his influence in the Liberal organisation; so the overthrow of Lloyd George was abrupt and complete.

How did this transformation occur? It is commonly thought that it was merely an aspect of the predictable decline of the Liberals, and that a Liberal prime minister was an anomaly in a predominantly Conservative government. Some observers have remarked that the 1922 crisis was bound to come eventually, and that the result would be the inevitable emergence of Labour and the Conservatives as the only significant parties. This interpretation seems plausible when viewed from today, but it did not correspond with the situation in 1922.

One must distinguish between Lloyd George's personal position and that of the Liberal Party. By late 1922 it was becoming increasingly unlikely that Lloyd George could remain prime minister without a major political readjustment. But this does not mean that the elimination of the Liberals as a major force was predetermined. In 1922 most politicians regarded coalition as a natural mode of governing and they did not change their minds when the Carlton Club Meeting overthrew Lloyd George. As this book shows, far from damaging the long-term prospects for coalition, the meeting actually made such prospects more likely.

The political situation of 1922 was fluid and confused, and the parties could have arranged themselves in several ways. The most probable was not a plain opposition of Labour to Conservatives, but a coalition of Liberals and Conservatives against a Labour Party strengthened by some left-wing Liberals. This remained the most likely arrangement, not merely before the fall of Lloyd George, but for some time after. Contrary to the expectation of a great many politicians, the election of 1922 stabilised the situation, and made coalition less likely. This book describes the distribution of political forces and the confusion of party alignments in 1922. It also examines the break-up of the Lloyd George Coalition, the general expectation of renewed coalition and the reasons why such a renewal did not take place.

The Coalition was born in 1916 in a crisis and lasted while the emergency lasted. The emergency did not end in November 1918, with the end of the war; rather there were many new and difficult problems in foreign and domestic affairs, as well as the old, but unsolved question of Ireland. They required firm but adaptable leadership, and it seemed that only Lloyd George could supply it. Thus his Government remained even though many of his followers disliked him.

In 1919 many of the old European guideposts had disappeared. The empires of Austria-Hungary, Russia and Turkey were no more, and in their places were smaller and less predictable successor-states. It seemed almost impossible to bring Russia back into the diplomatic circles of Europe, and to provide a just and acceptable peace with Germany. The Irish question, unsolved for generations, was now in an acute phase and urgently required settlement. At home, the Government had to deal with demobilisation, large-scale unemployment, rapidly rising prices and a militant Labour movement. Finally it had to redeem its 1918 election promises of social reform. The problems Lloyd

George faced were numerous and onerous, and between 1918 and 1922 he and his Government failed many times and succeeded many times; but the blame for the failures was generally attributed to Lloyd George personally, while the successes were often forgotten.

The establishment and maintenance of peace took precedence over domestic reform, for without peace any policy of social reconstruction would rest on an insecure base. Thus Lloyd George devoted most of his time to foreign affairs and to Ireland. Several foreign ventures failed or were misinterpreted, and he seemed to shift his ground on many others. Still he had a certain degree of success and, despite many false starts and mistakes, he settled the Irish problem for fifty years. However numerous electors and politicians were more interested in domestic policy, where his record was less successful.

The Coalition Government which set out to solve these problems had one of the largest majorities in modern times, but it was not a cohesive majority. Generally Lloyd George could count on most of his five hundred nominal followers to support him in a particular division, but on only a few to support him in every division. Fortunately for him, an even smaller handful opposed him consistently. The indiscipline of his followers weakened his position in the long term, though it did not seriously endanger his working majority. The M.P.s did not always identify their fate with his, and occasionally even his closest adherents voted against him. To be sure the M.P.s generally backed the Coalition, for they hoped Lloyd George would be able to carry on with his vast majority, enabling them to register individual protests from time to time.

Lloyd George's programme often contained elements drawn from right and left, as in 1920 when he supported coercion of Ireland at the same time as he was trying to restore diplomatic relations with Russia. Lloyd George disarmed his opponents on Ireland with his Russian policy, and his opponents on Russia with his Irish policy, and they did not combine to depose him. Another example of this division of opponents was the Amritsar debate of July 1920. General Dyer had been responsible for firing on an Indian crowd in Amritsar, and his dismissal had enraged the Conservative M.P.s, who voted 122 to 93 against the Government. Lloyd George was upheld in this division by the votes of Labour and Asquithian Liberal M.P.s who at the time vigorously opposed his repression of Ireland.

After 1918 the Coalition was in effect an alliance between the Conservative Party and Lloyd George. Wags described it as a deal between a flock of sheep led by a crook, and a flock of crooks led by a sheep. The Coalition Liberals had substantial strength in Parliament, but they could not be as effective in the country so long as Asquith continued to organise the Liberal machinery against them. Consequently the alliance between Lloyd George and the Conservatives was the mainstay of the Coalition. Despite his successful wartime leadership, numerous Conservative politicians distrusted Lloyd George, but they preferred him to a Labour government, which they regarded as the most likely alternative.

Except for Winston Churchill, more has been written about Lloyd George than about any other prime minister of the past century. Few of the biographies of Lloyd George have been adequate, and he remains an enigma. To some writers, he was an incompetent schemer, while to others he was always a sincere radical. There is evidence for either view, and for others as well. It is not our purpose to praise or to blame him, but to consider features of his character which contributed to his fall, such as his reputation for ambition and insincerity; his unorthodox methods of governing; his lack of interest in the commonplace men who comprised the vast majority of his parliamentary followers; and his tactless indifference to the fate of blundering colleagues.

Lloyd George was probably no more ambitious than many another politician, but whether he deserved it or not, he was widely regarded as a self-seeking plotter. Part of this reputation may have come from his rebellious activities in the 1890s. Soon after his first election to Parliament, he helped lead a backbench revolt against Gladstone over the Clergy Discipline Bill, and two years later he opposed Rosebery over Welsh Disestablishment, nearly bringing down the Liberal Government. Sir Edward Reed, Liberal M.P. for Cardiff, wrote concerning this second rebellion that Lloyd George had 'thrown back the cause of Welsh Disestablishment for many years', and that he had made the subject 'more or less ridiculous in the eyes of the Liberal Party'. However, Lloyd George may well have opposed the Government on these issues because he felt deeply about them, rather than because he saw an opportunity for self-advancement. Similarly, his admission to C. P. Scott that 'he was the disruptive element in the cabinet' of 1915–16 probably referred to his desire for more dynamic government war policy, not to his desire for the premiership. Nevertheless, many thought he would subordinate the national interest to his own, if the two conflicted, and political publicists wrote entire books, with little in common save their portrayal of Lloyd George as a man with great ambition and few principles.* A typical comment was that of 'Centurion', writing in 1922 : 'What Mr. Lloyd George seeks is still an enigma. Possibly his aim is to make himself a British Lenin; and after wrecking the Conservative Party, to pass over to the ranks of extremist Labour.'[1]

Many critics suspected that he changed his policies so often because of a fundamental lack of sincerity. He contributed to this impression by his manner of tackling a problem. When he determined to do something, he did his best to make his project work. When he spoke in favour of it, he would use all his many gifts of rhetoric and persuasion to convince the sceptics. Those who knew him said that these gifts were extraordinary, and even today, sixty years after most of them were given, Lloyd George's greatest speeches make exciting and persuasive reading. His vivid metaphors rouse hope, anger and a desire to work for his cause of the moment, the budget, Disestablishment or the war. Disenchantment with these speeches was an important reason why there was such a reaction against him later.

Not all his projects worked, and Lloyd George often saw this quickly. When they failed, he would drop them rapidly, using his powers of advocacy in the opposite direction. Such changes of policy were often less the result of insincerity than of changing conditions, and it should not be taken as proven that Lloyd George was insincere because he followed workable expedients rather than a consistent but unworkable plan. However, when he threw himself strongly on one side, then changed his mind and came out strongly on the other, it was easy to equate the change

* Examples of such books are : G. Raine, *The Real Lloyd George*, and 'Centurion', *The Man Who DIDN'T Win the War* (both by Conservatives); and Sir C. Mallet, *Mr. Lloyd George*, and J. M. Robertson, *Mr. Lloyd George and Liberalism* (both by Liberals).

with insincerity. Sir Geoffrey Shakespeare, one of his secretaries, said that Lloyd George's 'very resourcefulness made him the object of suspicion to the slow-witted'. This suspicion of his motives helped prepare the way for his fall. A typical view was that of the *Nation* in 1920 :[2]

> One has the sensation of giddiness in watching the whirligig of the Prime Minister's Russian policy. In November, a figure with smiling countenance, olive branches and out-stretched hands, whizzed past us. In December a warlike and threatening apparition succeeded him. In January a fresh rider heaves into sight, benevolent and gentle, and his hands are full of gifts. Will the machine go on turning? Will it come full circle again and show us once more the grim riders who are temporarily out of sight? What are the laws of its motion?

Some other charges against Lloyd George were that he did not pay sufficient attention to the details of his legislation, and that he changed policies radically when they needed little more than minor modifications. This resulted partly from his impressionistic attitude : Balfour was often surprised that Lloyd George was right as frequently he was, when he had such scanty information. 'If I had known as little as he appeared to do, I should certainly have done the wrong thing.' The most extreme examples of this during the period after 1918 were to be found in domestic affairs, which occupied him less than foreign policy; but the public held Lloyd George responsible for sudden shifts in important areas such as agriculture and housing. These changes alienated both the bewildered voters and the politicians who had defended the original programmes, and Lloyd George did not enhance his reputation or his position with his colleagues by treating legis-lation as a palimpsest, to be erased and rewritten at will.[3]

More often than had been the case with previous prime minsters, Lloyd George was personally involved with the reversals of his government, because he elevated the role of the premier-ship. He was a great innovator in the field of administration, his most notable creation being the cabinet secretariat, disparag-ingly known as 'the garden suburb' because of its temporary headquarters in the garden of 10 Downing Street. The secretariat was one of the main bases of the enhanced role of the prime minister, and a basis which has remained to this day. At the time, it aroused great hostility and helped to solidify opposition to him. He also tended to rely on unofficial advisers rather than on official opinion as expressed through the departmental civil servants. Lord Beveridge recalled the premier's conversation with one civil servant: ' "How long have you been here?" asked Lloyd George with a growl and a frown. "Since yesterday evening," came the answer, and the frown gave way to smiles.' Lloyd George once said that 'trade unionism is strongest among politicians', and when he brought blacklegs into politics as civil servants or even as cabinet ministers, it was natural that back-bench M.P.s with years of service would resent the intrusion of new talent. This was especially true of Conservative backbenchers who had been out of office since 1905.[4]

Perhaps Lloyd George could have avoided some of this resentment by befriending the M.P.s who made up his majority. This was not his temperament as he preferred clever men who knew their fields and were open-minded about them. Sir Basil Liddell Hart, the military expert, said that Lloyd George would 'squeeze the lemon' of people who knew their business. Usually the men he consulted were as unorthodox in their opinions as Lloyd George himself. For instance, when he appointed Sir Robert Horne as chancellor of the exchequer in 1921, he did so because Horne was 'the least orthodox of all the possibles, and the most indifferent to financial and economic orthodoxy'. About the same time, Lloyd George indicated his own views on economics to H. A. L. Fisher, his minister of education. When discussing some unemployment benefits which involved a loan of £12 million, Lloyd George suggested printing banknotes instead; but Fisher and other ministers persuaded him out of it.[5]

Lloyd George was impatient with the ordinary M.P.s, who were often men of modest talents. Yet it was important for him to build up a large personal following, as he could not rely on normal party allegiance to bind the M.P.s to himself. The Coalition Liberals were torn between himself and Asquith, while the Conservatives had no party tie to him at all. He had to make friends among the backbenchers, but even if he had to do so, he had little time for it. Between 1919 and 1922, he was obliged to attend more than twenty major international conferences; this does not even include the long series of Paris peace conferences in 1919.*

Nevertheless he was not always abroad, and if he had wished, he could have exercised his great charm on the backbenchers. One must therefore conclude that he did not bother. His treatment of J. M. Hogge was an example. Hogge had been elected whip by the Independent Liberal M.P.s, and he had much influence with the M.P.s who wavered between Asquith and Lloyd George. Hogge was neutral in this conflict, and open to persuasion, but despite this, he complained in 1921 that in ten years as an M.P. he 'had not yet had the opportunity of an ordinary friendly conversation with Lloyd George'. An even more striking instance of Lloyd George's coldness was his attitude to Austen Chamberlain, whom he appointed chancellor of the exchequer in 1919. Chamberlain noted in his memoirs that in the eight months after his appointment, 'I had only once seen him outside Cabinet'. Yet within two years Chamberlain became his right-hand man.[6]

Lloyd George relied heavily on a few Conservative ministers, Balfour, Birkenhead, Austen Chamberlain and above all Bonar Law. If Lloyd George had expected these men to check the Conservative backbenchers, he was mistaken. Both Balfour and Birkenhead were arrogant and often treated their fellow Conservatives like naughty children. Chamberlain had a reputation for aloofness, which was off the mark but still had a foundation, since he was so shortsighted that he could not recognise even close acquaintances at distances farther than two feet, while he was too vain to wear more than a monocle. Bonar Law was popular with all sections of Conservative M.P.s, but he resigned as Conservative leader in March 1921 because of ill-health. As his successor, Chamberlain did not keep as close control of the backbenchers, prompting Asquith to liken the Coalition under Lloyd George and Chamberlain to a pair of scissors with only one blade.[7]

Lloyd George did not even keep close ties with Wales, his only secure political base. In 1916 D. R. Daniel, a long-time associate of Lloyd George, compiled a memoir of their relationship. He mentioned that Lloyd George told him that 'his child-

* Harold Nicolson, *Curzon: The Last Phase*, 188–91, lists twenty-one major international conferences which Lloyd George attended.

hood days in Llanystumdwy were the unhappiest period in his life'. This saddened Daniel, who realised that he was 'a man of the city really, from the first time I knew him. London is his paradise'. According to Daniel, Lloyd George 'does not go to Wales often, nor does he like to stay there very long—not that his feeling was every very strong'. More important, he 'hardly ever sees the M.P.s or his old friends, and then only for brief moments'.[8]

Lloyd George was not gregarious, nor did he pretend to be. He 'could even say that he had no friendships which were not political. Outside the family circle he had few friends bound to him in a deep firm sense'. But if he did not feel friendship, neither did he feel anger for very long; many observers have commented on his inability to hold grudges. Both this and his failure to make friends were aspects of a distant nature which was unlikely to rouse deep attachments. Sir Geoffrey Shakespeare wrote that Lloyd George 'had little regard for the feelings of individuals as such'. The consequence was that although many admired Lloyd George's administrative energy, fewer sympathised with him personally.[9]

Frequently Lloyd George did not return loyalty. Normally he supported his subordinates solidly, so long as they were successful; but he could be swift and ruthless when they failed. His purge of Arthur Henderson from the war cabinet in 1917 was notorious: Henderson had attended a Socialist conference in Stockholm which had dealt with ways of ending the war. On his return the cabinet kept him waiting outside while it discussed his conduct; afterwards the premier dismissed him, and Henderson came out 'with a veritable hatred of Lloyd George'. He assured Lloyd George that he would continue to back the war effort, despite 'these embarrassing complications', but when the end of the war was in sight, Henderson played a large part in taking the Labour Party out of the Coalition, thus greatly weakening Lloyd George's bargaining position with the Conservatives.[10]

Lloyd George's treatment of W. Hayes Fisher in 1918 showed once more his ruthlessness toward his colleagues. Fisher, a Conservative M.P., was responsible for drawing up the electoral registers, and when Lloyd George decided on an early election, he found that because of a disorganisation, many servicemen would not have the vote. He then told Fisher that he had 'shown such lack of judgment and want of efficiency that I can no longer accept your services'. Bonar Law persuaded Lloyd George to tone down this curt note of dismissal, but only after dissension had arisen in Conservative ranks. Bonar Law did Lloyd George another service of this sort in 1918. Winston Churchill had hinted that he would take his own line in the 1918 election, and Lloyd George had drafted a 'bitter, wounding letter' to him. Bonar Law saw the draft and revised it to make it less pugnacious, and Churchill remained in the cabinet.[11]

Lloyd George did not seem to understand the feelings of the men he put out of office. Even Bonar Law, who gave him long and valuable service, found the prime minister uninterested in him once he was no longer of use. For several months after he retired in 1921, Bonar Law had no word from Lloyd George; eventually E. A. Goulding, a close friend of Law, shamed Lloyd George into writing Law a brief letter on politics. This lack of interest in his colleagues was not a major reason for his downfall, but it went far towards explaining why Lloyd George never regained office.[12]

Lloyd George had so many serious failings that one is inclined to ask, not why he fell, but why he retained power so long. The answer is that he was by far the best man for the shifting problems of the day, and the Coalition M.P.s realised it. Even the backbenchers he ignored tolerated him until he was no longer necessary. The condition of Europe, and of Britain within Europe, was unsettled in 1918. By 1922 it was much more settled, and much of the credit was due to Lloyd George. Nevertheless, the way he approached problems tended to disturb public opinion, as is evident from an examination of a few representative cases. The problems can be grouped under the headings of domestic, Irish and foreign policy.

The author of the 'People's Budget' and of the land taxes did not produce between 1918 and 1922 a consistent and effective plan of social reform. His Government started out in 1919 and 1920 with progressive policies, but when these policies received checks, the Government changed them radically or even cancelled them. Two instances of rapid change in domestic policy were the plans for low-cost housing and for agricultural price supports.

At war's end there was a large backlog of houses which the Coalition proposed to eliminate by its Housing and Town Planning Act of 1919. However, it did not fix housing prices, and private builders hesitated to construct houses because they feared a drop which would leave them with unsaleable high-cost houses. Their fears were justified, since housing prices declined by a third between 1920 and 1922. Not surprisingly, the rate of construction was low until prices became more settled. On 2 July 1921, a finance committee chaired by Lloyd George decided to halt the government's housing scheme. Dr Christopher Addison, the minister in charge of housing, protested to no avail, then resigned. Addison's successor Sir Alfred Mond, a millionaire chemical manufacturer, commented on the policy change that 'the newly married should be so happy that they can enjoy living in one room'.[13]

According to Lloyd George, Addison had to go. Whether he was succeeding or not, 'he was creating the impression of failure'. Even though Addison had helped him to power in 1916, Lloyd George evidently felt little claim on his loyalty, and Addison soon became a bitter critic of his Government.[14]

As with the housing programme, Lloyd George reversed his position on agriculture, alienating both the minister concerned, and an influential portion of the public. Lloyd George had long campaigned for agricultural reforms, and during the war he had seen the need to produce more food in Britain for strategic reasons. His Government tried to stabilise agriculture by fixing farm prices and wages. According to Sir Arthur Griffith-Boscawen, the under-secretary for agriculture, this was to be the 'permanent policy of the government', and as a sign of good faith the Government added a clause to the Agricultural Act which said that the whole Act could not be repealed for at least four years. But within six months, prices had fallen by a quarter. Farm prices fell even faster, making the government liable to a payment of £40 million. Instead it scrapped the price supports, and Griffith-Boscawen recanted his 'permanent' policy in the *Lloyd George Liberal Magazine*. Government spokesmen remembered the promise not to repeal the entire Act for four years, and referred to 'the repeal of Part I'. They refrained from mentioning that Parts II and III consisted only of a few technical provisions, such as a clause forbidding the removal of manure after the

1 'The Wizard who can't finish his tricks': Lloyd George in 1921, as seen by David Low

termination of a farm tenancy. In fact nothing of importance was left of the Act which had been intended to regenerate British agriculture.[15]

Griffith-Boscawen tried to mitigate some of the farmers' problems by suggesting a temporary farm subsidy, but Lloyd George rejected the idea, whereupon Griffith-Boscawen proposed immediate relief 'to those farmers who bought their farms relying to some extent on our promises'. This relief did not materialise either. Perhaps because of Lloyd George's rebuffs, Griffith-Boscawen was one of the two cabinet ministers who voted against the Coalition at the Carlton Club Meeting.*[16]

While the housing and agricultural programmes had many drawbacks, they were both sound in broad outline and progressive in nature. The agricultural price supports had been set at too high a level, but that did not mean that the basic notion of supports was foolish. Lloyd George could have tried to save the plans, and he need not have lost the support of the ministers who turned on him. Even the loss of a few ministers would have been comparatively unimportant if the M.P.s and public had continued to trust him, but they thought he had made the changes for mere expediency. This was not entirely accurate, as there had been valid economic reasons too; but most of the Press was hostile to him, and apart from his personal group, the party propagandists did not exert themselves in explaining the reasons for the changes. Thus disenchantment spread rapidly.

Though Lloyd George's vacillations in domestic affairs cost him some support, the blackest spot on his reputation came from his fluctuating and often brutal treatment of Ireland. In many other fields, it is arguable that he regarded a particular issue as insignificant, or that he had definite views which he revealed only gradually. No such explanation excuses his Irish policy, for the Irish question could scarcely be regarded as unimportant, and it seems that he really did veer from one position to another. This veering may be why he succeeded where so many had failed: if he had been a convinced Home Ruler, the Conservatives would have opposed him on Ireland from the start. On the other hand, if he had believed sincerely in repression, he would not have granted self-government.

* The other was Stanley Baldwin. Lord Curzon, though a member of the cabinet, and opposed to Lloyd George, was not present at the meeting.

In February 1918 he had favoured conciliation of Ireland, and told H. A. L. Fisher that the Bishop of Raphoe was 'the biggest man out of Ireland since Parnell'. He suggested an Irish settlement consisting of 'a single Parliament, perhaps sitting alternatively in Belfast and Dublin'. After the German offensive of March 1918, Lloyd George tried to get more troops by applying conscription to Ireland. At this point he was still conciliatory to the Irish, and was willing to grant Home Rule in exchange for conscription. The Irish nationalists opposed his plan strongly, and Lloyd George reacted with characteristic vigour. On 29 April Fisher found

> L.G. furious against the priests, thinks English public opinion would applaud violent enforcement of conscription. I say, 'No, it would be revolted'. B. Law enters. I repeat my point; he agrees. Adds that personally he was against introducing conscription, but the Tories would have withdrawn support if he hadn't. . . . L.G. wants the aeroplanes to disperse crowds.

By mid-June, Lloyd George wanted to abandon Home Rule, saying that 'the real leaders of Irish opinion—men like de Valera and Arthur Griffith' were involved in a conspiracy against England, and that the Roman Catholic Church was also involved. To introduce either Home Rule or conscription would lead to a 'political Passchendaele'. After this, his position on Ireland was heavily influenced by his dependence on Conservative opponents of Home Rule.[17]

The post-war record in Ireland was regrettable, but probably could not have been avoided. After 1918 the British controlled little of Southern Ireland, and the administration was often in nationalist hands. As ordinary British forces proved incapable of dealing with the situation, the Government introduced auxiliary police to cow the Irish rebels into accepting the Government of Ireland Act of 1920. This act provided separate legislatures for the North and South; if the two agreed, they could merge in an All-Ireland Council. Of course there was little chance that they would do so, but the plan would thrust responsibility for Irish affairs into Irish hands. The North accepted the proposal, but the South did not, and terrorism continued. The brutality was great on each side, but the odium fell on Lloyd George, since the rebels were underdogs fighting for their homeland, while the 'Black and Tan' lawlessness was condoned by the Government. Even Sir Henry Wilson, the chief of the imperial general staff, and subsequently a right-wing Ulster M.P., felt that if Lloyd George wanted to murder rebels, 'then the Government ought to murder them'. It should not hide behind the pseudo-legality of the Black and Tans. Moderates of all parties were scandalised too.[18]

In June 1921 the nationalists agreed to a truce; the Conservatives rightly suspected that Lloyd George was considering coercing Ulster, to rid himself of the Irish problem for good. Bonar Law told him that if Ulster were included forcibly in an all-Irish parliament, he would rebel. Lloyd George backed down, and persuaded the Southern Irish to accept the situation, on the veiled understanding that this could lead to union later.

Diehard Conservatives felt that yielding to the Irish was treason, and their revolt forced the new Conservative leader Austen Chamberlain to use up much of his stock of goodwill in persuading his party organisation to trust the Government to preserve the rights of Ulster. Although Chamberlain got his vote of confidence at the 1921 Conservative conference, he alienated many diehards; but Bonar Law retained his position as champion of Ulster, while at the same time preserving his reputation among moderate Conservatives.

Except for a brief flare-up in 1922, the Irish question was now shelved until the 1970s; it was Lloyd George's greatest achievement, but it was also the greatest single cause of his overthrow. The bloodiness of the solution appalled radicals and moderates, while the fact that the Southerners obtained virtual independence infuriated right-wing Conservatives. Few felt proud of the settlement which had done so much damage to the political credibility of Lloyd George.

In contrast to Ireland, where his position was fickle, and to some extent irresponsible, his foreign policy was constant, though often devious. He gave the impression that he had no consistent foreign policy, and indeed he sometimes acted as if treaties were like pieces of domestic legislation, which he could revise at will. But it is misleading to accuse him of inconsistency in foreign affairs : he changed many details of his plans, but not the aims. Those who helped frame his foreign policy testified to the consistency of his goals and even of his methods. Thomas Jones, deputy secretary to the cabinet, wrote that his objectives 'were not only moderate and conciliatory, but stable. Contrary to public opinion, he was steadfast in pursuing them'. Viscount d'Abernon, British ambassador to Germany from 1920 to 1926, echoed this view, and said that popular impressions of Lloyd George's changeability were 'never shown in the course of the conferences on reparations. On the contrary, the line or the policy taken from the first was adhered to steadfastly'. Most other writers who knew Lloyd George's foreign policy from inside agreed with Jones and d'Abernon. Nevertheless there was good reason for outsiders to regard Lloyd George as capricious, because, as d'Abernon said, the limiting factor was not what Lloyd George thought right, but what 'he thought it safe to put before the House of Commons'.[19]

Because he did not have a party majority, Lloyd George felt unable to announce all his plans to a predominantly Conservative commons which might repudiate him. He also seemed to have little faith in the good sense of the public in questions of foreign policy, and he rarely showed them his hand in advance. In his speeches, he gave his listeners what they wanted to hear, while in his diplomatic dealings, he frequently worked in different directions from his stated public policy. Lloyd George was not a liar in the strict sense : that is, he rarely told complete falsehoods, but he did tell half-truths which gave the wrong impression. If he had advertised his plans for reconciliation with Russia and Germany in 1918, he would probably have alienated many Conservative M.P.s before putting the plans into operation. Even a cursory examination of contemporary periodicals shows that anti-German and anti-Bolshevik sentiment remained high in 1922, especially in Conservative circles. If Lloyd George told half-truths, at least he did so in the cause of peace. His reputation suffered, not because his foreign policy was bad, but because his methods of presenting it were nimble rather than honest. His Russian and Turkish policies illustrated his varying statements about stable and moderate aims. In both cases, he sought peace in a chronic trouble-spot, but such success as he had came at a heavy cost to his own political fortunes.

His Russian policy developed from the wartime decision to prop up anti-German forces and to prevent the Germans from seizing munitions. In effect this intervention supported the anti-Bolsheviks in the civil war. With the end of the war came also the end of the original reasons for intervention, but through most of 1919 it still seemed possible that one of the anti-Bolshevik groups could take power in Russia, and premature withdrawal would have serious consequences for the forces which had thereto had a moral commitment from Britain. Many Conservatives agreed with Colonel J. G. Jameson, M.P. for Edinburgh West, who said in April 1919 that Britain should 'strike a blow at the vitals of Bolshevism'. Lloyd George did not reject this demand outright, but he did reply that indefinitely prolonged intervention would be 'the greatest act of stupidity that any Government could possibly commit'. He went further in the cabinet when in August 1919 he denounced a proposal as 'an organised campaign against Bolshevism', and as such 'dangerous'. He told his cabinet colleagues that when peace came 'the Bolsheviks would not wish to maintain an army, as their creed was fundamentally anti-militarist'.

Despite his covert opposition to the post-war intervention, he agreed to limited extensions of aid to the anti-Bolsheviks in both April and August 1919. Evidently he wished to demonstrate to the convinced anti-Bolsheviks in Britain that it was futile to hope for a White victory. He made gestures towards them, anticipating that they would eventually realise the folly of their demands. In the cabinet Winston Churchill pressed for an anti-Bolshevik crusade, but Lloyd George 'would give Denikin [the White leader] one last "packet" so to speak, and he suggested that the Secretary of State for War [Churchill] should state what the contents of the "packet" should be, and estimate its cost. We should say to Denikin : "You must make the most of it." '[20]

He told Churchill to make his maximum demands, so that Churchill and others would realise the futility of the White cause when the 'last packet' proved insufficient. His cabinet generally supported him : in July 1919, during a cabinet speech by Churchill favouring increased intervention, Curzon passed H. A. L. Fisher a note saying 'What a dangerous man he is !' According to Fisher,

L.G. thinks Winston is probably a greater source of danger than of strength in his Gov.—Says he is like the Counsel that a solicitor employs (not to speak but to be quiet). He would be dangerous on the other side.

L.G. says that Henry Wilson told him we should need at least a million men to take Moscow.

Lloyd George went so far with Fisher as to say that he did not want Denikin to win. However he did not reveal this sentiment to the public. In November 1919 he stated publicly that Britain had sent millions of pounds worth of material to the Whites, 'and not a penny of it do I regret'. At that very moment he was preparing to disengage; by February 1920 he proposed a trade agreement with Russia. He was not shaking hands with murderers, he said, but saving them by trade where it had proved impossible to save them by force. By 1920 it was apparent that the Soviet regime had won the civil war. Churchill still believed that recognition of the Soviets 'was to take sides against Russia as a whole in favour of a band of dastardly criminals'; and some right-wing Conservatives agreed with Lieutenant-Colonel Martin Archer-Shee, that they 'would rather the Germans, or some other inferior race' handled any trade with the Russians. Most other groups were more realistic. Even if Lloyd George had wanted to overthrow the Bolsheviks, he was unlikely to get much support for such a policy. Conveniently for him, in May 1920 the dockers refused to handle a shipment of arms for Poland, intended for use against the Russians. Abandonment of the Whites was the only feasible policy, even if it did entail the loss of some Conservative support. Lloyd George now acknowledged the policy of conciliating Russia. Curzon, no friend of Lloyd George, defended this in Bonar Law's cabinet in November 1922, when he told the ministers that the ex-premier had 'worked indefatigably and sincerely to reach agreement with Soviet Russia'. Nonetheless the popular impression was that Lloyd George had been remarkably flexible. So far as the Conservative M.P.s were concerned, the chief significance was not that he backed one policy or the other, though that was important; but that he seemed to change his mind, and that he did not appear to have much confidence in their judgement.[21]

Much the same happened with respect to the Turkish question, where Lloyd George's desire for peace was viewed by the public as irresponsible surrender to Greek expansionism. During the

Chanak crisis of August and September 1922 Lloyd George threatened to use force against the Turks. This restored peace for a while to the most troubled area in south-eastern Europe, but his policy alarmed many, and critics frequently referred to it as an example of his recklessness. Although his handling of the Chanak affair was not the sole cause of his fall, it contributed to it. More important in the long run, a second Turkish crisis in mid-November gave Bonar Law an opportunity to show that he could deal with a major foreign crisis, but in this case quietly. This helped him greatly, coming as it did at the very end of an election campaign.*

To the public, the most noticeable aspect of Lloyd George's Turkish policy was that it changed. The *Nation* expressed the view of many when it wrote that 'some policy in the Near East must be relatively right. And if a policy is well chosen, it is the best part of prudence to keep it'. Yet this idea of a 'right' policy is unhelpful in a fluid situation. In this case, when Venizelos was Greek prime minister, a pro-Greek policy made sense, because Venizelos did not press his luck in Asia Minor too far, and because he was pro-British. When King Constantine displaced Venizelos in 1920 a pro-Greek policy became less advisable, as the Greeks became much more expansionist, and Lloyd George adopted a position of benevolent neutrality. The return of Venizelos in late 1922 made a pro-Greek policy realistic once more. Changed conditions dictated the changes in Lloyd George's policy. If he wished to be consistent in this question, he had three choices. He could support massive intervention, to cow both Greeks and Turks. This was not feasible, because Britain was too war-weary in 1921–2 for threats of such intervention to be credible. On the other hand he could ignore the dispute altogether, even if it threatened European stability. His final choice was to support moderate Greek expansionism, while opposing extreme policies, and this was the course he followed.[22]

Sometimes Lloyd George had a consistent policy, but an inconsistent explanation of it. His post-war attitude to both Russia and Germany fell into this category. In neither instance was it politically advisable to clarify his intentions from the beginning, or to explain why he had disguised his aims. In 1922 wartime

---

* The crisis of August and September 1922 is examined in more detail in Chapter 4, while that of November is examined in Chapter 8.

passions remained high in some circles, and the Press often pounced on small scraps of evidence to discredit his policies. In July 1922 Northcliffe's *Daily Mail* denounced the high level of cigar smoking in Germany. If so many Germans smoked cigars, the *Daily Mail* thought they could pay higher reparations, despite what Lloyd George said. The German question did not often arise in the 1922 election, but where it did, the anti-German candidate benefited. In Bosworth, Major Guy Paget, the Conservative[23]

saw that the Socialist candidate had been telling them that they ought to love the Germans. Well, that advice would be more valuable if it came from a man who had fought against the Germans. 'I have had that experience,' said the Major, 'and I don't love the German. I think he is a filthy swine [applause] and I am happy in my own mind to think I can make him uncomfortable.'

The electors apparently agreed with Paget, for they gave him the highest percentage obtained by a Conservative candidate in the constituency in any election between 1895 and 1966, and moreover the Labour percentage dropped slightly, though it went up in nearby seats.

Lloyd George acknowledged the strength of anti-German sentiment in public statements, even though behind the scenes he worked for reconciliation. He told the delegates to the Genoa Conference in April 1922 that unless there was a moderate peace, 'within his own lifetime Europe would again be plunged into a welter of blood'. In this connection it is revealing to note the gradual transformation of J. M. Keynes. In 1919, Keynes had been Lloyd George's most potent critic, and his book *The Economic Consequences of the Peace* had become a bible for those seeking a less punitive peace treaty. By 1922, Keynes, though still a critic of Lloyd George, had come to realise that the prime minister was 'secretly sensible'. In a book which received far less attention than *The Economic Consequences*, Keynes said that Lloyd George was 'protecting Europe from as many evil consequences of his own Treaty as it lay in his power to prevent, with a craft few could have bettered, preserving the peace, though not the prosperity of Europe, seldom expressing the truth, yet often acting under its influence'.[24]

Keynes was the prisoner of his own propaganda : although he debamboozled himself about Lloyd George, he did not debamboozle the public. His earlier book harmed Lloyd George's reputation and influence in the Liberal Party as much as anything, and paved the way for his fall in 1922.

Lloyd George was not leading a party government, and even if the Conservative M.P.s did not oppose him, they rarely explained his policies to their constituents. This basic weakness in his political position reinforced Lloyd George's existing tendency to make disingenuous statements about his plans, and by 1922 he was exhausting his stock of credibility. Perceptive men such as Keynes understood his difficulties, but the public was not as aware. Lloyd George could have countered this if he had retained the strong newspaper support which he had had when he took power in 1916. However, despite his lavish bestowal of honours on journalists, the Press was almost solidly against him by the time he fell.

In normal times, newspaper proprietors are unable to depose a Prime Minister : Lord Beaverbrook discovered in 1930 how difficult it was to depose Baldwin as Conservative leader even though he had twice led his party to defeat. Baldwin could count on party loyalty, but the unusual political environment of the early 1920s gave the Press more influence, as the crosscurrents caused by the Coalition weakened the bonds which usually tied newspapers to political parties. Newspapers felt more responsibility for airing criticism, as Parliamentary opposition was very weak; and the suspension of normal party conflicts made such criticism easier and more effective, as well as more respectable. Consequently, all issues of politics were put up to debate, not just a selection of them.

An overwhelming majority, at least 79.1 per cent of the electorate, had never voted before,* and they wanted information about politics. This enhanced the role of newspapers, especially

---

* In December 1910, some 7,705,602 had been eligible to vote, but only 5,234,293 had done so. The civilian male death rate for England over the period 1910–18 was 154.6 per thousand. Assuming that the voters of December 1910 died at the same rate as the male population as a whole, it follows that 4,472,180 voters of 1910 were alive in 1918. This represented 20.9 per cent of the 1918 electorate, which totalled 21,392,322. If military deaths are counted, it is evident that the proportion of eligible voters in 1918 who had voted in December 1910 was even less than 20.9 per cent.

in foreign affairs, for which the Press was practically the only public source of information. The war had been over less than four years, and the public was concerned to prevent such wars in the future. The visits of Lloyd George to international conferences provided a combination of human and political interest which hostile newspapers could use against him if his policies suffered reverses.

The Prime Minister could not be accused of ignoring the Press, for in his rise he had cultivated and relied on journalists. He even scheduled his major speeches for weekends so they would get double coverage in the Sunday Press, and in the Monday editions of daily newspapers. After he became Prime Minister, Lloyd George gave honours to nearly all the important newspaper proprietors. Those who already had honours, such as Lords Astor, Burnham, Northcliffe, and Rothermere, went up a grade to Viscountcies, while those without peerages became barons, such as Lords Beaverbrook, Dalziel of Kirkcaldy, Riddell, and Russell of Liverpool. Editors and proprietors of politically important provincial newspapers received knighthoods : some were Sir Robert Bruce, Sir John Findlay, Sir Leicester Harmsworth, and Sir Arthur Sutherland. This list is by no means exhaustive. Between them, these men and others receiving honours from Lloyd George controlled four-fifths of the national daily and Sunday papers, and six of the eight most important provincial ones. The other two major provincial newspapers were the *Manchester Guardian*, whose editor, C. P. Scott, rejected honours; and the *Yorkshire Post*, whose editor took office only in 1919, and thus did not qualify for recognition of wartime services to journalism.

Despite this, many newspapers turned on Lloyd George. Some had opposed him for years : the Cadbury Press supported Asquith after 1916, and drenched Lloyd George with 'cocoa slop', as he complained during the Maurice debate of May 1918. At the time he could still count on most other newspapers, but he soon offended the most important single journalist, the brilliant, but erratic and hypersensitive Lord Northcliffe. Lloyd George had once paid particular attention to Northcliffe. During the 1909 budget controversy, when Northcliffe had been particularly objectionable, Lloyd George had cast aside precedent to show him some of the draft proposals for the budget which he was to present a few days later. This flattery paid off during the Marconi affair of 1912–13, when Northcliffe held back from the general Conservative attack on Lloyd George. In 1915 Northcliffe had a hand in the shell scandal attack on Asquith, which helped bring on the first wartime coalition; and he also lay behind some of the manoeuvres which gave Lloyd George the Premiership in 1916. Perhaps he thought he had a blank cheque on Lloyd George's political account, for in 1918 he told Lloyd George to make him a delegate to the peace conference. According to Lloyd George he also tried to vet the list of ministers in the reconstructed government. Lloyd George 'told him to go to hell . . . Northcliffe was a great man, but he could not be allowed to dominate the Prime Minister'. Almost at once Lloyd George appointed Lord Riddell, proprietor of the *News Of The World*, to be one of his chief aides during the peace conference, and he also discussed in detail the composition of his new cabinet with Riddell.[25]

Northcliffe began a crusade against Lloyd George's 'pro-German' policy. At first the Premier considered bringing a libel action against him, but he settled for crushing him in the Commons. He told the M.P.s that Northcliffe had debased *The Times* into nothing more than 'the threepenny edition of the *Daily Mail*'. Northcliffe was trying to divide the British and French; not even Northcliffe's 'diseased vanity' justified 'so black a crime'. The M.P.s, most of whom disliked Northcliffe, gave Lloyd George their support, but it was a hollow triumph, for when Northcliffe stepped off Lloyd George's bus, *The Times* and the *Daily Mail* stepped off with him. So did Northcliffe's brother, Lord Rothermere, and his papers, the *Daily Mirror* and the *Sunday Pictorial*.[26]

Lord Beaverbrook also turned away from Lloyd George: Beaverbrook said they had fought in 1918 and again in 1920, but that their split did not become final until 1922, when the proprietor of the *Daily Express* helped persuade Bonar Law to bring down the Coalition.[27]

The Northcliffe, Rothermere, and Beaverbrook newspapers, accounting for over half the London daily circulation, were especially influential, as they blended political information with slickness to a remarkable degree. These newspapers were typified by the *Sunday Pictorial*, which Rothermere used as a personal base for condemning Lloyd George. Beginning in August 1919, he denounced Lloyd George frequently, though he rarely discussed the political parties behind him. Instead he held the Premier personally responsible for high government spending, ineffective domestic programmes, and eccentric foreign policy. By early 1921, Rothermere found that the most effective cry was 'anti-waste'. Running with his support, Sir Thomas Polson won the safe Conservative seat of Dover as an Anti-waste candidate in January 1921. Two weeks later, Rothermere formed an Anti-waste League, which took an axe as its symbol, to signify the attack on government spending. The government took no particular notice of the Dover loss, as distinct from its other by-election losses. However in June 1921 it lost two more by-elections to the Anti-waste League.

Lloyd George was preoccupied at that moment: his Government had just averted a general strike, and was beginning the final series of negotiations for the Irish settlement. There was also a conference in London on reparations, and another in Paris on the Graeco-Turkish dispute. H. A. L. Fisher noted, 'the PM is dead tired and wants to throw a sop to anti-waste'. This sop consisted of an economy committee under Sir Eric Geddes, wielding the 'Geddes Axe' in an attempt to appropriate Rothermere's symbol as well as his idea.[28]

Most by-election candidates, including some Labour supporters, raised the cry of anti-waste, but the most important effect of the anti-waste victories of June 1921 was on the Conservatives. There had been many reasons for Conservative dissatisfaction with the Government, but in by-elections before June 1921 the Conservative candidates had run as committed supporters of the Coalition. Between June 1921 and the fall of Lloyd George in October 1922, twenty-three by-elections had Conservative candidates.* Only five of them stood as Coalitionists, while eighteen did not. Lord Rothermere had demonstrated that open support of the Coalition might cost Conservative candidates even the safest seats.

The anti-waste campaign continued in 1922, although it had achieved most of its stated goals, for the Government reduced spending dramatically. Moreover Lloyd George and the Coalition were discredited as vote-getting forces in the eyes of many Con-

* Excluding uncontested ministerial by-elections.

servatives. During the 1922 election the Anti-waste League played only a small part; this was an aspect of the general decline of the influence of the Press during the election. The Coalition fell so shortly before the election that the new Government had no time to create a record, good or bad. It also made a secret of its plans, if it had any. Thus Rothermere and the other Press lords had few convincing arguments to use against the new régime.

By 1922 Lloyd George's well-publicised changes in policy had given him a reputation for insincerity which he never shook off. Many suspected him and, apart from his ministerial colleagues, few politicians felt close ties to him. He did not even seem to be an electoral asset, which may have been what told against him in the end. The Conservatives might have hesitated to strike him down if they had depended on his help at election time, but as it was, while he brought them many Liberal votes, he also drove away some Conservatives. Many Conservative M.P.s wanted to use him while avoiding the taint of his unpopularity: as later chapters show, it was probable that they would react blindly against him, then take fright and finally revive some form of coalition. They might even have formed another coalition with Lloyd George, though this is more debatable. Coalitions were in view, not because the Conservatives wanted Lloyd George, but for other reasons.

Politicians do not readily form coalitions, if only because there are fewer offices to go round than in ordinary party governments. But they will put up with coalitions if conditions are right. To have a coalition, as the Duchess of Omnium said, politicians must first know one another. In 1922 the Conservatives were at least on speaking terms with both Liberal factions, and a *rapprochement* with either or both was possible. Another condition for prospective coalitionists is that there should be no fundamental divergence of principle; and apart from free trade no major open difference was apparent. The third and most important condition is that there must be some positive reason to coalesce. The Liberal Unionists had had Ireland, while the Conservatives and Coalition Liberals had had the emergencies of the war and post-war years. In 1922 an important development made future coalitions not only possible but likely. This was the rapid growth of the Labour Party.

Labour entered 1919 with only 60 seats in Parliament and a fifth of the popular vote; but it retained a strong organisational base in the trade unions, and the party did well in municipal and by-elections: between 1919 and 1922 it gained 14 seats in by-elections, and nobody knew how far it would repeat its performance in the general election. Nor did anyone know what Labour would do to society if, by chance, it won. The record of the two Labour Governments of 1924 and of 1929–31 was not particularly socialist, let alone Bolshevist, but the Conservatives in 1922 were not to know that Labour in office would be rather mild. On the other hand they had solid ground for their fears. In January 1919, at the very time that the German Government was suppressing the Spartacist revolt, Britain had two general strikes, one in Glasgow, the other in Belfast. The Belfast strikers formed a soviet which sent an 'embassy' to Londonderry, but the Glasgow strike was more spectacular. For several days, a hundred thousand strikers held the city, and did not disperse finally until troops (later supported by tanks) occupied it. Even more menacing was the threat of a strike by the 'triple alliance' of miners, railwaymen and transport workers. Although such a strike was proposed and called off in 1920 and again in 1921, it remained a possibility. During the 1920 crisis General Page Croft, Conservative M.P. for Bournemouth, actually formed an amateur defence force, which he placed at the service of the Lord Lieutenant of Hertfordshire. This force was fully enlisted within two weeks of its formation. In 1921 the Government formed an even larger force with similar aims.[29]

With this background, it was not surprising that Conservative candidates played on fears of Bolshevism during the 1922 election campaign. Their central office issued posters proclaiming that 'Lenin wants you to vote "Labour"'; 'Russia lies in ruins', 'Lenin and Trotsky are helping the "Labour" Party to POWER', 'The Bolsheviks stole the women's wedding rings' and so on. According to G. F. Hohler, Conservative M.P. for Chatham, Labour was 'pledged to destroy the present machinery of industry. . . . It will bring compulsory military service; it will bring an end to liberty; it will bring an end to free elections; it will bring terror and hunger'.

Sir Arthur Bewicke-Copley, Conservative candidate for Doncaster, went farther, describing the Labour programme as 'no

God, no religion, no king, no money, no commerce, no happiness, and no safety; also for marriage to be done away with and children to become the property of the state'. Oliver Locker-Lampson, Austen Chamberlain's private secretary, while touring his Birmingham constituency, had a mascot in the form of a 'Bolshie' hanging from a miniature gibbet. Even the stage showed interest in Bolshevism : a play, *The Beating on the Door*, opened at St James's Theatre in the middle of the 1922 election. Perhaps prudently, it took a non-committal stand.[30]

At first glance, it might seem that the widespread apprehension of socialism would benefit the Conservatives rather than the Liberals, because of the Conservatives' clearer commitment. However many Conservatives feared Labour so deeply that they contemplated long-term alliances with the Liberals to keep Labour out. This gave the Coalition leaders reason to hope that they could preserve their regime. In 1920 Lord Birkenhead proposed an alliance of anti-socialists to fight the 'greed, envy, and malice' of the 'English Communists'. While his proposal was almost entirely negative, it might yet be sufficient to stave off the fall of the increasingly unpopular Government of Lloyd George. The relative positions of the Liberal and Conservative Parties changed greatly during the war, and this indicated a Liberal decline, though how much of a decline was uncertain. It also remained to be seen whether Lloyd George would be able to make the most of the remaining Liberal strength to forge a permanent pact with the Conservatives.[31]

2

Liberals and Conservatives in the Early Twenties

Tactics! Tactics! Ladies and gentlemen, the country is tired of their tactics. It would have been better for them if they had less of tactics and more of reality. But they have lived for some years on tactics and now they have died of tactics.

Sir Henry Campbell-Bannerman referred in 1905 to the Conservatives, but spoken twenty years later his words could with greater justice have been applied to the Liberals. In 1914 the Liberals formed the Government, but by 1925 they were a fragment of forty M.P.s without major influence on either Government or Opposition. Their fall was the most dramatic change in party fortunes in the past century and a half, and there have been many interpretations of it, most of which have stressed underlying defects in the Liberal position. It is a simple matter to list these defects, and the factors favouring the Conservative resurgence. There can be little question that the Liberals faced many problems after the war, but there was a future for them if they accepted a lesser role than they had had previously. As late as 1923 the Liberals won practically as many seats and votes as Labour, who formed the Government. This demonstrated that they were not finished; but, to use Campbell-Bannerman's phrase, they needed more of reality. The Liberals were facing decline, not disaster, which is what their leaders gave them. On the other hand the Conservatives faced challenges too, but chance and effective leadership transformed their position of marginal improvement into more than two decades of overwhelming dominance. This chapter considers the basic position of the Liberal and Conservative Parties, and the actions of their leaders between 1919 and 1922; the remainder of the book examines in greater detail the development of Conservative opinion in the turning-point of the 1920s, the crisis of 1922.

In considering the differences between the Liberal and Conservative Parties which preserved one instead of the other, one may ask whether one party was just unlucky, or whether it was doomed by some important flaw. As this book indicates, the Conservatives had many weak points, but Liberal or Labour blunders prevented those weaknesses from being fully exposed in 1922, while Liberal failings were bared, not only by Conservative and Labour supporters, but also by Liberals. The most important differences between the Liberals and Conservatives lay in their leadership. Neither Conservative leader would split his party, but each Liberal leader did so. Contrary to general opinion, Lloyd George's motives were political, while Asquith's were more personal; also, as this chapter shows, Lloyd George's actions resulted partly from Asquith's vendetta, and not wholly from his own projects for transforming the political system.*

With united leadership, the Liberal problems after the war would have been much less serious than they actually were. The 1918 redistribution cost them some seats, and more important, the Labour Party was unwilling to remain a minor partner, though this Labour rivalry can be stressed too much, as the Labour surge was gradual, despite the tripling of the electorate in 1918 and the extension of the franchise to the lower ranks of the working class. Since Labour was slow to win the new voters, the Liberals had an opportunity to consolidate their ground. In any case, although the Labour Party was almost certain to expand after the war, it did not follow automatically that Labour expansion necessitated the almost complete destruction of the Liberals. Indeed right-wing Liberals could rely on increased Labour strength as a valuable bargaining counter in framing electoral pacts with the Conservatives.

As noted in the first chapter, only a fifth at most of the 1918

* After this book was written, Dr Roy Douglas published an article discussing the 1918 election. He pointed out, as I have done, the significance of Asquith's refusal to join Lloyd George's Government in 1918. Cf. *English Historical Review* (1971) 328–30.

electors had voted in December 1910. Family traditions may have influenced the party choice of some new voters, but because numerous families in 1918 had no voting habits at all, there was a higher proportion of uncommitted voters than in previous elections, and many seats elected M.P.s of all three major parties between 1918 and 1924. The overall election results showed that the new voters tended marginally to support Labour : between 1918 and 1924, although electoral qualifications did not change, the turn-out rose by 5.8 million, and the Labour vote by 3.1 million. Evidently the newly enfranchised voters at first hesitated, then gradually established more or less fixed voting patterns. But because the evolution was gradual, all three major parties had an opportunity to win the new voters before they committed themselves.

In this period of confusion, seemingly ephemeral factors influencing the first votes of new electors were important in setting political patterns. Such things as the failure of a party to nominate a candidate in a given constituency over a period of several elections could hinder that party's long-term development even if many other factors favoured it. For example Labour did not contest either the 1922 or 1923 elections in Birkenhead East, but shared the two seats in the borough with the Liberals. When Labour eventually nominated a candidate in 1924 and 1929, it found the existing pattern of Liberal-Conservative competition too hard to break, and despite the working-class nature of the seat, Labour did not win it until 1945. A crisis such as a war was required to break the voting trends established years before. This happened in scattered seats throughout the country, but before the Liberals could confirm their position in a significant number of constituencies, they had to determine what their future would be.

There are several sorts of political party : governing parties, factions surrounding a leader and sectional groups. A governing party is large enough to rule alone, or sometimes in combination with minor allies. In either case it advances its own programme if in office, or provides an alternative government if in opposition. Before 1914 the Liberals and Conservatives had been such parties. A faction around a leader cannot form a ministry of its own because of its smallness, but it may fill offices when allied to a larger party, as the Peelites had done, and as the Lloyd

George Liberals did between 1919 and 1922. The sectional group agitates for some policy or section, such as trade unions, agriculture or regions. Such groups normally have a fairly secure, if limited electoral appeal, and they may provide governing parties with a temporary majority, as the Irish Nationalists and Labour had done for the Liberals before 1914. One problem of the Liberals after 1918 was that they did not decide which type of party they wanted. The distribution of Liberal assets and liabilities left each choice open to the party, but mainly because of the distractions of the Liberals into leadership quarrels, they took up none of the choices until 1931, by which time it was too late.

Liberal losses to Labour after 1914 are sometimes attributed to intellectual changes which caused a 'revolution in ideas'. According to this view, Liberal social doctrines were purely political answers which did not suit an era in which the main questions were economic. However if any policies were dated, they were those of the Conservative Party, whose programme of exaggerated patriotism, *laissez-faire* plus tariffs and reform of the house of lords hardly engaged the sympathy of a majority in the early 1920s. Although more relevant, some Labour doctrines were not clearly thought out, and many Labour spokesmen did not appear to understand them.

On the other hand the Liberal Party included many original economists and social theorists, such as Keynes and Beveridge, or at a lower level Ramsay Muir, Lloyd George and Sir Alfred Mond. What economic debate there was in Britain tended to take place inside the Liberal Party, and the foundations of post-1945 economic policy are to be found in Liberal programmes of the 1920s rather than in those of the Conservatives or Labour. Ideas did hamper the Liberals, but not in the way one might expect. While many Conservative programmes were vacuous, the more positive Liberal ones frequently antagonised voters who sympathised with the general Liberal position. A curious example of this was the attitude of some Liberals to nationalisation, with which the party flirted in 1920. The 'Liberal anti-nationalisation committee' warned voters that their party was proposing a state tobacco industry, and that cigarettes would soon, like French cigarettes, contain 'socks, gloves, nails, and even mice'. Such disputes over economic policy would not have hurt Liberal chances much in normal times, and in a way they were a sign

of intellectual vigour. However they occurred in a party already
divided seriously over leadership, and they tended to accentuate
divisions.[1]

The influence of the war, unlike the supposed revolution in
ideas, had a noticeable effect on Liberal fortunes. Several Liberal
M.P.s and candidates left their party for Labour during the war,
and several more were refused nomination by their constituency
parties in 1918.[2] But the Liberal flock had often bleated a dis-
cordant litany before 1914, even over a war, yet it had recovered.
The existence of a strong Labour Party, not all of which was
deeply committed to the war, offered an alternative to Liberal
dissidents.* Nevertheless some of the wartime seceders and most
of the post-war ones might have rejoined the Liberal Party had
it been definitely in opposition from 1919 to 1922. The Labour
Party was not entirely attractive even to longtime socialists in
those years : during the annual Labour Party conferences, con-
situency and union delegates often referred to the 'shocking' and
'confused' behaviour of their M.P.s Two Labour M.P.s, Ben
Spoor and William Graham, thought their colleagues 'altogether
deplorable' and contemplated retirement from politics or joining
the Liberals. Some ex-Liberals were also disenchanted. E. T.
John, who had been Liberal M.P. for Denbigh, said that his
new party made 'an exceedingly poor show in Parliament'. Sir
Leo Chiozza Money went further. Money was a prominent
social reformer who had been a Fabian for years, although he
did not leave the Liberals for Labour until 1918. Four years later,
Beatrice Webb found him[3]

> raging abuse at the Labour Party and quite incoherent in his
> abuse. 'I have sacrificed my political career in vain,' he
> shouted at us. 'I might have been a Privy Councillor, a
> Cabinet Minister, a *leading* Cabinet Minister, if I had not
> come over to the Labour Party to be insulted and ignored by
> a lot of boozy and illiterate men.'

The Labour Party was hardly threatened by a few disgruntled
supporters, although these remarks show that the advance of
Labour was not entirely smooth. However Labour was pre-
empting Liberal strength, especially in mining districts where

---

* I am at present preparing a book on Liberal seceders which deals with
this and related topics in greater detail.

there had been cleavages between the two parties before the war. Once Labour decided to oppose the Liberals in these con- situencies, the Liberals had little chance to defend their position; but the mining constituencies were unusually homogeneous, and the working class elsewhere was more divided and thus more difficult for Labour to convert. Even so the Liberals won more mining seats (39) than Labour (31) in 1918, and held an average of nine in each of the following three elections, despite strong Labour attacks. In non-mining industrial areas, the Liberals did much better, a fact which could have made them invaluable to the Conservatives as allies. Though it was hard for the Liberals to accept this limited role, careful manoeuvring by the Liberal leaders could have exercised a moderating influence on the Conservatives; and the Conservative governments of 1922–3 and 1924–9 needed such a moderating influence. Two things which gave the Liberals additional bargaining power in their dealings with the Conservatives were their wide appeal and their ability to find effective and popular candidates.

The Conservatives normally predominated in only two main types of seat, ones with large agricultural or middle-class votes. The Liberals had much strength in most types of constituency, but were dominant in none, perhaps because they did not con- centrate their effort on any one social group or area. Thus the Conservatives had a sizeable electoral redoubt, which the Liberals lacked. In the elections of the 1920s, the Liberals won a great variety of seats, including some which had eluded them in every election between 1885 and 1910.* During the period 1918–29 the Liberals won 281 seats one or more times. In the same five elections Labour won 304 seats at least once, that is, only 23 more than the Liberals. Yet Labour formed two governments, while the Liberals did not even form the official opposition once.

The Conservatives regularly triumphed in middle-class and agricultural seats, but fared badly in industrial ones. Their only industrial strong points were Liverpool, where the Irish issue remained; and Birmingham, where the Labour Party was both badly organised and influenced by its far left wing. Even in these

---

* Some seats the Liberals won between 1918 and 1929 which they had not won between 1885 and 1910 were: Ashford, Basingstoke, Blackpool, Chichester, Holderness, Horncastle, Hull Central, Lonsdale, Oxford, Shrews- bury, Tiverton, Wavertree, West Derby (Liverpool) and Worcester.

two cities there was an underlying trend to Labour after 1918, and in Liverpool there was also a brief Liberal surge in 1923. The Conservatives did poorly in other industrial areas: of the 45 seats in Great Britain which had fewer than 10 per cent middle-class voters, the Conservatives won only five one or more times in the 1920s. The Liberals in contrast won 19 in the same elections. This does not mean that the Conservative working man was imaginary. He existed, but not in sufficient numbers outside Birmingham and Liverpool to elect Conservative M.P.s with much frequency. On the other hand Liberal working men were more numerous, as M.P.s and trade union officials* or as voters, and they were the basis for a Liberal claim on the Conservatives.

Another claim was the drawing power of many Liberal candidates. Perhaps in some periods, few candidates are worth more than 500 votes, as a party agent said in 1955, when the two-party system operated with a regularity not found in the 1920s. Ideological differences between the main parties were also relatively uniform from one constituency to another in the 1950s. Quite apart from the consideration that an average of one seat in six was decided by fewer than 500 votes in both 1922 and 1923, there were many variations during the 1920s in local party alignments and even in the ideological basis of party differences. In some places the Conservatives backed the Liberal candidate against Labour, while in others Labour supported the Liberal against the Conservative. Constituencies where this happened in 1922 are listed in Appendix II, but the phenomenon was also noticeable in the other elections of the 1920s.

Other evidence for the personal influence in particular candidates may be found in the election results for the twelve two-member constituencies. Voters in these constituencies could mark their ballots for either one or two candidates. If they 'plumped' for one, their vote would count only once. Splitting their votes would swell the total of another candidate, perhaps putting him ahead of the voter's first choice. Where a party nominated two candidates, it would be natural to expect a high degree of

* Some Liberal trade unionists who were also M.P.s were: J. G. Hancock (Belper; financial secretary, Notts. Miners' Association); Barnet Kenyon (Chesterfield; general agent, Derbyshire Miners' Association); John Ward (Stoke; founder, Navvies' Union); J. Havelock Wilson (South Shields; President, Sailors' and Firemen's Union); and others.

cohesion, which would lead to each candidate getting roughly the same vote. This did not always happen, as several instances from 1922 show. In Brighton one Conservative polled 1705 votes more than the other. In Derby J. H. Thomas won 4538 more than his Labour running mate, and came first while his colleague came last. The Asquithian Liberal in Oldham received 3636 votes more than his partner, while in Sunderland 3410 more voted for one Conservative than for the other.

These examples illustrate the importance in the 1920s of individual candidates. Personal qualities were more important to the Liberals than to the other parties, since the Liberals occupied an intermediate position in which individual candidates could appeal to their right or left as they chose. Their choice naturally influenced the other parties, and often led them to support the Liberals over a period of three or four elections. J. M. Kenworthy, who stood on the left of his party, received Labour support in Hull Central in four successive elections; right-wing Liberals with prolonged Conservative support were more numerous. Four among many were Sir Beddoe Rees (Bristol South), H. C. Hogbin (Battersea North), Trevelyan Thomson (Middlesbrough West) and John Leng-Sturrock (Montrose District).

Many Liberal candidates staged strong election campaigns, but in different constituencies from one election to another. In 1922, apart from sitting Liberal M.P.s who were running again, only twenty-seven seats had the same Liberal candidates as in 1918. This did not give the others, who changed constituencies or who ran without previous experience, much time to establish themselves locally. This lack of continuity was emphasised by the frequent elections of the early 1920s, and local Liberal parties were generally too disorganised to smooth the transition from one candidate to another.

This lack of continuity was one reason the Liberals won seats only once or twice. Ineffective organisation in most constituencies forced the Liberals to depend on strong personal campaigns by their candidates. A conspicuous example of this was Oxford, where Frank Gray visited every working-class house at least once. He won this hitherto safe Conservative seat in 1922 and 1923, although he was unseated in 1923 for corrupt practices, and the Liberals never came close in Oxford again. Elsewhere, when active Liberal campaigners won, they then had to spend most of their time away from their constituencies, attending Parliament; few of them received sufficient publicity to counter-act the effect of their enforced absence. Conservative candidates generally ran partisan, as distinct from personal campaigns, had much stronger organisations, and therefore did not suffer as much from absence from their constituencies.[4]

The Liberal failure to hold seats they won can be seen clearly in Table 1, which shows that although they won 281 seats in all in the five elections between 1918 and 1929, they took only a score all five times. The maximum the Liberals won in a single election was 163, in 1918. In the early 1920s circumstances favoured them first in one group of constituencies, then in another. Thus they won many mining constituencies in 1918 but not later; many agricultural seats in 1923 but not in 1918 or 1922; and many textile seats in 1922 and 1923 but not in 1918. If their fortunes had coincided in one election, the Liberals would have won 200 to 250 seats instead of their maximum of 163. Conservative seats changed less frequently.

Table 1   Seats won, 1918–29*

Times won	Conservatives	Liberals	Labour
5	154	22	49
4	105	19	63
3	76	34	48
2	54	69	53
1	56	137	91
nil	157	321	298

* This table excludes Northern Ireland because of boundary changes in 1922.

Pre-war industrial discontent with the Liberals, wartime secessions, losses from redistribution and many other influences whittled down Liberal strength, but whether taken singly or together, they added up to a retreat rather than a rout, if the Liberals could find a new ally to replace Labour. The Conserva-tives were willing to be such an ally, though their demands were high; and wise tactical planning by the Liberal leaders could have minimised some, though not all, of their party's strategic weaknesses. The quarrel between the two Liberal leaders made such planning virtually impossible.

Historical opinion tends to accept that of the two Liberal leaders it was Lloyd George who broke his party, and that Asquith merely picked up the pieces after the 1918 election. The reality was different. Lloyd George certainly took the main overt action which split the Liberals, when he distributed 'coupons' to Conservative opponents of Liberal candidates in 1918. However Asquith forced him into this position mainly, it seems, for reasons of personal revenge. Lloyd George suggested compromises to Asquith, who rejected them, and in so doing forced Lloyd George into dependence on the Conservatives. This in turn cancelled most of Lloyd George's options. If the united Liberal Party had been behind him, he could have resisted many Conservative demands, for instance, for harsh treatment of Germany and Ireland. With the Liberal organisation against him, he could resist only by the devious and unattractive methods outlined in chapter 1.

Lloyd George has been unfortunate in his biographers. He left no political party to resurrect him historically, while he did leave many enemies in each major party, who spent much effort on discrediting him. Even his son's biography exposed Lloyd George as a womaniser without scruple, moral or political. Recently, in a book dealing with the Liberal decline, Trevor Wilson described Lloyd George as 'a compulsive, restless intriguer' who had marked 'deficiency in political judgment'. In this view Lloyd George emerges not only as unscrupulous and immoral, but also as a bungler who 'knew neither his ultimate objective nor the means of attaining it'.[5]

In particular Professor Wilson singled out the distribution of 'coupons' in 1918 as one of Lloyd George's political mistakes. He attacked the myth that Lloyd George awarded these coupons on the basis of whether or not a Liberal M.P. voted for him in the Maurice debate of May 1918. As Wilson demonstrated, the real basis for handing out coupons was a pact Lloyd George made with the Conservative organisation in late October 1918, by which the Conservatives would support 150 Liberals in return for Lloyd George's support elsewhere. Wilson concluded that Lloyd George put himself in the Conservatives' pocket and had nobody but himself to blame for the consequences. Indeed, looking back four years later, when the couponed Conservatives had deposed him, Lloyd George may have regretted his 1918 bargain; however, in 1918 he had sound reasons for making it.

Lloyd George had many failings, but he was not a political *ingenu* who schemed for scheming's sake. He was a realist who understood rapidly changing problems, especially those of the Liberal Party. His chief liabilities, so far as the Liberals were concerned, were that he was not notably loyal either to individuals or parties, and that he was single-minded. The question of his loyalty has been considered in chapter 1; it is sufficient to mention here that he was not the only back-stabber in politics in 1922. His single-mindedness was a greater drawback. Whether he was concerned with social reform as in 1910, or with waging war, or with framing the peace as in 1919–22 or with land reform as in 1926–9, he concentrated his energy on one subject, tending to ignore others.

This single-mindedness and the dynamism which accompanied it worried orthodox politicians, both Liberal and Conservative; but it was valuable in a time of international crisis, and Lloyd George was unusually sensitive to foreign developments and had the courage to deal with them forcefully. However despite his imposing parliamentary majority, Asquith's opposition deprived Lloyd George of the basic strength which would have come from a coalition in which one party balanced the other.

Even before 1914, to adapt Bagehot's phrase, Asquith had been the 'dignified' and Lloyd George the 'efficient' part of the Liberal machine. Asquith had provided the aura of respectability which Lloyd George never obtained, while Lloyd George had provided the drive. Asquith had a manner rather than a purpose, and was well suited to fighting in a situation where party lines were prearranged and clearly defined. His lack of imagination did not make him at home in the political flux of the post-war years, and in addition his apparent willingness to indulge personal grievances against Lloyd George outweighed many of his good points. Between 1916 and 1923, as A. J. P. Taylor has said, Asquith resembled 'an ageing heavyweight who has been knocked out by a younger, more agile, opponent'. In this case, the fight destroyed both men concerned, as well as the party they held in trust.[6]

The quarrel began in 1916 when Lloyd George replaced Asquith as prime minister. There are three views of the 1916 crisis : that it was caused by Lloyd George's lust for power and office; that Lloyd George simply wanted to wage war more effectively by keeping Asquith as premier while he exercised the real power himself; or that Asquith 'deliberately resigned office as a manoeuvre to rout his critics'. It was probably a combination of the last two, but regardless of the interpretation of this crisis, the two leaders definitely split, and there was no quarrel over basic aims.[7]

Although he tried to weaken Lloyd George's Government by mild criticism, Asquith at first refrained from direct public attacks on a popular government in wartime. His criticism then and later was not grounded in major differences in principle, and was explicable only in terms of personal revenge. Nevertheless until 1918 both Asquith and Lloyd George hoped to capture the united support of the Liberal Party, and they did not run rival Liberal candidates in by-elections. This hesitation was more on Lloyd George's side, as the Derby by-election of December 1916 showed. The Derby Liberals leaned heavily towards Joseph Davies, Lloyd George's secretary; but the Liberal headquarters in London was still controlled by Asquith, even though he had ceased to be prime minister. It issued an edict that Davies should not be nominated under any circumstances, and Asquith's personal secretary went to Derby to enforce this decision. Even though a majority of delegates supported Davies, the association nominated a follower of Asquith, who won the by-election without a contest. The episode showed that Liberal headquarters had a decisive role in nominating candidates, that Asquith still controlled it and that he would use all his resources to eliminate Lloyd Georgians from important positions in the Liberal Party. Asquith maintained this attitude right up to the election of 1923, when he and Lloyd George had a temporary reunion. The Derby affair also demonstrated Lloyd George's unwillingness to force a fight, because even if he won the fight, he would split the party and gain only a barren heritage. He preferred to wait until Asquith recognised his defeat and handed over the party as a unit.[8]

But Asquith did not know when he was beaten. He apparently thought Lloyd George would be unable to form a ministry in

1916, and even when he did form it, Asquith still believed he had the confidence of the Liberal Party and the country, and because of this illusion, he persisted in his vendetta even though it was plain that it would merely ruin the Liberal Party without doing anything either for Asquith or the Asquithians. Of all the causes of the Liberal débâcle after the war, one of the most important was Asquith's neglect of the realities of public opinion. According to Sir Robert Donald, one of his strongest supporters, Asquith was[9]

> not in touch with public opinion, and had only prejudiced sources of information. He complained of the Press attacks, but he never took account of the Press himself. . . . He took no pains, either personally or through his secretaries, to keep in touch with the newspapers which were his supporters. They had to support him in the dark.

Several times before the 1918 election, Lloyd George tried to effect a reconciliation with Asquith, but he failed each time. In 1917 he used Lord Reading as a go-between, and in 1918 Lord Murray of Elibank. After a conversation with Lloyd George in September 1918, Murray offered Asquith the lord chancellorship if Asquith would agree to an immediate election, the extension of conscription to Ireland and the passage of Home Rule with the exclusion of Ulster. Elibank said that Lloyd George was 'not master in his own Government, the greater part being Conservatives. He wishes to be in the position of issuing orders; at present he can do nothing without negotiations'. In addition to the chancellorship, Lloyd George offered to let Asquith nominate two of the six principal secretaries of state, and six under-secretaries. According to Lloyd George, these suggestions had come from some of Asquith's supporters who wished to reunite their party; he added that Bonar Law, as Conservative leader, accepted this arrangement, but that Asquith did not. Elibank recorded that Asquith rejected this proposal, saying that there was no need for an election, 'and that my information that L.G. would sweep the country by no means tallied with his own'. He said Asquith really opposed reunion because he did not trust either Lloyd George or Balfour. Elibank concluded his aide-memoire with this observation: 'Unless I am very much mistaken . . . I have been present at the obsequies of the Liberal Party as I have known it.' [10]

Not content with rebuffs to intermediaries, Lloyd George met Asquith in person. On his return from the meeting, Asquith told his wife that[11]

> he had been received with a friendliness that amounted to enthusiasm and asked where he stood. Mr. Lloyd George then said :
>
> 'I understand you don't wish to take a post under the Government.'
>
> To which my husband answered that that was so. . . . At this Mr. Lloyd George looked a little confused. He was walking up and down the room, and in knocking up against a chair a pile of loose books were thrown to the ground. Hastily looking at his watch and stooping to pick up the books, he said he would consider my husband's proposal.

The evidence of Elibank and Mrs Asquith shows that Lloyd George was not the only cause of the Liberal split. He tried several times, right up to the 1918 election, to bring Asquith into his Government, on condition that Asquith should accept his primacy. Lloyd George's other conditions could have been renegotiated, and in any case the projected conscription of Ireland was irrelevant once the war was over. But Asquith was not more prepared to accept Lloyd George's primacy than he had been in 1916; on the contrary he made it clear that he would fight Lloyd George. Lloyd George expected Asquith to act like himself, to drop grudges where they prevented his own advancement and hampered the future of his party. It was not the first time, nor the last, that Lloyd George made this mistake, and it accounts for his confusion at the meeting described by Mrs Asquith. He did not want to destroy Asquith; rather he wanted his support, but he was even less willing to let Asquith destroy him. From that moment, if he wished to keep power, Lloyd George was forced to fight with the Conservatives against Asquith and his followers. It was not until this point that his previous arrangements with the Conservatives took final shape, and that Lloyd George issued coupons to his Liberal and Conservative allies.

The division over the Maurice debate of 9 May 1918 provided
Lloyd George with a convenient public excuse for his attack on
the Asquithian Liberals in the election. During 1917 and 1918
Asquith openly crossed swords with the Government on only a
few major issues. By far the most important of these debates
concerned Major-General Sir Frederick Maurice's* accusation
that Lloyd George had deliberately withheld troops from Haig,
thus exposing the army to disaster. However if Lloyd George had
really considered this vote in Parliament as a final or complete
break, he would hardly have negotiated with Asquith only four
months later. Lloyd George clearly used the division as an excuse
to cover his attack on the Asquithians after his plans for reconciliation with Asquith had been frustrated in September.

Trevor Wilson argues that Lloyd George did not award
coupons on the basis of the policies of the Liberal candidates,
but on the basis of the agreement with the Conservatives in late
October to limit the total number of Liberal coupons to 150.
However almost all the Liberal M.P.s denied the coupon offered
Lloyd George partial support at most, as a few examples indicate.
The Liberal M.P. for Islington West, Thomas Lough, said he
would support Lloyd George, though he had previously been
his opponent. *The Times* described Lough's methods of support
as 'to say the least, peculiar'. J. W. Wilson, in Stourbridge, said
Lloyd George should receive 'very strong support', but at the
same time, he refused to be a 'voting machine'. Many other
instances could be cited, where Liberal M.P.s who had previously
been fence-sitters at best announced 'independent', 'partial' or
'general' backing for Lloyd George during the election campaign.
Lloyd George was 'a little suspicious in some cases of the sudden-
ness of the conversion'. He might have added that the 'general
support' offered by most former Liberal M.P.s was usually just
a euphemism for outright opposition.[12]

Numerous Liberal candidates who had not been M.P.s supported Lloyd George, but nevertheless had coupons issued against
them. This might seem to be a clear case of Lloyd George yielding to Conservative pressure. However most of these Liberal
candidates were contesting former Conservative seats and Lloyd
George opposed them because they were breaking the electoral
truce between his faction and the Conservatives, a truce which

* Maurice was director of military operations at the time.

was fragile enough in any event. It is unrealistic to suggest that Lloyd George could have restricted his intervention in the election to opposing every Liberal who had voted against him, while keeping out of other seats. He was not trying to purge his enemies; grudges rarely entered his calculations. To strengthen his position in the new Parliament he had to back Conservatives in the seats they already held. If he had supported Liberals in the former Conservative seats, or if he had remained neutral, the Conservative M.P.s would have felt free to support or oppose him at their pleasure. By giving them coupons, Lloyd George ensured that they would have a moral obligation to support his policies. The Conservatives would have retained most of their old strongholds anyway, even if Lloyd George had not issued coupons, and by issuing coupons to Conservatives in these places, he obtained guarantees of future support without doing much harm to the Liberal Party. It is unlikely that he thought in terms of an overwhelming tide against the Asquithians. The Conservative central office did not, at any rate in a prediction they sent Lloyd George on 17 December 1918, a few days before the election.[13]

The 1918 election lowered Lloyd Georges' stock, but in early 1918 only Asquith and a few of his closest followers seemed ready to maintain internal party strife. Lloyd George evidently banked on the reunion movement, and he did not break completely with his old party until 1920. In 1919 he still thought his overwhelming control victory would eventually give him control of the party organisation. Nearly all Asquith's leading associates were beaten in 1918, as was Asquith himself; and for six months after the election, Asquith did not receive a single invitation to speak to a local Liberal association. Asquith did not know whether he had the support of the majority of Liberals in the country, and the election results indicated the opposite; but he would not let Lloyd George take over the party without further fighting.[14]

Before Parliament met, and before the Liberal M.P.s knew whether they would form one parliamentary party or two, Asquith appointed a house leader and a chief whip. He did not consult the M.P.s about his, and some of them objected, as they had already chosen their own chief whip. Asquith was within his constitutional rights when he appointed the two officials, but as he had just been rejected by a large section of the Liberal Party, he could have asked his party whether it wanted him to carry on.[15]

From the opening of the new Parliament, Asquith made it plain that he would oppose the Government, whether or not he had serious grounds for disagreement with it. In April 1919, while Lloyd George was still planning his reconstruction policy, Asquith accused him of betraying the ex-soldiers and of undermining free trade. Asquith proclaimed his policy to be the maintenance of an independent Liberal group, but his other plans seemed virtually identical to Lloyd George's. Asquith confirmed the essentially frivolous nature of his opposition to Lloyd George in June 1919. The Government decided to retain some wartime customs duties on a few goods such as musical instruments, clocks and motor cars. The Asquithians at once issued a pamphlet (*How the U-Boats 'Protected' You*) comparing these duties with the wartime 'protection' by submarines against imports. The issue was small in itself: the duties had been imposed originally by Reginald McKenna during Asquith's regime, and Lloyd George was actually reducing them. As time passed, the Asquithian Liberals had many valid reasons for denouncing Lloyd George's administration, over Ireland, the Treaty of Versailles and many other matters. However it is worth noting that their early criticisms, though strong, had little basis, and that Asquith was unwilling to give Lloyd George even a short time to demonstrate his Liberalism. If he had been willing, it is doubtful whether Lloyd George would have yielded to as many Conservative pressures as he did.

The Coalition Liberals abstained from the parliamentary vote on these duties, because they refused to let the Asquithians pose as the only true Liberals. This often happened during the Parliament of 1919–22. As Winston Churchill remarked, the Conservatives would listen carefully to a united Liberal Party which would speak to them *puissance à puissance*.[16] They would also listen to a coherent splinter group which would compromise on one thing to gain concessions on another; but they were much less patient with a group which might at any moment desert the Government on an important issue. Each time the Coalition Liberals abstained or voted against the Government, the Conservative M.P.s felt less inclined to go on with the arrangement.

Thus the maintenance of a separate Independent Liberal group in the commons directly undermined the influence of Lloyd George and his section with the Conservatives; of course this had been the intention of many Asquithian Liberals.

The Coalition Liberals wanted reunion badly, and tried to win over the Asquithians. This failed, and since they would not leave the Coalition, they still had the alternative of joining with the Conservatives in a new party; but they did not want to go as far as fusion with the Conservatives. The Coalition Liberals persisted in the illusion that they could hover indefinitely between the Conservatives and Asquithians, retaining ties with both without being repudiated by either. It was a case of 'how happy they could be with either, were t'other dear charmer away', and it was as difficult to maintain, if it could be maintained at all. At first the Coalition Liberals were probably right in counting on Conservative goodwill. Even after the Carlton Club Meeting of October 1922, most Conservative M.P.s were willing to accommodate the Coalition Liberals, but the Conservatives could not be expected to wait for ever while their allies made up their minds.

As usual Lloyd George ran ahead of his party. In January 1919, before Parliament opened, he spoke of 'the necessity of reuniting the Liberal Party'. Once Parliament assembled, and it became obvious that Asquith could consider reunion only on his own terms, Lloyd George became more hesitant. In February he decided not to try for the Liberal leadership. By September he wanted to form 'a new progressive party', and he informed his Liberal colleagues that 'Liberalism has no future'. A few months later he added that the Coalition label was only slightly better: 'The Coalition may be the best punch in the world, the sugar, the lemons, etc., but there are no fillers', and the only thing was to set up a new party.[17]

Lloyd George often sensed the reality of a political situation before others, and in this case he outran his Coalition Liberal colleagues. He realised that the Liberals were unlikely to form any more governments on their own, but he wanted to preserve Liberal principles, and even more, he wanted to preserve his own position. Asquith made it clear that the Coalition Liberal could not hope for quick reunion in November 1919, when he rejected advances from some Liberal backbenchers:[18]

Three [Coalition] Liberal members for Leeds came to me furtively this morning, in Nicodemus fashion, to implore me to reunite the Liberal party. They were good, well-meaning men, un-confined, and yet not professing 'free' Liberals. I reminded them of Alphonse Karr's reply to someone who advocated the abolition of capital punishment : 'Que messieurs les assassins commencement.'

The Coalition Liberal ministers still hoped for reunion despite these rebuffs and on 18 March 1920 they opposed a suggestion by Lloyd George for fusion with the Conservatives. Perhaps they hoped that this would in some way certify their Liberalism, but six days later, Asquith announced that Liberal headquarters would oppose Coalition Liberals even if nominated by their local Liberal associations. Two months later, in May 1920, both the National Liberal Federation in England and the Scottish Liberal Federation condemned the Coalition Liberals at stormy meetings.

Neither meeting was as popular and representative as some later accounts suggested. Both contained delegates who supposedly represented the constituency associations; but even before the war, many of these bodies had been phantom associations at the best of times. During the wartime political truce, most Liberal associations did not meet even if they had been active before 1914. The North Cumberland Liberal Association for instance did not even have executive meetings between 1914 and 1918. Regional Liberal groups such as the Lancashire, Cheshire and North-western Liberal Federation, said that the wartime political truce made its annual meetings 'purely formal', and it returned its executive without bothering to hold elections. After the war many Liberal associations which had been dormant took a long time to revive. In Hereford the *Manchester Guardian* correspondent found that the Liberal organisation had 'been allowed to lapse', and was 'virtually non-existent'. This was a common occurrence, and it meant that the Liberal headquarters, controlled by Asquith, could name its own delegates to the National Liberal Federation meetings, since the N.L.F. rules allowed the national executive to fill vacancies in delegations of inactive associations. This clause allowed one faction to pack the N.L.F. meetings with its supporters if it controlled the executive, as the Asquithians did. Thus it is impossible to say how many delegates

to the N.L.F. meeting of May 1920 represented active constituency parties, and how many were Asquith's nominees. Some
may even have been nominees of other factions. The Skipton
Liberal Association opposed nationalisation strongly, and hoped
to prevent the N.L.F. from adopting it as party policy. It sent
letters to distant Liberal associations, suggesting that Skipton
would supply delegates if the other associations could not come.
Even when the delegates actually came from the constituency
parties they did not always represent the opinions of their
members. For example, shortly after the N.L.F. meeting of May
1920, the executive of the Wansbeck Liberal Association condemned the Coalition by 5 votes to 2; but a general meeting
of the members repudiated their executive by 70 votes to 10,
whereupon the agent resigned and emigrated to Canada. This
indicates that the Asquithian claim that the N.L.F. spoke for
English Liberalism as a whole was at least disputable.[19]

In Scotland the situation was similar. In October 1918 the
executive of the Scottish Liberal Federation decided to disband
its general council, as the local parties which had appointed it
'had practically ceased to exist'. In 1919 and 1920 its minutes
recorded that 'little was being done in the way of organisation'
because of sectional feeling in the party. Despite this disorganisation, the Federation held a general meeting in May 1920, at
which several Coalition Liberal M.P.s for Scottish constituencies
were present, including Winston Churchill and R. R. Munro
(secretary of state for Scotland). Munro proposed that the meeting
refer back the executive's report against the Coalition Liberals,
but he was hooted down, and only fifty or sixty supported him,
while 'there was a very large show of hands against'. However
the meeting rejected, by 100 votes to 80, an Asquithian proposal forbidding any association with the Conservatives. The
Asquithians later maintained that this second vote, which had
gone against them, was fraudulent. Several members of the
executive, including the chairman and vice-chairman, resigned
in protest against the virtual exclusion of the Coalition Liberals.
The rump executive then changed the constitution to enable it
to interfere with local affairs, and it repudiated the previous
theory that the Liberal Party was a federation of autonomous
local associations.[20]

Supporters of Asquith may have outnumbered supporters of

Lloyd George in both England and Scotland, but manipulation of the party organisation made this uncertain. Therefore the Coalition Liberals did not need to reconsider the question of fusion with the Conservatives immediately. If they had been repudiated truly by the whole Liberal Party, they would have been more willing to accept Conservative advances, but it was easy, and perhaps accurate, to represent the May 1920 expulsions as the decision of an autocratic clique. Most Liberal associations with Coalition Liberal M.P.s supported the Coalition and such seats accounted for a majority of pre-1914 Liberal strongholds; while most seats where Asquithian Liberals had lost in 1918 had been areas before the war of relative Liberal weakness. Although there were some exceptions, this meant that the Lloyd George Liberals could maintain that they represented more Liberal voters, even if not as many associations as the Asquithians.[21]

If either Asquith or Lloyd George had been the obvious choice of most Liberals, the party split would have been much less serious than it became. However both leaders had a strong following, and neither had the support of an overwhelming majority. Following the 1920 expulsions, Lloyd George's followers set up a separate organisation as an insurance policy to make it harder for Asquith to capture the entire party behind the scenes. This reaffirmed the party split even though most Liberals wanted reconciliation.

The quarrel over leadership distracted Liberals from the problems of their party, that is, determining future policies and alignments. The split was not primarily over doctrines but over personalities, and neither side was committed definitely to one set of policies as against another. Difficult decisions about such problems as nationalisation were frequently postponed, and even more important, decisions about electoral arrangements with other parties were left incomplete. In 1922 the Liberals had many options, too many perhaps for their own good. In March 1922 Charles McCurdy, Coalition Liberal chief whip, told Lloyd George that he had[22]

the choice of three possible plain statements : —
1. The Coalition is finished. National unity no longer exists except among the leaders. I deeply regret it but I accept the fact and my Liberal Ministers are no longer members

as they owned business premises outside the constituencies in which they lived. From 1918 to 1929 the Conservatives owed between 5 and 17 seats to these 'business voters'. No election in this period was decided by seventeen seats, but they aided the Conservatives, especially in 1922, when Bonar Law held his seat in Glasgow Central because of the business vote. If he had been defeated, the Conservative leader might have retired, and even if he did not retire he was not certain to win a by-election. Three of his ministers lost their seats in the general election and ran in by-elections in seemingly safe seats in Liverpool, Surrey and Middlesex. All three were defeated. With the unsettled condition of the Conservative Party in late 1922, one can attribute many developments to the existence of the large business vote in Glasgow Central.[23]

The agricultural constituencies were less dependable for the Conservatives, as only 22.8 per cent of them voted for the Conservatives in every election of the 1920s; in contrast 43 per cent of the middle-class ones did. Nevertheless farming districts were good fighting ground for the Conservatives, as were the seats in Northern Ireland. Taken together they did not normally vote so solidly for the Conservatives as to provide a party majority, but they did give a secure base from which to conduct negotiations with other parties. Labour was just beginning to develop such a base in 1922, in the Scottish and South Wales coalfields, and in the slums of Glasgow and London, but the Liberals had no such strongholds except for a handful of seats in rural Wales and Scotland. They were constantly fighting for survival and each election was vital to them. Parties with a great electoral bastion such as the Conservatives had can afford to step down in a few constituencies where they might win, if by doing so they gain worthwhile concessions elsewhere. Thus in Glasgow in 1922 they supported the Lloyd George Liberal in Partick, though they would probably have won the seat if they had contested it. They held back because the Lloyd George Liberals supported them in other Glasgow seats. Altogether in 1922 the Conservatives stayed out of 132 constituencies. The Liberals could not fall back on a large redoubt as could the Conservatives, or to a lesser extent Labour. To make a respectable overall showing as a prospective governing party, they had to fight nearly every seat where they had much chance; they could afford fewer electoral concessions than the Conservatives, except in seats where they were so weak that their support counted for little anyway.

The Liberal predicament was worsened by the redistribution of 1918, which abolished numerous Liberal seats and created many new Conservative ones. The total number of M.P.s rose by 37, and the redistribution gave the Conservatives 28 more seats in England, Scotland and Wales than they had held in December 1910, as against a combined Liberal and Labour gain of only 8. Thus the redistribution made a net change of 20 seats in favour of the Conservatives.[24]

Ironically, the passage of Home Rule in 1921 substantially increased Conservative strength too. In 1918 Ireland elected 26 Conservatives and 79 Home Rulers. With the passage of the Irish Treaty, Northern Ireland was reduced to only 13 seats (including one university seat), of which 11 voted Conservative in 1922. This was 15 fewer than they had won in Ireland in 1918, but their opponents lost 77, making a net change in favour of the Conservatives of 62. This change was roughly the size of Bonar Law's majority in 1922, so that if the Conservatives had not agreed to Home Rule in 1921, they would have had only a bare majority, or none a year later.

The 1918 redistribution, Home Rule and retention of plural voting did not alone destroy the Liberal Party, but they helped. Some factors aiding the Conservatives over the Liberals were based on long-term social influences. However these particular Conservative gains resulted from political decisions. Practically any system of minority representation, introduced along with all the other electoral changes, would have produced Liberal gains to offset these Conservative ones. Moreover systems which ensure minority representation generally provide some built-in continuity of personalities, and this would have mollified another Liberal weak point, their rapid turnover of M.P.s and candidates.

Another influence favouring the Conservatives which need not have done so was the war, which created a gap in the continuity of party conflict, and made many old rivalries seem irrelevant. This increased the opportunities for failure if a party was badly led, since party loyalties were eroded to some extent as well. In the case of Sir Hubert Gough, the gap in political continuity favoured the Liberals. In 1914 Gough had been the chief figure in the Curragh incident, when some army officers had threatened to resign rather than impose Home Rule on Ulster. Gough later wrote that 'one of the chief results of the war had been to bring about some change in my opinions on Ireland'. In fact they were so changed that he turned down an invitation to run as a Carsonite in an Ulster constituency in 1918, and ran instead as an Asquithian Liberal in a 1921 by-election. But Gough's case was unusual, and the break in continuity generally favoured the Conservatives. Before the war many moderate voters had been repelled by the party's diehard attitude to such matters as Lloyd George's 1909 budget; after 1918 the Conservatives were more careful, though they were still capable of blundering, as Baldwin showed in 1923, over the American war debts question and over the dissolution of Parliament. But in 1922, for the time being, the Conservatives got round the possibility of making mistakes by doing scarcely anything. Bonar Law admitted during the 1922 election that his approach was 'purely negative'. This did not drive people away during the campaign because the previous decade had been so full of positive actions. On the other hand this attitude was unlikely to gain converts if it was prolonged indefinitely, and the Conservatives needed something else to win voters.[25]

The Conservatives had not won an election on their own since 1874, though they had won in 1886, 1895, 1900 and 1918 with the support of Liberal factions. They could not count on such support indefinitely, and many Conservatives, remembering their past weakness, considered that they needed some sort of alliance to win future elections. They were far from winning a majority of votes: in 1918 they won slightly over a third of the votes cast in an election affected by a surge of patriotism, and they got only 38 per cent in 1922, counting independent Conservative votes with ones for official Conservative candidates, although in many cases they opposed each other. This compared unfavourably with their disastrous showing in 1906, when they had taken 43.7 per cent. The Conservative leaders recognised the many difficulties of their position, and tried to restrain their followers from stirring up partisan feelings, lest Labour take office on a split anti-socialist vote. Not all Conservatives were willing to co-operate with the Liberals, and according to Sir William Sutherland, one of Lloyd George's organisers, the far right wing of Conservatism wanted to 'hoist the old Tory flag as a sort of Jolly Roger'.[26]

If this attitude had been more widespread, the Conservatives could easily have stumbled out of the Coalition before securing sufficient electoral support to form a stable government. The leaders of the party and most M.P.s were more moderate : in 1918 Bonar Law told Balfour that 'our Party on the old lines will never have any future again in this country'. Then and later, many prominent Conservatives agreed with him. In early 1922 Lord Derby said, 'If we attempt to stand alone without the help of our Liberal allies, we are bound to be beaten'. Derby was not a member of the Coalition Government, and his remark was not special pleading. Lord Peel, secretary of state for India in both the Lloyd George and Bonar Law governments, wrote shortly before the Carlton Club Meeting that if there was a break in the Coalition, 'the results will be deplorable'. He expected Labour to add up to 250 seats to the 77 it held at dissolution. In September 1922 Austen Chamberlain predicted that the Conservatives would get at most 290 seats, and perhaps only 252. Earlier in 1922, in a confidential memorandum prepared for the Conservative chiefs, the party's central office said they could count on 317 seats; but this included such hopeless ones as Leigh, Bethnal Green South-west, Tradeston and St Rollox, which the Conservatives did not win in any election from 1922 to the present. Even counting such seats, the Conservative organisers conceded that they would be hard pressed : Sir Malcolm Fraser, the party's principal agent, said they should 'knock off' 10 per cent of the estimated wins; Sir Arthur Griffith-Boscawen said the central office always deducted 20 per cent from its predictions, and 40 per cent for Wales, but whichever rule was applied, the estimate foresaw the Conservatives in a minority.[27]

The Conservatives did not contest 132 seats in 1922, as they preferred Liberals in most of them to the risk of letting Labour in on a divided free enterprise vote. This meant that they had to win two-thirds of the seats they did contest, just to have a majority of one; and this in turn meant that the Conservatives needed a very clear idea of the seats which they could leave uncontested. However the Conservative organisers had some strange ideas about the distribution of electoral strength outside

the south-east and the middle-class areas of London. Their
estimate of January 1922 contained no fewer than 152 mistaken
predictions, for an overall error of 25 per cent (not counting the
university seats). Their errors were most numerous in Wales,
Scotland and northern England, where they made 59 mistakes
out of 143, for an error of 41 per cent. In eastern London,
central Scotland, the West Yorkshire textile district, northern
Staffordshire and southern Wales, the Conservative central office
was more often wrong that right. This was hardly an example
of pinpoint accuracy, and it revealed how out of touch the
Conservative organisation was with public opinion. Yet it was
the basis of Conservative campaign planning.

The prediction seriously overestimated Lloyd George Liberal
support, and listed 96 seats as 'safe' for the Premier's followers.
It also listed 42 others as reasonably secure, for a total of 138;
yet in the election the Lloyd George Liberals actually took only
47 constituencies. The Conservative predictions were based on
estimates by local party leaders, and this shows that they regarded Lloyd George as a much more potent electoral force
than he was; and this in turn made them hesitate to break with
him. Even when they did leave the Coalition, the Conservatives
felt they needed his help, and that of other Liberals, so acted
as a brake on their own party's militant supporters to prevent
them from stirring up the embers of pre-war conflict.

The factors mentioned so far in this chapter were important
in bolstering the Conservatives and hampering the Liberals;
but the attitudes of the Liberal and Conservative leaders were
also vital to the development of their respective parties. It is
difficult to believe that the Liberal decline would have been so
precipitous if Asquith and Lloyd George had come to terms
earlier, and the Conservative leaders had this example of the
disastrous effect of personal squabbles in front of them at all
times, and they tried not to destroy their own party's unity.

The great question for the Conservatives was whether the
moderates could hold their party together, and at the same time
enforce electoral co-operation between Liberals and Conservatives at the constituency level. In both Liberal and Conservative
Parties, disruption could come from the leadership or the party
organisation. In many places the Liberal organisation strongly
desired unity even after the 1918 election, but the actions of the

leaders made this almost impossible. In the Conservative Party, the organisation caused much trouble, but the activities of the leaders minimised its consequences. Their success in maintaining party unity and at the same time winning an important election was to some extent accidental, and to examine this it is necessary to consider first the role of the two Conservative leaders, then the distribution of strength within the organisation and finally, the nature of the dissident groups in the party.

R. T. Mackenzie has written that Conservative leadership has been less stable than that of the Labour Party, and his interpretation has impressive evidence : only four leaders have been deposed by their followers during this century, Balfour, Austen Chamberlain, Neville Chamberlain and Lansbury. Three were Conservatives, and one Labour. However this does not mean that Conservative leaders have had less power than Labour leaders, only that they have had a different sort of power. The Conservative leaders have been pre-eminent in their party, so they have attracted greater personal blame for failure than Labour leaders, who could usually fall back on the internal structure of their party for support if things went wrong. It is significant that the only Labour leader to be deposed, Lansbury, fell because of a trade union revolt. The unions were reluctant to grant power, and slow to take it away; but the Conservative and Liberal leaders have exercised more direct control over the party machine than Labour leaders, and have usually quelled revolts by using their wide powers. In the Conservative pressure-cooker, there has been so safety valve, and protests against the leaders have either subsided or built up a formidable head. This was especially noticeable under Austen Chamberlain in contrast to the quiet leadership of Bonar Law.[28]

Chamberlain had the qualities of a competent, if second-rate, administrator rather than those required of a party leader in a time of flux, and he had been numbed, first by fifty years' intellectual servitude to his father, then by several more years' servitude to Lloyd George. This made it difficult to determine whether he had his own principles, and if so, what they were. To the backbenchers he seemed to have little initiative, and if he had shown them that he could control Lloyd George, they would have trusted him more. As it was, he did frustrate Lloyd George on several occasions, notably during the election scare of January

1922, but to use his own words, he 'did not find it worthwhile' to let his own followers know that he had opinions of his own. Another failing of Chamberlain was that he was incapable of filling in for Lloyd George during the latter's frequent absences at international conferences. Whereas Bonar Law had often replaced the premier with few adverse results, Chamberlain fumbled badly, as in a debate on teachers' pensions, when Lloyd George was at the Genoa Conference.* [29]

Any Conservative leader would have difficulties in a coalition with a non-Conservative premier, for he would have to detect signs of dissatisfaction among the M.P.s, and to cajole the party organisation into backing policies which they might not like. Chamberlain did neither. He had several advantages: most Conservative leaders have either been in opposition and thus without patronage; or they have been prime ministers with an administrative load. Chamberlain had the patronage, and his departmental duties as lord privy seal were insignificant. But as his friend Lord Birkenhead said, he lacked bonhomie, a currency 'with which great statesmen can easily finance a large political business'. [30]

Chamberlain rarely tried a personal approach to his supporters in the country. *Gleanings and Memoranda*, the official monthly Conservative news bulletin, reported all the important party meetings, such as the annual conferences of the regional associations. According to these reports, Chamberlain attended only three of the twenty-six major gatherings of his party organisation held during his leadership. This meant that he had little contact as leader with his militant followers in the countryside, although he was relying on them to back a coalition for which many of them had little enthusiasm. This failure to attend party meetings undermined Chamberlain's own position and that of the Coalition he supported.

He was equally careless in his relations with the Conservative M.P.s. Chamberlain was elected leader in March 1921, but took two months before he addressed the backbenchers. Even then he did not speak to the Conservative M.P.s as such, but the New Members' Coalition Group, which contained numerous Liberals. When he did speak to his supporters, Chamberlain was not always clear. Birkenhead said his rigidity 'almost verged upon

* Cf. chapter 5.

pedantry' but this pedantry was not always precise, and views which may have been well defined in Chamberlain's own mind often seemed vague to his followers. As chapter 5 shows, he was not committed as blindly to Lloyd George as he seemed to be, but he did not make this clear to his party. It said much for the loyalty of the M.P.s that they did not depose him sooner than they did; as it was, his tenure as Conservative leader was the shortest of the century.[31]

Chamberlain could be blunt and high-handed. Early in 1922 a Glasgow M.P., Gideon Murray, wrote a letter to the Press calling for 'rehabilitation of the Conservative Party'. Murray and Chamberlain had never discussed the Coalition, and Murray admitted that if they had, he would not have sent this letter. However Chamberlain refused him further information on parliamentary business, and Birkenhead, Chamberlain's ally, even cut Murray socially. Soon after this, the Glasgow Conservatives repudiated Murray. Such persecution was uncommon, but even if it was deserved, it lowered Chamberlain's stature in the eyes of M.P.s. His attitude at the Carlton Club Meeting did not create a good impression either. The meeting was basically an attempt to by-pass the annual party conference, which Chamberlain believed would repudiate his policies. To make his position more secure, he excluded several Conservative M.P.s, some of them on dubious grounds. At the meeting itself, he ignored attempts to adopt a compromise. Chamberlain needlessly challenged the M.P.s to accept what seemed to them to be shifting and indefinite views on the future of the Coalition, or to reject him as leader. He could have won them round by adopting a comfortable deception, or even by outlining his real views, but he made the party think it would have to commit suicide to satisfy him, and it refused. The strange thing is that it did not have to commit suicide, as Chamberlain's real views were compatible with those of his followers.[32]

Chamberlain made three contributions as Conservative leader. He persuaded it to support the Irish negotiations in November 1921, although the party was divided over the question, and almost single-handed he united the Conservatives against himself and against the Coalition. This ensured that all sections of his party, not just a few on its right wing, would oppose him. His third contribution came after his defeat, when he refused to lead a revolt against Bonar Law. After the 1922 election, a core of fifty-four M.P.s remained around Chamberlain, who could have wrecked an already weak government; but they did not, nor did they wage guerrilla warfare on their opponents during the election campaign. If Chamberlain had yielded to pique, he might have wounded his party as Asquith and Lloyd George had wounded theirs. His main colleagues were angry with their rejection, and spoiling for a fight. Sir Robert Horne spoke privately about two Conservative parties, while Balfour said in public that he M.P.s who had ended the Coalition were not gentlemen. Many other supporters of Chamberlain were restive too. However Chamberlain's best-known quality, loyalty, came into play, and he advised his supporters to stick to their party. For instance he told Sir Robert Newman, M.P. for Exeter, who was running as an independent Conservative, that 'The future is obscure to me, but I have no intention of leaving our party or of joining any new combination. Don't cut yourself off from your old friends'.[33]

Incapable of leading a party in a storm, Chamberlain could recognise defeat and arrange his affairs accordingly, for his own benefit and that of his followers. Within two years most of them were back in office, and on reasonably good terms with the victors at the Carlton Club Meeting. Much of this was due to Chamberlain's refusal to put personal feelings first.

Bonar Law was a leader, not just a man who held the office, as Chamberlain did. Practically everyone who knew him remarked on his ability to win friends and to keep them. The memoirs of his political opponents almost invariably praised him. J. M. Kenworthy, an Asquithian Liberal, said he was an 'honest upright man' and the 'ablest of all the Conservative elder statesmen of my time'. Lord Snell, a Labour peer, said Law was 'unreservedly liked on the Labour benches', and Ben Tillett described him as 'the most remarkable personality it has been my own good fortune to meet . . . a gentle and Christian soul. . . . I never knew many man that so readily and so courageously offered the soft answer that turneth away wrath'. David Kirkwood, the Clydeside rebel, called Bonar Law 'one of the greatest men I ever met, very able and very sincere'. J. R. Clynes, another prominent Labour M.P., said Law 'put the good of his country before the good of his party'. Other writers paid tribute not merely to his honesty and friendliness, but to his ability as well. Sir Arthur Griffith-Boscawen said that whenever a minister blundered during the Lloyd George regime, he would turn to Bonar Law, who would extricate him. Griffith-Boscawen called this 'doing a Bonar'.[34]

Bonar Law kept in close touch with the backbenchers, and up to his first retirement Lloyd George relied on him to keep the Conservative M.P.s quiet. His loyalties were undivided, and the M.P.s knew that he supported Lloyd George, but that if the premier presented a real threat to Conservative principles, he would put his party ahead of personal ties.

Bonar Law coped easily with changing situations, as he demonstrated in 1922, when he outmanoeuvred Lloyd George several times. His able handling of the campaign may not have been decisive in winning the election, but it boosted the morale of the Conservatives who had deposed Lloyd George. Bonar Law's flexibility also ensured that the fall of Lloyd George did not lead to a complete break-up of the electoral pacts with the Lloyd George Liberals which were helpful to many Conservative candidates.

Asquith described Bonar Law as 'the unknown prime minister', but his verdict was unjust. Bonar Law was one of the most popular premiers since Gladstone, among men of all parties, just as Lloyd George was one of the most suspect. While he did not initiate any major social reform or new direction in foreign policy, Bonar Law held his party together in the greatest crisis it had faced in decades, and he provided an easy transition from the frenzied years of coalition to the era of Baldwin and MacDonald.

Behind both Chamberlain and Bonar Law was Sir George Younger, a jaunty and confident Scottish brewer of seventy-one who was chairman of the Conservative organisation from 1916 to 1922. Younger resembled the archetypal Tories to whom Disraeli gave the advice: 'Above all, no programme'. Certainly he believed in Tory principles, but in his view the chief principle was party survival. A man of sound practical sense, he was interested in tactics rather than in political theology. According to the Liberal *Daily News*,[35]

One or two prejudices occasionally darken a disposition that is naturally merry and bright. He does not love 'those Radical fellows'—it is pure joy to note the scorn he can impart to that word 'Radical' [i.e., Liberal]; and temperance reformers are on his short list of dislikes.

Younger did not underestimate his own influence, and was proud of his role in the crisis of 1922. Lord Beaverbrook described him as[36]

a charming companion, though somewhat taken up with the stories about his encounters in the past with one or other of the Conservative leaders. He would say, for instance, quite emphatically, 'I told Austen what to do, and of course, he did it.' Or, 'Bonar Law, of course, acted on my advice'.

In late 1921 Younger told Chamberlain that 'doubtless the P.M. can act on his own view if he pleases to flout us, but we can smash his hopes easily'. A few weeks later Sir William Sutherland, one of Lloyd George's organisers, crossed him, and Younger informed Chamberlain that 'Sutherland has got it in the neck. So will L.G. when I visit him'.[37] These comments indicate Younger's strong will, and his clear sense of priorities. He hoped to maintain the Coalition, but would not lift a finger to preserve it at the expense of the party he knew and understood. Like Bonar Law and Chamberlain, he cared too much about his party to let it go the way of the Liberals. In 1922 the Liberals had no zealous organisational chief like Younger, who was prepared to shove aside factional disputes of the party to ensure the maximum representation for his party. Younger's chief contribution in the election lay in what he refrained from doing. Under his auspices there was no purge of Chamberlain's supporters after the Carlton Club Meeting, as there might have been if he had been less careful. In the 1922 election, Lloyd George tried to provoke Younger by attacking him personally, but Younger refused to disrupt his party by entering a feud.

This chapter has compared the positions of the Liberal and Conservative Parties in the period just before the 1922 crisis, and it has indicated that the Conservatives had many advantages, particularly in their leadership. Nevertheless the leaders could not hold their party together if the organisation or the M.P.s rebelled, and this could have neutralised many of the Conservative advantages. In 1902 Ostrogorski predicted that the mass organisations would make M.P.s subservient to their local parties, and that the local parties would therefore be able to impose ill-advised policies on their more sensible representatives. This never happened, and Ostrogorski's worries might seem groundless. Generally the party leadership offsets the influence of local parties to some degree, especially if the local parties are both unco-ordinated and leaderless. However in 1922 the power of the leadership was attenuated, and Ostrogorski's forecast almost came true. The reluctance of the party zealots to accept their leaders' views about continued coalition could have had a lasting and detrimental effect on Conservative fortunes.[38]

3

The Conservative Constituency
Parties and the Coalition

According to Bonar Law, the Coalition fell because of 'a deep-rooted' feeling in the constituencies. He felt that the party organisation deposed Lloyd George, and that the M.P.s merely assented to this constituency revolt. The purpose of this chapter is to determine how far Bonar Law's belief was justified. It examines first the relationship between the Conservative leaders, the M.P.s and the local parties; then the question of whether the local parties were representative; and finally the extent of the constituency revolt.[1]

It is impossible to determine whether the local parties represented popular feeling accurately, as there was no contemporary survey of opinion. However the feelings of the rebel groups do not seem to have been as widespread as has sometimes been thought. Nor need the revolt have had the consequences it did, for there was little co-ordination of local party revolts, although a few minor dissident groups co-operated. Nevertheless the party leaders help provide co-ordination by challenging the malcontents directly. Most local parties were basically sensible, and firm but careful leadership could have avoided many difficulties in 1922, perhaps without ending Lloyd George's career and certainly without bringing down the Conservative leaders. Many consequences of this crisis were avoidable, as was the crisis itself. Chapters 4 and 5 pursue the arguments presented in this chapter, and discuss factions in the parliamentary party and the sequence of events which led the Conservative M.P.s to pull down the Coalition.

In the 1920s only a handful of Conservative M.P.s openly conflicted with the united pressures of their leader and organisation. A few did so successfully. This happened in Westminster and Harrow in 1922, and in Exeter in 1929. In each case the sitting M.P. stood as an independent Conservative and defeated the official candidate. In 1922 some forty-two strongwilled M.P.s formed a group known as the Diehards, but they were only a tenth of the parliamentary party, nor did many of them conflict with their constituency associations, although they did conflict with their leader. Generally if a Conservative M.P. or candidate quarrelled with both his leader and his organisation he could write off his political career; but if the leader and organisation were at odds, the situation was more complex.

The main power of the Conservative leaders over the M.P.s was patronage, but in 1921 and 1922 patronage had to be distributed between two parties, a requirement which frustrated many ambitious Conservative backbenchers. Moreover the appeal of jobbery at the end of a Parliament is less than at its beginning, as the jobs cannot last long. In the last year of the Coalition, this was more the case than ever. After several by-election reverses, the premier appointed few new ministers, because at that time such appointments required by-elections. The Government also feared by-elections resulting from elevations of M.P.s to the peerage, and it told them not to expect peerages.[2]

At the level of electioneering, the power of the leaders was usually only moral. The leaders and the central organisation under their control could supply or withhold speakers, pamphlets and sometimes money, but this did not always thwart determined rebels. For instance before his fall in 1922, Austen Chamberlain denied all these things to Gervais Rentoul and Reginald Clarry, independent Conservative candidates for Lowestoft and Newport. Both men got Diehard M.P.s to speak on their platforms, and they also received publicity in the Northcliffe and Rothermere newspapers. Both won, as did many other Conservatives in 1922 who had little or no organisational or financial support from their party headquarters.[3]

Withdrawal of funds did not always bring Conservative candidates to heel, especially where the candidates paid well for the privilege of running. The Conservative M.P.s often subsidised their local parties, and although they usually observed a decent reticence in public about these contributions, a few instances have come to light. Duff Cooper paid his local party £300 a year, while Sir Edward Nicholl in the first ten months of 1920 alone spent more than £6,000 in local donations. Sometimes the M.P. was sponsored by an outside organisation : the British Commonwealth Union, an organisation of employers, subsidised Sir Allan Smith in Croydon South, and paid his 1919 by-election expenses of £1,421. This organisation sponsored several other Conservative M.P.s, and a few 'patriotic Labour' candidates as well. In March 1922 T. Davies, Conservative M.P. for Ciren-cester and Tewkesbury, said he would stand independently of the Coalition in the future, and that to preserve his independence he would run his campaign entirely on local funds. These were but a few instances of the widespread tendency of Conservative M.P.s and candidates to depend on their own financial resources, or on groups outside the official party organisation.[4]

After the Second World War, Conservative M.P.s were forbidden to subsidise their local parties, and this tended to increase the power of both the leader and the local parties in relation to the M.P.s. The pre-war subsidies had made the M.P.s to some degree independent of the narrow cliques which often dominated constituency party executives; but even granting this, the constituency parties had some important powers, which they used often enough in 1922 to show that they were real, not just theoretical. They could repudiate M.P.s, and they could sometimes force prospective candidates to adopt a particular view on coalition with other parties. They also decided whether or not to nominate a candidate.

Although local parties could dismiss sitting M.P.s they did so only occasionally, and then often for personal or financial reasons unconnected with party policy. The Conservatives in East Fulham rejected Sir Henry Norris for a mixture of reasons : in April 1922 the secretary of the local party told Norris that his readoption 'would involve an increase' in his subscription of £200 a year. Norris offered £300 if he could control the agent, but his executive found another candidate instead, and Norris refused to support him. A similar thing happened to Sir George Elliott in Islington West, though the amounts involved were not published.[5]

In 1922 several constituency executives removed their M.P.s

because of their attitudes to the Coalition. Most of those deposed were anti-coalition, although C. L. A. Ward-Jackson (Leominster) alienated his executive because he supported the Coalition. He then contested Harrow, where the local party had deposed Sir Oswald Mosley because of his anti-coalition attitude. Two Glasgow Conservatives, Gideon Murray and T. B. S. Adair, also lost their seats because they opposed the Coalition. In 1923 several Conservative M.P.s who supported free trade were repudiated by their associations; one case was particularly interesting. In Rochdale the prospective Conservative candidate was a free trader, and refused to run. His replacement was a strong tariff reformer, N. Cockshutt, who had been candidate in 1912, but who had been deposed because he had rejected Bonar Law's extreme position on Ulster. Thus Cockshutt had lost his position in 1912 because he deviated to the left, then regained it in 1923 because he deviated to the right of his party.[6]

Despite these examples, repudiation of M.P.s was uncommon for any reason, though the M.P.s realised that it was always a possibility and usually tried to pacify discontented groups inside their local associations. Prospective candidates were more vulnerable to pressure from constituency executives, as they did not have the prestige accruing to a sitting M.P., and had to work harder to gain the confidence of the local party officers. The problems of Lord Deerhurst in Worcester were an example of this. In May 1922 a member of the Worcester party executive informed Deerhurst that as prospective Conservative candidate he must be independent of any coalition, 'no matter whether under the leadership of Conservative or Liberal'. Deerhurst pointed out that this would have prevented him from supporting either Lord Salisbury's government after 1895, or the wartime coalition. He added, 'Practically continuously since 1885, the government of the day has been either a coalition government or has been supported by a coalition of parties'. He did not agree to the demand and resigned his prospective candidacy. Little more was heard about the matter until a garden party a month later, at which a Diehard was introduced as the new candidate. The electorate rebelled at this, and voted Liberal in 1922; it was the only time between 1885 and 1970 that Worcester failed to elect a Conservative. If many other constituency parties had imposed the Worcester conditions, the

Conservatives would have had too little room to manoeuvre, and this would have magnified the importance of such splits as existed in the party in 1922.[7]

The local parties held a third power, which was more significant in 1922 than in any election since. This was the right to decide whether or not to contest the election. The Conservative central office acknowledged this power, but at the same time tried to prevent the local parties from nominating candidates against sitting Lloyd George Liberals in several places. For instance in Bedford the local Conservatives nominated Major Guy Paget against the Lloyd George Liberal M.P. Pressure from the central office led to Paget's withdrawal, but the local association refused to yield to this pressure, and nominated a new candidate, who won the seat.[8]

The central office usually worked through regional organisations. The Conservative leaders and central organisation had little direct power over the local parties. They could expel persistently rebellious groups, but almost never did so. However in a number of seats the party leadership exercised influence indirectly. Where there was only one organisation for a group of seats, such as a small county or a multimembered borough, the leaders sometimes persuaded this organisation to accept electoral pacts with the Lloyd Georgians, even when the Conservatives in one constituency in the group opposed such pacts.

This happened in Bristol, where the local Conservative organisation covered all five seats. The city had returned three Lloyd Georgians in 1918 and two Conservatives, and the local party executive decided to maintain this in 1922. A Diehard, W. Wilkins, who was not a member of the Conservative Party, but only of a Conservative drinking club, decided to oppose the Lloyd George Liberal in Bristol North. The central Bristol organisation refused their support, and Wilkins did not run. In Leicester East, a local schoolmaster intended to stand against a Lloyd George Liberal, but there too there was a central organisation for the city's three constituencies, and it persuaded him to withdraw. In Scotland the Conservative organisation prevented at least one constituency, Rutherglen, from nominating a candidate, and it even convinced some Diehards to abide by its rulings. Gideon Murray, though deposed in Glasgow, received an offer from some Dundee Conservatives who disliked Winston

Churchill. Murray declined, saying that he abided 'by the majority decision of the Scottish Conservatives'.[9]

Some M.P.s resented the influence of city or county organisations in their constituencies. Sir Arthur Steel-Maitland, a strong opponent of the Coalition, did not like his position, where the central Birmingham party controlled the agents. In 1923 he tried to get his own, 'under our direct control', perhaps because of his protracted dispute over the Coalition with the leading Birmingham Conservative, Austen Chamberlain. Similarly, in Portsmouth North Sir Bertram Falle maintained a personal Conservative organisation in direct conflict with the central Portsmouth party. In 1922, the latter did not support Falle in the election.[10]

Thus the local parties usually had the final voice in repudiation of sitting M.P.s, new nominations, and local electoral arrangements. Regional bodies occasionally controlled these things, but even then the M.P.s sometimes successfully supported decentralisation of authority. This was potentially dangerous to the Conservatives, as it put several significant powers in the hands of local groups which did not always act in harmony with their party's best interests. The example of Ilkeston showed how an unrepresentative group could frustrate the party's overall aims.

In Ilkeston, the Conservative association had been suspended during the war and had not been revived, as there was a Lloyd George Liberal M.P. There were several Conservative clubs in the towns of the constituency. One of them, at Heanor, decided in private to oppose the Liberal, who up to then had had the support of the Conservative central office, as well as that of the moribund local association. On the other hand, the Ripley Conservative Club continued to support the Lloyd Georgian during the campaign. One might question whether the views of a private group in one town represented the feelings of Ilkeston Conservatives, but their candidate ran, giving the seat to Labour, who barely edged out the Lloyd George Liberal. The Conservative trailed badly.[11]

Sir Malcolm Fraser, principal Conservative agent, and consequently well-informed on the situation, said that the local Conservative parties were disorganised in all the Coalition Liberal seats, not just in Ilkeston. The absence of organisation made it easier for dissident groups to nominate their own candidates against the Coalition Liberals, and to maintain that theirs were the official candidates.[12]

Some Conservative seats also had weak organisation, and this gave dissidents more influence than their numbers warranted. In Daventry the Conservatives had suspended their village associations during the war, and had not reorganised them because the Coalition Liberals objected to a party machine, as distinct from a Coalition one. Conservative opponents of the Coalition spread rumours of an impending independent Conservative candidate against the M.P., E. A. Fitzroy. There was no accurate way for Fitzroy to assess their strength, because of his constituency party's disorganisation, and although he favoured the Coalition, he gradually edged away from the Government, and then voted against it at the Carlton Club Meeting. Almost immediately afterwards, he called for continued active co-operation between the Liberals and Conservatives.[13]

Even where the constituency associations were relatively active, the members of their executives were not always representative of the membership, let alone of Conservative voters. In many places the local officers held their posts for decades. A few examples illustrate this : E. Bourne (treasurer, Evesham, 10 years), A. E. Lord (treasurer, Bewdley, 28 years), H. G. Ricardo (chairman, mid-Gloucestershire, 24 years), Sir George Dixon (chairman, Knutsford, 37 years) and J. Page (chairman, Kidderminster, 40 years). These long terms resulted from the desire of the local parties to have prominent local men on their executives; they were rarely, if at all, chosen for their views on the Coalition, and their views could easily have been different from those of the ordinary party members. Nevertheless these local officers had considerable power, and quarrels between the M.P.s and their constituency parties usually involved the executives rather than the general membership.[14]

The local executives were probably unrepresentative in another way, that is, in respect to their views on party policy. Most observers believe that the active members of Conservative associations are much more militant than either the M.P.s or voters. Moreover the memberships of local parties are and were often small. In a detailed study of Newcastle-under-Lyme politics, Bealey, Blondel and McCann said that in the 1920s, the local Conservative party had a nominal roll of between 1200 and

2000 members, 'but the members did not meet and did not even have a place to meet'. They also concluded that the active Conservatives in Newcastle were unrepresentative of their party at large. G. W. Jones, in a book on Wolverhampton, said that the only role of the Wolverhampton East Conservative party was to nominate a candidate, which it did 'with difficulty only close to elections'. In 1929 some members of this party even proposed disbanding, because the association never had more than 25–30 members. A. H. Birch, describing Glossop in the 1920s, spoke of 'the remoteness of the pre-war Conservative organisation from the mass of the people'. R. T. Mackenzie estimated that only 1–3 per cent of Conservative Party members could be called 'active', and Peter Paterson called the party 'a ramshackle edifice in which every possible interest is represented, all claiming the highest degree of autonomy, a system that works because, like the Victorian society in which it was designed, everyone knows his place'. Only about sixty people, wrote Paterson, choose each Conservative candidate.[15]

In a book on candidate selection after 1945, Austin Ranney showed that in almost every case where a Conservative association dismissed its M.P., the executive made the decision without consulting the members. The M.P.s sometimes forced the issue to be debated at general meetings, and in five places* the members upheld the M.P. against the executive. In two,† they upheld the executive, and in Bournemouth East, they were almost evenly divided, 3763 voting for the executive and 3671 for the M.P. An incident took place after the publication of Ranney's book which confirms the trends he noted. The Harrow East executive repudiated Commander Anthony Courtney, by 32 votes to 4, but the party members upheld him by 454 to 277.[16]

Most informed observers, then, have been sceptical about the theory that the local parties adequately represent the opinions of their membership. If this could be applied to the situation of 1922, one must question interpretations such as Bonar Law's which stressed the significance of pressure from the local associations. If these bodies were unrepresentative, it is

* Aberdeenshire East, Dorset South, Ipswich, Southall, and Woolwich West.
† Carlisle and Hampstead.

difficult to maintain that the National Union of Conservative Associations was representative either, since it consisted of selected individuals from the local executives.

In addition, while there may have been widespread Conservative dissatisfaction with the Coalition, it rarely took the form of public rebellions against sitting M.P.s. If there had been an extensive grassroots revolt, it would have had more frequent open manifestations, since the purpose of the revolt was to rouse public opinion against the Government. Yet barely a dozen of the more than 250 newspapers used in preparing this book contained accounts of attacks by rebel Conservative groups on their M.P.s Perhaps constituency militants exerted pressure in private, but the scarcity of public attacks indicates that they were unwilling to go very far against the M.P.s and leaders, if the M.P.s and leaders stood together.

The constituency rebellions which did appear cast further doubt on the representative nature of the movement. Most local revolts which were reported were unimpressive. That in Huntingdonshire consisted of a meeting in the grounds of the White Hart, a public house, attended by two police, several children, and a handful of drinkers, the total coming to twenty-five. The Imperial Conservative Association spearheading the revolt in Plymouth, had sixteen members. A Diehard meeting in Hexham, held in the middle of town on market day, had two speakers from Lord Salisbury's Conservative and Unionist Movement, and a small handful of listeners. Rebel Conservatives in Swindon held 'a poorly attended meeting'. The other reported constituency revolts were similarly insubstantial.[17]

But although there was little evidence of a major public revolt in the Conservative Party in late 1922, there was even less evidence of a spontaneous surge of opinion towards retaining ties with Lloyd George. The Diehards existed, even though their popular support was limited. On the other hand Conservative M.P.s rarely saw Coalition Liberal groups. Apart from some phantom associations in London, hardly any Conservative seats had organised Coalition Liberal parties, and those which did exist rarely held non-political meetings with the Conservatives. The *Lloyd George Liberal Magazine* recorded practically every Coalition Liberal activity in Britain between 1920 and 1923, but it listed only seven social gatherings where the Lloyd Georgians

appeared with Conservative M.P.s. This had happened in the
days of the Conservative alliance with the Liberal Unionists too.
J. A. Bridges, at one time Austen Chamberlain's constituency
manager, said of the Liberal Unionists that[18]

> Our ways were not their ways. Smoking concerts, for instance,
> which we found so serviceable, were, I feel sure, an abomina-
> tion to the Liberal Unionists. I have seen a few of them there,
> but if not always like skeletons at a feast, they never seemed
> comfortable. They gave the idea of condescending to what
> they considered a regrettable waste of their valuable time. We,
> on the other hand, thought their political tea parties, attended
> by people we did not know, and perhaps had never heard of,
> jejune affairs.

It had taken the Liberal Unionists and Conservatives twenty-
six years to fuse their parties. The same situation faced the
Coalition Liberals after 1918 : it was difficult to co-operate at
election time with their old rivals, and they neglected social
co-operation, which was almost as important. J. R. P. Newman,
who voted against the Coalition at the Carlton Club Meeting,
complained of this. He had often wondered, he said, why no
Coalition Liberal had volunteered to throw in his lot with the
Conservatives so long as the Coalition continued. He and other
Conservative M.P.s were faced with a situation where they saw
few Coalition Liberals, and presumed the premier's party to be
weak in their constituencies, but where they saw and heard the
Diehards. The Diehards may have been few in number, but they
were invariably noisier than the Coalition Liberals, or than
moderate Conservative Coalitionists.[19]

One strong point of the anti-Coalition Conservatives was the
National Union, a body of about 3000 delegates from the
constituency parties which supposedly represented Conservative
opinion in the country. More likely it represented the views of
the staunchest party militants: a few years later Sir Samuel
Hoare, a leading Conservative opponent of the Coalition in
1922, wrote to a colleague about the National Union. He said
that 'the delegates who attend are, of course, the keen partisans'.
He realised that they were not necessarily typical Conservatives;
but the National Union had some standing, because of the active
role most delegates played in elections.[20]

The National Union was expected to repudiate the Coalition at its November 1922 meeting, but this expectation was based on the known opinions of the Union's executive members. Diehards M.P.s and their close associates comprised fourteen of the forty-four active members of the executive. Attendance at executive meetings was never complete, and at the most important meeting of 1922, held on 18 October, thirteen of the fourteen Diehard M.P.s and sympathisers were present. Convinced Coalitionists were fewer on the executive, and they attended less regularly, so the Diehards influenced this group disproportionately, simply because they were more persistent than the Coalitionists.*

This chapter has shown that the local parties had substantial electoral power, and considerable influence over their M.P.s. These powers were naturally greatest at election time, and from the beginning of 1922 there was a constant atmosphere of electioneering which emphasised the role of the constituency associations. Nevertheless a handful of miscellaneous constituency troubles need not have brought down the Government. Most people expected the National Union to vote against the Coalition, but even if it did, the National Union was not running the country nor was it responsible to the electorate. It would have been a serious blow to the Conservative leaders if the Union had voted against them on a major issue, but it need not have been fatal. The M.P.s were both constitutionally, and really, responsible for party alignments, and the party leaders rightly left it to the M.P.s to determine the future.

* This paragraph is based on the attendance lists of the executive which were published monthly in *Gleanings and Memoranda*. There were more members than forty-four on the executive, but as they did not attend any meetings, they did not appear on the lists.

4

The Conservative M.P.s and the Coalition

The Coalition fell after an adverse vote by the Conservative M.P.s, and an account of the 1922 crisis must consider why they voted as they did. Another question to consider is whether the M.P.s were divided over the principle of coalition, or whether they rebelled for a variety of passing reasons, none of which conflicted with the basic intent of the leaders to combine Liberal and Conservative forces. This chapter shows that there was one fissure in the parliamentary party, but that only one M.P. in ten rejected the Government completely. The rest mostly voted against the Government at the Carlton Club Meeting because they opposed one or two aspects of government policy or party leadership, not because they repudiated coalitions in general. An analysis in this chapter of the individual M.P.s shows that the division between moderates and Diehards was greater than that between the pro- and anti-coalitionists. This suggests that, although most M.P.s were discontented with the Government in late 1922, more efficient leadership by Chamberlain could have preserved it.

Several long-term factors favoured the Conservatives after the war : they at least provided a clear alternative to Labour, which the Liberals did not. Nevertheless long-term factors are not always decisive if a party makes many short-term blunders, as the Conservatives had done between 1909 and 1911. In 1922 they might have fumbled again, if they had reacted blindly to Lloyd George, or if they had rejected a major reform. Moreover their trap would be deeper than before the war, as there were many working-class voters in 1922, and because the Irish issue was no longer available to trump social legislation.

In 1922 most Conservative M.P.s feared to break completely with Lloyd George, since they regarded their Liberal alliance as essential if they were to remain the governing party. Few of them liked Lloyd George's brand of Liberalism, but they would have been more enthusiastic had the Coalition Liberals been subordinate allies, rather than dominant ones, as they seemed to be under Lloyd George. While the disappearance of the Liberals may have been on the cards, that was not how it appeared to most politicians of the time. A number of them, including Lloyd George himself, talked of the imminent decline of the Liberals, but it was risky to eliminate the Liberal Party from serious political calculations, and few anticipated the very rapid decline of both the Liberals and Lloyd George. Consequently even Conservative opponents of Lloyd George generally regarded their alliance with him as useful, though perhaps regrettable. Despite this, they broke it.

They faced a difficult choice. By forcing out Lloyd George and his faction, the Conservative M.P.s risked a quick election defeat by a Liberal-Labour combination; by continuing the Coalition, they risked losing office anyway, because of the unpopularity of government measures. Or they could draw away from the Coalition, supporting it independently, trying to in- fluence an essentially non-party government in which their leaders however held office. To some extent this actually hap- pened under Lloyd George, for instance in debates over alien pilots (1919), India (1920) and teachers' pensions (1922). In each case, numerous Conservative M.P.s voted against the Government, and in two of the three, the Government lost. But these divisions, though possibly guides to the future, were isolated incidents, and what most dissident Conservatives envisaged was a larger degree of independence than they had had between 1919 and 1922.

This would have been a major shift in the parliamentary system, and it would have undermined the principle of cabinet and party solidarity more than the 'agreement to differ' was to do in 1932: the 1932 agreement was restricted to one issue, free trade, and the Samuelites were far less important in 1932 than the Conservatives had been a decade before. Increased freedom of action for the Conservative backbenchers would also have undermined cabinet responsibility, as the Government would not necessarily have to resign because of a defeat on one measure, but only when it lost the confidence of the M.P.s generally. The question arose of what could be considered a 'real' defeat. In July 1921, when the Government lost a vote over the taxation of co-operatives, Austen Chamberlain, the house leader, decided that it was not a 'real' defeat, and did not even adjourn the commons for one day, as was customary. In the teachers' pensions debate of 1922, the Government lost when one of its own whips, T. A. Lewis, voted with the Opposition; but he kept his post and the Government did not fall.[1]

At the time of the Carlton Club Meeting, many Conservative rebels hoped for loose whipping along the lines described. Two days before the meeting, Samuel Samuel, M.P. for Putney and a strong critic of Lloyd George, predicted further coalitions along the lines of French governments, with the Conservatives being the predominant group. Bonar Law's victory made such group government unnecessary, but in late 1921 it seemed improbable that Bonar Law would lead a rebellion against his own successor, or that such a rebellion would succeed even if he did lead it. It seemed more likely that Conservative-Liberal relations would remain undefined, as they had done for the previous three years; but several influences worked against this state of moderately comfortable indecision. One was the activity of anti-coalition groups inside the Conservative caucus; another was the divisive role of Austen Chamberlain.[2]

In March 1922 Sir William Sutherland, one of Lloyd George's closest advisers, said that there were three types of Conservative M.P.: the Diehards, a 'purely blood and iron group' opposed to coalition policies and out to get Lloyd George; the 'old Tory group', which approved government policies but preferred a Conservative régime; and a third group representing industrial seats, which supported the Coalition. But not all Conservative supporters of the Coalition stood for business interests, nor were the others all country squires, which was in effect how Sutherland labelled them. This can be seen by examining the vote at the Carlton Club Meeting. The Conservative M.P.s, and their attitudes at the meeting, are listed in Appendix I. Altogether 273 Conservative M.P.s voted at it, and 102 more were eligible.* Division lists on parliamentary votes are less useful guides to the M.P.s' attitudes, since the divisions generally concerned specific policies, rather than the general principle of coalition government.[3]

The Diehards were those signing one or both of the published Diehard manifestos of mid-1922, or those who stated publicly that they were Diehards. Most of them voted against the Government frequently between 1919 and 1922, and they were particularly committed to opposing Irish Home Rule. Distinctions between various groups of non-Diehards were less clear than Sutherland indicated. Some Coalitionists were long-time M.P.s sitting for safe seats and holding comparatively unadvanced views; some progressive anti-Coalitionists sat for industrial seats. There were some differences in the occupations of the M.P.s, as Table 2 shows. The M.P.s backing the Coalition were more likely to be businessmen than were the Diehards, while the Diehards were more likely to be landowners than were the other anti-Coalitionists. These were trends rather than clear-cut divisions, and one must beware of making too much of this because there were many exceptions; in addition a few M.P.s had no apparent occupation, as listed in *Who's Who* and similar references. Such M.P.s have been excluded from the table. But despite this necessary imprecision, it is evident that the Coalitionists by and large represented the business groups which

Table 2   Occupations of Conservative M.P.s, 1922

Occupational group	Diehards	Non-Diehard opponents of Coalition	Supporters of Coalition
Govt service, military, landowners, peers etc.	61.9%	37.8%	20.9%
Professional men	26.2	26.2	32.6
Businessmen	11.9	35.5	43.0

* There were also five Conservative M.P.s ineligible to vote at the meeting: Lord Robert Cecil, Reginald Clarry, J. M. M. Erskine, T. A. Polson and M. F. Sueter.

were coming to play an increasing role in their party, while the moderate anti-Coalitionists, and still more the Diehards, stood for important, but declining interests.

During the Parliament of 1919–22 the Diehards were the only clear Conservative faction. Most of them were nonentities, their parliamentary organisation never amounted to much and they rarely won the support of many other Conservative M.P.s on motions of non-confidence in the Coalition. Diehard organisation in the constituencies was divided, and in most cases very weak. Yet these same Diehards exercised considerable influence, because they rebelled openly and got away with it. Their relationship with the other Conservative M.P.s resembled that of the Asquithians in relation to the numerically far stronger Coalition Liberals. Both small groups, the Diehards and the Asquithians, could take frequent stands based on party principle, and then ridicule the Coalitionists of their own party who outnumbered them, but who were held back by loyalty to their leaders or by the realisation that there had to be occasional compromises if there was to be any government.

Chamberlain had few ways of disciplining the Diehards: most sat for safe seats and were thus almost invulnerable to threats of withholding speakers and organisers. Very few were likely to gain advancement in office because of personal drawbacks, so Chamberlain could not use patronage to divide them. Thus the Diehards spoke freely and voted against the Government time after time; the Coalition Liberals rebelled too, though not so often as the Diehards, especially in the last year of the Coalition. Moderate Conservative M.P.s understandably sought looser discipline, but there was a difference in their attitude towards the Coalition Liberals and to the Diehards. They knew that there were few organised coalition groups in Conservative constituencies which would offset local Diehards, however small the Diehard groups were. Most coalition groups were active only in seats held by Lloyd George Liberals, and this was one reason why so many Conservative M.P.s made overtures to the Diehards without actually joining them. Austen Chamberlain stood in the same relation to his parliamentary followers as the moderate M.P.s did to their constituency associations. Chamberlain needed another organised faction of M.P.s which supported the Coalition strongly, to counter Diehard influence: if one had

existed, he could have acted as arbiter between it and the Diehards, so seeming to be above factions. But although many
Conservative M.P.s backed the Coalition, few were willing to
risk an intraparty fight for it. Consequently Chamberlain had to
lead the fight himself, and he appeared to be splitting the party
when he did so.

Who were the Diehards, and what did they stand for, if
anything? How extensive was their influence in the constituencies,
and could the other M.P.s have resisted it if they had tried?
Table 2 indicates that the Diehards were predominantly landowners and those engaged in the official services, with three-fifths
of all Diehard M.P.s falling into those categories. The Diehards
also had more political experience than average. Excluding those
elected in by-elections after 1918, 25 of the remaining 33 had
sat in Parliament before 1918 and 4 of the other 8 had contested
at least 2 elections before 1918. Thus only 13 per cent (4 M.P.s)
were new to politics. In contrast, 43 per cent of all M.P.s elected
in 1918 were entirely new to Parliament, and many of the new
men had never been candidates before. Thus the Diehards had
more experience, and perhaps longer political memories, than
the typical Conservative M.P. There was also a much higher
proportion of Irishmen in the Diehard group than in the rest
of the parliamentary Conservative Party. At least 21 of the 42
Diehard M.P.s were Irishmen or had close Irish connections,
such as Irish parents. The main Diehard grievance against the
Coalition was that it had granted Home Rule to the 26 counties,
and the Irish background of so many Diehards was probably
the determining factor in their revolt. But while other Conservatives sympathised with their Irish colleagues, it is unlikely that
they felt as strongly about Ireland as did the Diehards.[4]

Though the Diehards had above-average parliamentary experience, only one of the forty-two had ever held a ministerial
post : A. C. Morrison-Bell had been a parliamentary secretary.
Even after the Carlton Club Meeting, Bonar Law took only four
Diehard M.P.s into his Government, all of them in minor offices.*
This was no accident, for most Diehards were too extreme to be
acceptable as members of governments, though a few of them
had considerable talents. Vice-Admiral Sir Reginald Hall had a

* Lord Salisbury, the leading Diehard peer, was also in Bonar Law's
Government, as lord president of the council.

clear and original mind which had served him well as director
of naval intelligence during the war. Sir Henry Wilson had
schemed his way to the top in the wartime military-political
infighting, and two other Diehards, Sir Charles Oman and Sir
John Marriott, were well-known historians. However only one
Diehard made much impact in Parliament, Sir Henry Wilson,
and he was an M.P. for just over three months before his
assassination in June 1922. The rest were inconspicuous, or
Parliamentary curiosities such as Sir Frederick Banbury, whom
Birkenhead described as a 'converse Cassandra' because his
prophecies of doom were always wrong. Another was Martin
Archer-Shee, who informed the commons in 1921 that the
cavalryman 'is as a rule drawn from a more intelligent class,
perhaps, than the infantryman'. This provoked an immediate
reaction from other Conservative M.P.s who had been in the
infantry. Sir Henry Page Croft, another Diehard, demanded in
1921 that the Coalition expel the 'hordes of Bolsheviks' who were
flooding into Britain. This 'absolute riff-raff of the world' was
making the country unsafe. The largest group to which he
referred was American. Sir Archibald Salvidge, the leading Liverpool Conservative, described the Liverpool Diehard Sir Reginald
'Blinker' Hall as

> a perfect enigma. He seems to live in a world of his own,
> entirely peopled by spies. Everyone who is not a Tory is either
> a German, a Sinn Feiner, or a Bolshevist. Mention any
> politician of the left, and 'Blinker' nods and blinks mysteriously,
> and utters, 'Wait a bit sir, I'm watching him. I'll have his
> hide.'

In Diehard eyes, Britain could get 'vast wealth' from Germany,
and even if it turned out not to be vast, at least they could get
'every penny which it is possible to get'. The Diehards, if given
'fifty thousand additional men and a free hand' could eliminate
the 'murder junta' from Southern Ireland in a few months.
Many Diehards apparently believed that Lloyd George and his
cabinet spent their time entertaining murderers. A North Dorset
Diehard revealed that 'Lloyd George was actually shaking hands
and dining with the very man who entered the cellar in Russia
and shot the Czar and Czarevitch with his own hands'.

Table 3   Diehard voting, 1919–22

Date	Number	Subject	Diehard votes Against Govt	For Govt
1919				
Mar. 24	16	Ireland [local government]	2	9
May 23	33	Protection of dogs	9	8
May 27	37	Ireland [local government]	8	4
Aug. 5	84	Ministers and Secretaries Bill	7	9
*Oct. 23	113	Alien pilots	20	3
Oct. 28	116	War emergency laws	3	14
1920				
Mar. 31	77	Government of Ireland	16	10
Jul. 6	188	Automobile tax	9	7
*Jul. 8	196	Punjab disturbances [Dyer]	23	3
Jul. 12	202	Excess profits tax	16	7
Nov. 3	349	Agriculture Bill	10	2
*Nov. 9	356	Ministry of health	15	2
*Nov. 9	357	Ministry of health	18	0
Dec. 8	391	Ministry of health	10	4
Dec. 9	398	Limit on national expenditure	15	14
1921				
Apr. 20	81	Disbandment of cavalry regiments	8	3
Apr. 21	83	Civil service estimates	7	5
Jul. 6	227	Railways	7	3
Aug. 9	335	Railways	8	10
Aug. 15	350	Auditor-general's salary	8	4
*Oct. 31	361	Ireland	32	3
*Nov. 3	367	Criminal investigation	24	0
1922				
*Mar. 22	54	Army estimates	19	1
*Mar. 23	59	Ireland	28	1
*Apr. 5	78	Coalition government	29	1
*Jun. 13	137	Cabinet secretariat	18	2
Jun. 21	167	Excess profits tax	10	7
*Jun. 26	176	Ireland; death of Sir H. Wilson	37	2
Jun. 28	184	Law practices	9	2
Jul. 13	224	Legal fees in income tax cases	8	12
*Aug. 1	270	Irish Constabulary	20	1

* Divisions marked * represent significant Diehard cohesion against the Government.

Table 3 shows that the only significant Diehard rebellion during 1919 came on the alien pilots question, when a majority of other Conservative M.P.s also rebelled. In 1920 there were two significant divisions (356 and 357 were the same issue). These concerned the Punjab disturbances and the ministry of health. Again most Conservatives voted against the Government on these issues, so the two divisions did not set the Diehards apart.

Diehard views developed little during 1919, 1920 and 1921. Even some issue which became prominent later had clear roots in an earlier period. For instance the 'honours scandal' of July 1922 had been foreshadowed by several debates prompted by Diehards, during Asquith's régime, and again in the first months of Lloyd George's premiership. In the 1918 election Sir Henry Page Croft's 'National Party' had campaigned against the sale of honours, and in 1922 the issue was hardly new to Croft or to other Diehards. However it took a catalyst to spark latent discontent over honours and other issues into a full-fledged rebellion. The catalyst was the Irish Treaty of December 1921.[9]

On 31 October 1921, thirty-two Diehards supported a motion of non-confidence in the Government's handling of Ireland. Virtually all other Conservative M.P.s supported the Government on the issue, which marked the real beginning of the Diehard revolt. In the next nine months, the Diehards showed increasing cohesion, and directed their attacks more often against the Government than they had done in the preceding three years. Five of the eight main Diehard divisions concerned Ireland,* and two more were general attacks on the Coalition. This shows the Diehard involvement with Ireland; and the fact that few non-Diehards joined them in these divisions demonstrates how cut off they were from their party.

Although they may have had grievances, few Conservative M.P.s wanted to join an extreme group, and during the 1922 election they generally avoided taking strong partisan positions. In contrast the Diehards tried to keep party bitterness alive. The Conservative voters did not appear to approve of organised dissidence in either. There were fourteen contests between official and independent Conservatives: in three of them (Dover, Isle of Wight and Richmond), the conflicts concerned personal rather

* 1921 (361 and 367); 1922 (59, 176, 270).

than political issues.[10] In the remaining eleven seats, the 'defending' Conservatives (that is, sitting M.P.s, and where there was
no sitting M.P., the official candidate) in almost every case won
a large majority of the Conservative votes. The figures were:

'Defending' Conservatives	186,945	76.1%
'Attacking' Conservatives	58,680	23.9%

All eleven constituencies were safely Conservative, and party
splits were unlikely to cause defeat. Conservative unity could
have been expected in marginal seats, but these figures show that
the splits were limited in safe seats too. The 'defending' Conservatives were either strong Coalitionists or Diehards, but the
Conservative voters backed them, apparently regardless of their
attitude to the Coalition, and only a small minority supported
the attacking forces.

The importance of the Diehards, and of similar groups such as
the Anti-waste League, was exaggerated by their concentration
in London. Diehards held over half the seats in the residential
area of western London where most M.P.s lived during sessions
of Parliament. In the area bounded by Hampstead, Chelsea, and
the City of London, there were eleven Conservative seats, six
of them held by Diehards. Conservative M.P.s representing
distant constituencies, and who lived in this, the Diehards'
greatest stronghold, may have overestimated Diehard strength
because of this. On the other hand the Lloyd George Liberal
organisation was active in many parts of the country, but not in
western London. The Conservative M.P.s might have discounted
the Lloyd Georgians less if they had seen the active local parties
in eastern Lancashire and elsewhere, but according to Sir
Malcolm Fraser, 'knowledge and experience are largely directed
by the area in which they have existence. South Kensington in
its isolation is not greatly affrighted by the Socialism of Poplar'.[11]

Four-fifths of the ani-Coalition vote at the Carlton Club
Meeting came from non-Diehards, and it is essential to determine
why so many moderates rebelled, when they had supported the
Government for several years. There are various approaches to
analysing the rebellion of 19 October 1922. One can examine
the social and economic background of the M.P.s who voted for
and against the Coalition, to see whether there was a connecting

factor. In the case of many Diehards, Irish affiliations were such a factor. One can also examine the policies of the non-Diehards, to see whether specific policies or issues alienated the M.P.s. Finally, one can examine electoral considerations such as the previous voting history of the seats held by the individual M.P.s.

According to Sir William Sutherland's analysis mentioned earlier in this chapter, social differences were important; but Table 2 shows that such differences were tendencies, not clear-cut distinctions. Many businessmen voted against the Coalition, and many landowners supported it, though the general trends were the other way. Religious affiliations do not appear to have been decisive either. It is difficult to determine the religion of most of the M.P.s, but at least eight nonconformist Conservatives voted at the Carlton Club Meeting. One would have expected them to back the Coalition strongly, to retain ties with the majority of nonconformists in the Liberal Party. In fact they supported the Coalition by only 5 votes to 3, which shows that nonconformity, at any rate, was not much of a guide to the cleavage of October 1922. Much the same applied to the former Liberal Unionists, 12 of whom voted at the meeting, 7 for and 5 against the Coalition. The ties of these M.P.s to the Chamberlains, and their previous experience with at least a form of Liberalism did not seem to count for much.

While social background may have influenced some M.P.s, then, it did not apparently provide a key to the behaviour of the majority. Was their opposition perhaps directed against particular government policies? Again this may have been so with a few M.P.s, but not with all. The crisis of 1922 was unusually open, and even though some M.P.s may have played down their personal dislike of Lloyd George, their speeches generally indicated what they regarded as the key issues. Historians are generally limited to the relatively small group of M.P.s who write memoirs or leave manuscripts, but the public nature of this crisis makes it possible to reconstruct a representative sample of Conservative M.P.s to determine what their opinions were.

Many writers on the 1922 crisis have stressed the importance of disputes over one policy or another; but an examination of a large number of speeches shows that it is unhelpful to isolate any single failure of policy and to label it as the reef which sank the Coalition. In this examination we shall consider the views

expressed by 38 Conservative non-Diehard opponents of the
Coalition, exactly one-quarter of the total. Many gave more
than one reason for their break, but these reasons all fell into one
of three categories : specific government policies (mentioned by
8 as major and by 8 as minor reasons),* opposition to Coalitions
or to Liberals (7 major and 1 minor) and problems of party
leadership (27 major and 1 minor). That is, most of them rebelled
because of personal antipathy to Austen Chamberlain and Lloyd
George rather than because of government policies. Moreover

*Table 4   Reasons given by Conservative M.P.s for ending the
Coalition*

Issue†	MPs saying issue was major reason for their break	MPs saying issue was minor	Total MPs referring to issue
Category I Party leadership			
Lloyd George/desire for			
Conservative P.M.	16	—	16
Conservative unity	10	1	11
Chamberlain's poor leadership	6	—	6
Total in Category	**27**	**1**	**28**
Category II Specific policies			
Turkey	3	4	7
Agriculture	3	2	5
Extravagance	—	5	5
Ireland	2	1	3
Kaiser not hung	—	2	2
Beer taxes	—	2	2
Indian reforms	—	2	2
Honours scandal	—	—	nil
Housing and social reform	—	—	nil
Russia	—	—	nil
Total in Category	**8**	**8**	**16**
Category III Other reasons			
Against coalitions in general	6	—	6
Against Liberals	1	1	2
Coalition not close enough	1	—	1
Total in Category	**7**	**1**	**8**

* Duplications within categories have been eliminated from these figures;
however several M.P.s mentioned reasons falling into two or three categories.

† Several M.P.s mentioned more than one issue in a given category, and
these duplications have been eliminated in the category totals.

many of those who did mention specific policies really broke because quarrels over the policies revealed the gulf between themselves and their leaders. It is interesting to note that the policies mentioned were dispersed, and that no M.P. in the sample mentioned the honours scandal or Russia, and that only 6 said they opposed coalitions in general.[12]

The division lists of the 1919–22 Parliament confirm that there was no major divergence over policies between non-Diehards who voted for or against the Coalition on 19 October. A good example of this was the alien pilots division of 1919, which was the first major Conservative rebellion. Some 43 M.P.s voted who backed the Coalition in 1922. They divided 27 against, and 16 for the Government. The non-Diehard anti-Coalitionists voted 43 to 26 against the Government. That is to say, each group voted in a ratio of 5 to 3 against the Government. The Diehards, on the other hand, split 20 to 3 against the Government. This was typical of the other major divisions during the period.

Yet another way of showing that issues such as free trade were not decisive at the Carlton Club Meeting is to see how the Conservative free traders voted. If any group had close ties to the Liberals over a major political issue, it was this group; yet they voted 8 to 4 against the Coalition. This analysis does not mean that the M.P.s were uninterested in political issues, only that they were unwilling to smash the keystone of post-war political alignments because of disagreements over one or two policies.

The emphasis most of the M.P.s laid on the failures of party leadership indicates that they were unlikely to trust Lloyd George with supreme power once he gave it up, even if he retired for a short while to rejuvenate himself. Several political leaders advised him to do so in 1922, and he contemplated following their advice. Another conclusion is that the Conservatives were not deeply divided over questions of policy, and this in turn indicates that they would accept many things if their party had the appearance of power. In a predominantly Conservative government, Lloyd George might have held an important but subordinate post, as Joseph Chamberlain had done before 1906, or as Winston Churchill was to do in 1924. In 1922 Churchill was if anything even less popular in Conservative circles than Lloyd George. This came out in a conversation between Sir Archibald Salvidge and

Sir Alexander Leith, the Conservative leaders in Liverpool and the north-east respectively. Salvidge recounted that[13]

> I happened to be sitting on a couch chatting with Winston. Shortly afterwards Leith came to me and putting his hand upon my shoulder said—'Salvidge, you did very well at [the 1921 party conference in] Liverpool, don't spoil it'. I thought his manner patronising not to say offensive. I asked him what he meant and he replied, 'Oh, it's all right. I saw you talking to that fellow'. I said 'What fellow?' and he answered 'Churchill'.

Other Conservatives regarded Churchill as Leith did. He admitted himself that even as a young man, the orthodox had regarded him as a vulgar seeker after publicity; this general mistrust had changed to hatred when in 1904 he had switched parties. His dispatch of warships toward Northern Ireland during the Curragh affair of 1914, and his later involvement in the Dardanelles expedition had added to this unpopularity; yet within two years after the fall of the Coalition, Churchill had re-ratted—no mean feat in itself—and had become the second man in Baldwin's Conservative Government. Lloyd George's eclipse was complete because his old rivals thought he would take no place but the first. In 1916 Asquith had refused to serve under anyone else, but there was a difference in that Lloyd George still had much to offer after 1922, while Asquith had been a spent force even before he had lost office.[14]

This examination has so far indicated that the divergence between non-Diehard Conservatives was not primarily over policies, or the result of different social backgrounds, though both had an influence. Electoral considerations were more important. No fewer than 61 of the 86 Conservative M.P.s voting to retain the Coalition sat for constituencies which had been Liberal or Liberal Unionist in one or both of the 1910 elections. The only area of pre-war Liberal strength where the Conservatives re- pudiated the Coalition was the West Yorkshire textile district, where four M.P.s voted against, and one for the Coalition. Even in West Yorkshire, though, the decision to abandon the Coalition was made by only 'a small majority' at the July meeting of the Yorkshire Conservatives. Few Coalitionists came from London, and all but two of those who did sat for constituencies in the outer suburbs. The two exceptional M.P.s represented Mile End and Rotherhithe, which had both voted Liberal in the last pre-war election. This close connection between the past voting record of the constituencies and the result of the Carlton Club Meeting suggests that the basis of strong Coalition support was expediency, and that where the M.P.s knew there were many Liberals, they hesitated to repudiate the Coalition. The exceptional seats, where Conservatives sat for traditional Conservative areas and still voted for the Coalition included two where the M.P. was a former Liberal, three where he was in Lloyd George's Government, and another where the M.P. was Birkenhead's brother.[15]

Altogether 273 Conservative M.P.s voted at the Carlton Club Meeting, of whom 35 were Diehards.* A further 67 had close personal ties to the Government based on the former allegiance of their constituencies, jobs or other factors. Only 20 of the remaining 172 non-Diehards voted with Chamberlain, or less than an eighth. This shows that Chamberlain had managed to alienate nearly all the backbenchers who had no special reason to stick up for the Liberals.

The backbenchers might even have tolerated Lloyd George, if Chamberlain had seemed to influence him as Bonar Law had done. However they reacted to Chamberlain as the French M.P.s reacted to Aristide Briand : they had deposed Briand because he had seemed to be too much in Lloyd George's pocket. In Britain Chamberlain's insubstantial character made the Conservatives look elsewhere for a defence of their party's interests. The moderate M.P.s who toppled the Coalition wanted to continue their alliance, but did not want to be tools of Lloyd George or any other Liberal. The government defeat in April 1922 over teachers' pensions brought home to the M.P.s just how weak Chamberlain was. He could not even tell the difference between a purely technical defeat and a serious one, nor did he have the stamina to ignore it. Instead he waited until Lloyd George telegraphed him instructions from Genoa. This showed once more that Chamberlain was Lloyd George's lackey; but in

---

* All reckonings in this book of the vote at the Carlton Club Meeting are based on Austen Chamberlain's list. There were several differences between his list and J. C. C. Davidson's (cf. Appendix 1), and it has not been possible using contemporary sources to resolve all these differences.

fact he was not a lackey. Austen Chamberlain was the worst possible leader in 1922, one who sometimes led, and sometimes did not. A purely nominal leader would have given more responsibility to Lloyd George, and this would have forced Lloyd George to spend more time mending his political fences. A strong leader might have headed off rebellion. Chamberlain did neither : sometimes, as at the November 1921 party conference, and in the January 1922 election scare, he took strong decisive action. At other times, as in April 1922, he seemed at a loss. By October 1922 nobody could be sure whether he would stand up for his party, or betray it. More than anything else, then, Austen Chamberlain's fluctuating attitude to affairs in the last year of his leadership decided the outcome of the Carlton Club Meeting.[16]

5

The Ebb of Coalition

The Coalition did not falter because of one blow, but languished over a year and a half. Although it faced periodic troubles in its ranks from 1918 onwards, these crises were unimportant until the election scare of January 1922. From January to October, the atmosphere of constant political intrigue widened rifts between the Conservative leaders and their organisation, and this eventually toppled Lloyd George. In late 1921 and 1922 his ministry suffered setbacks which could have happened under any regime whether or not it was a coalition, but which took on added seriousness because the Conservative leaders did not communicate effectively with their followers, and thus allowed mutual trust to evaporate. Lloyd George had a strong personal following, but his party organisation was often sketchy, and this made him dependent on the Conservative machine in many constituencies. Even so, this organisational drawback counted seriously only because the Conservative leadership proved weak. There were few basic policy conflicts between the Conservatives and Coalition Liberals at this time : free trade was contentious, but most Coalition Liberals accepted limited tariffs disguised as 'safeguarding'. A notable division on 31 July 1922 concerned duties on imported fabric gloves. The Coalition Liberals supported this tariff by 45 to 27, and even the Conservatives were divided on this question and on others. The two wings of the Coalition acted together, and although the Conservatives wanted more offices, this desire could have been settled without breaking up the Coalition.

Thus as 1921 opened, there were few clouds on the Coalition horizon. Lloyd George's prestige remained high, except with

Liberal and Labour men who repudiated his brutality in Ireland; but many of them were beginning to realise that his German and Russian policies were less reactionary than they had previously supposed. Then during 1921 and 1922 diverse strands of the Coalition programme snapped, with consequent loss of prestige for the premier. Even this need not have caused a final break if the Conservative leadership had remained in the firm grip of Bonar Law; instead it passed into the nervous and fumbling hands of Austen Chamberlain.

Beatrice Webb described Chamberlain as 'morally as well as intellectually unaware, and equally unaware of the subtler nuances of truth and of untruth'. She was often a harsh critic, and L. S. Amery, for one, regarded his longtime colleague as 'almost morbidly sensitive to the suggestion that he might be failing in personal loyalty'. But one need not be disloyal to communicate effectively, and many times during his leadership, Chamberlain did not outline his ideas clearly to his followers. He admitted this, evidently not realising the gravity of the admission, in several letters preserved in his private papers. His position was not always easy to understand, but he faced a possible conflict of loyalties in 1922, and he served both Lloyd George and his party badly by failing to interpret their position to each other. In addition to this failing, Chamberlain showed little ability to handle men, and tended to dismiss genuinely discontented Conservatives as frustrated cliques; nor did he organise his own supporters. Instead he allowed them, and indirectly himself, to be humiliated at several party meetings in early 1922, at each of which he probably could have had his way.[1]

Chamberlain was not Lloyd George's toady. He had definite ideas about the future of the Coalition, and hoped to become prime minister after an election which the Conservatives would win by riding on Lloyd George's coat-tails. He had rationalised this in his own mind as a form of loyalty to Lloyd George, but he did not explain this to the M.P.s, who thought he intended to keep Lloyd George on as premier. During 1922 Chamberlain changed his views on this topic several times, or at least he appeared to change them. In reaction many Conservative M.P.s drifted away from him gradually, and Lloyd George could not push his own plans, since he depended on the Conservative leader, indecisive though he was.

There were four major crises in the history of the Coalition, only one of which concerned a government policy. The other three were different acts of the same crisis, as all dealt with the mechanics of representation within the Coalition. There was far less opposition to the idea of coalition than to the confused and varying plans for its maintenance. The year 1922 was one of electioneering, cabinet splits and indecision. The bickering received wide publicity, and even those Conservative M.P.s who hoped to maintain an alliance with the Coalition Liberals observed their leaders' uncertainty about the future. Much of this uncertainty came from Chamberlain's attempt to please both Lloyd George and the Conservative activists at the same time, without getting either to make real concessions. Another problem, which was not wholly his fault, was the public discussion of the nature of the Coalition by Conservative organisers at the highest level. Many troubles could have been avoided if this dissension had been kept quiet; but when Sir George Younger pledged the Conservative organisation against an early election in January 1922, Chamberlain found it difficult to repudiate him, especially as he had prompted Younger's actions himself.

Latent discontent in the Coalition in early 1921 had no real focus, though Horatio Bottomley led a handful of disgruntled M.P.s, among them Colonel Claude Lowther, Conservative M.P. for Lonsdale, and Sir Cecil Beck, Coalition Liberal M.P. for Saffron Walden. But despite Bottomley's public appeal (before his conviction for fraud in 1922), he had little influence in the commons. In January 1921 Lord Rothermere founded his Anti-waste League, but its parliamentary influence was also limited. In general the Coalition remained strong, and many important Tory groups praised it at their annual meetings. For instance at the quarterly meeting of the Lancashire Conservatives, Lord Derby, one of the most powerful figures in the party, said 'they would make a mistake if they tried to resume normal party government'. Derby later told Sir Philip Sassoon, Conservative M.P. for Hythe, that 'Lloyd George is very popular', and he told Bonar Law that 'I do not think you need have any fear of there being any break in the Coalition in Lancashire'. The only internal problem concerned Sir George Younger's statement on 20 January 1921 that he expected the Coalition to last its full term; four days later, he suggested holding an early election once the Government introduced an economy budget along with lords reform. On 4 February he denied that he had suggested an election; perhaps he had only been venting his views on two subjects he regarded as important, but his role exactly a year later in regard to an early election in 1922 gave his 1921 remarks a retrospective significance.[2]

The chief event for Coalitionists in early 1921 was Bonar Law's retirement. At first his successor Austen Chamberlain had much support, and Lloyd George anticipated eventual fusion of the Conservative and Coalition Liberal groups. 'Toryism', he believed, was dead. 'No Tories in the cabinet—all Liberal-minded men.' The open split in Liberal ranks, noticeable at the National and Scottish Liberal Federation meetings in 1920, impelled the Lloyd Georgians to strengthen their position, and they set up numerous local organisations, at any rate in their own seats. By early 1921 Lloyd George had good reason to support fusion of these groups with those of the Conservatives, and they might have been ready for him. His victory over the miners in the coal strike which began on 31 March strengthened his position among Conservatives. The miners had intended to collaborate with the railwaymen and transport workers, but Lloyd George persuaded the other unions to stay at work, and in June the miners' strike collapsed. Even the *Morning Post*, his severest critic among Conservative newspapers, admitted that 'of late, Mr. Lloyd George has taken a line which Conservatives can unreservedly applaud'. In May Austen Chamberlain hoped to combine 'in one party men of different traditions' to avoid perils 'more insidious' than those of the war; but he did not say what the future of the Coalition would be. Also in May Lloyd George told the Kent Conservatives that he had not changed his coat; all Coalitionists were changing theirs to those of a new party. Thus the main party leaders, at any rate, seemed to desire fusion.[3]

Several poor by-election results indicated that the premier might be losing his popularity. Anti-waste candidates took Hertford and Westminster-St George's; both victors were right-wing candidates in constituencies with the habit of electing Conservative dissidents. A loss to Labour in Heywood-and-Radcliffe was more important, since the Lloyd Georgians had worked hard to elect one of their own. Another significant development in June 1921 was a meeting of backbench Liberals, eighteen from each faction. The chief Coalition representative, John Wallace, M.P. for Dunfermline, told the meeting that there was 'now no suggestion of fusion between Coalition Liberal and Conservative organisations'. Nearly all those attending the meeting favoured immediate Liberal reunion. Reunion did not come at that time, but the Conservatives saw that the Coalition Liberals could not always be trusted and in conjunction with the by-election losses, that they might not even be vote-getters.[4]

Several Liberal ministers were also drifting away from the Coalition at this time. Edwin Montagu reportedly voted against the Coalition candidate in a by-election, and he was known to oppose Lloyd George's pro-Greek policy. Winston Churchill was moving towards the Conservatives : Lord Beaverbrook attributed this to Churchill's failure to become chancellor of the exchequer when Austen Chamberlain gave up the office to become Conservative leader. At a cabinet meeting in August 1921 H. A. L. Fisher noted[5]

The whips' request to members to co-operate in autumn campaign. Winston says doubtful if he can co-operate. A significant hint. PM and AC look with consternation. PM makes an appeal to Cabinet. Asks me later what Winston is after. WC had told me before how dissatisfied he was with conduct of our finances. We ought to have taxed war capital.

In mid-1921 the Government reversed itself on several major domestic issues, the Agriculture Act and the housing programme. On 14 July Christopher Addison, until recently in charge of housing, resigned. Lord Beaverbrook regarded this as a milestone in Lloyd George's relations with the Tories, since they saw that the premier could be bullied into dropping his old associates. In fact Lloyd George was not sorry to be rid of Addison, and Tom Jones, one of the premier's assistants, told Bonar Law, 'Addison has left us and we do not miss him'.[6]

Nevertheless July 1921 was a turning-point for the Coalition, not because of Addison or agriculture, but because of the Irish truce, which went into effect on 11 July. This led directly to the treaty of December 1921, which shelved the Irish problem for almost half a century. On 18 July Martin Archer-Shee, a Roman Catholic Conservative opponent of Home Rule, seceded from the Coalition because of the concessions to Sinn Fein, and Colonel John Gretton followed him three days later. On 19 August the Government revealed that it would concede control over the armed forces to the Southerners; this worried many Conservatives, especially when de Valera's reply was truculent. The reaction of numerous Conservative M.P.s was also truculent, and eighteen of them, only one of whom sat for an Irish constituency, denounced Lloyd George's offer as instituting 'a Sinn Fein army'. These eighteen M.P.s formed the core of the 1922 Diehard group. This was the first time that a sizeable fragment of the Conservative Party had repudiated the general policy of the Coalition, but the adjournment of Parliament shortly afterwards meant that Gretton's group was unable to gather much strength. On 31 October, during a debate on negotiations with the 'alien and unscrupulous mountebank', as one rebel Tory described de Valera, the Diehards attracted only 45 votes to the Government's 441.[7]

On 3 November, the Diehards jousted with two Coalition Liberal ministers, Sir Hamar Greenwood, chief secretary for Ireland, and Edward Shortt, the home secretary. Greenwood was a Canadian who had once been a circus 'barker'; the Diehards ridiculed him and mimicked his accent. They then turned on Shortt with 'explosive vehemence', as the *Manchester Guardian* correspondent described it, because of his dismissal of Sir Basil Thomson, the director of special intelligence. The Diehards regarded Thomson as a defender of Ulster, and his probable successor as a Sinn Fein sympathiser. Sir Reginald 'Blinker' Hall, the famous spy-catcher, attributed Thomson's dismissal to 'the extremists' and 'secret enemies'. Shortt then announced the withdrawal of General Byrne, the prospective replacement for Thomson, and on this, the Diehards said that they had achieved their objective.[8]

The overwhelming government majority of 31 October showed that most Conservative M.P.s wanted to settle the Irish question quickly, but the much smaller majority of 3 November (146 to 43) showed that they would not give Lloyd George unlimited freedom of action. Lord Derby, a good barometer of Conservative opinion, said he would 'stick to Lloyd George as long as he does not use any compulsion' on Ulster, but he added that the Government might see coercion as the only solution.

Bonar Law urged Lloyd George to let Ulster determine its relations with Southern Ireland, and he told a journalist that 'nothing will move me from my present position'. Parliament prorogued on 10 November, with the Irish negotiations in progress, and with Lloyd George's definite assurance that lords reform would have high priority in the succeeding session.[9]

The Diehards announced their intention to fight the Government at the annual Conservative conference on 17 and 18 November. Over 2000 Tories assembled in Liverpool for the largest conference their party had held to that date. The Diehards proposed four motions condemning the Government for negotiating with rebels, then withdrew them in favour of a less immoderate resolution by Gretton criticising 'the long-continued ascendency of crime and rebellion in Ireland'. Gretton, chairman of a Staffordshire brewing firm, was an unyielding and lugubrious speaker who had 'manifestly steeled himself to the counteracting of new ideas'. He rejected any settlement which coerced Ulster or ignored the Southern loyalists, and other Diehards followed him. General Prescott-Decie thought the murder gang could be suppressed rapidly if the military were given 'full powers and not interfered with', while Martin Archer-Shee said that the negotiations had broken down and that the Conservatives should form their own government.[10]

During a break, Sir George Younger, Colonel Leslie Wilson, and Sir Archibald Salvidge held a private council, after which Salvidge proposed an amendment to Gretton's resolution, expressing the hope that the Irish negotiations would bring peace. He took advantage of the break to still emotions raised earlier in the debate. During his three-hour speech Salvidge said that 'the real issue is whether you condemn or support your own elected leader'. An uproar followed. The Diehards, he said, would not die at all, but many young Englishmen would, if the Diehards got their way. A score of delegates supported Gretton, while nearly 2000 backed Salvidge. Lord Derby told Lloyd George that the debate 'went well on the surface', but that there was disquiet beneath. Younger thought that the Diehard resolutions could have been fended off easily, and that 'any intractable attitude on the part of Ulster will be bitterly resented'. On the other hand the Diehard Lord Salisbury felt that the Coalition was unpopular at the meeting, and that the delegates felt strongly about Ulster; while the *Manchester Guardian* described the vote as 'a nervous and somewhat hesitating rally to the leaders of the party'.[11]

On the evening of 17 November, Chamberlain gave one of the best speeches of his career. One correspondent described it as 'magnanimous throughout even to the bitterest of his Diehard opponents'. It was one of the few times during his leadership that he stood clearly for an important principle, and placed himself unmistakably on one side. During his year and a half as leader, Chamberlain's position was generally vague even on the relatively few issues he dealt with, but his speech on this occasion persuaded many, even though it used up part of his stock of goodwill.[12]

Chamberlain spoke bluntly about Conservative suspicions of Lloyd George. He was convinced that even the Diehards would accept the Government's Irish proposals, but he could not give details as the negotiations were still in progress. 'I have no quarrel with the Diehards. They are men of sincere conviction and strong faith. All I ask of them is that they should wait.' He guaranteed that the Government would give Ulster free choice, and in a daring comparison, he reminded his listeners of his own opposition to the unification of Southern Africa during his Diehard days before the war:

I thought it a rash and wicked thing to do. If we could have seen further into the future, if I could have voted in that division with the fuller knowledge I have today, I should have known that that great act of faith was not, as I thought it, the destruction of our policy, but its completion and fulfilment.

However he blundered before and after this speech, Austen Chamberlain showed himself capable of strong leadership on this occasion; but even so, his fumbling was evident. He refused to prophesy the future: 'Sooner or later, sooner rather than later, the decision must be given' to form a new party or to dissolve the Coalition. He did not tell his audience what political alignment they could anticipate, apart from a remark that until the problems of European peace were settled, the Conservatives could not stand alone. This speech could be read in several ways, and was, for Chamberlain did not say whether he would fight for fusion, for continued coalition in the next Parliament or for mere electoral co-operation.[13]

Eighteen days later, at 2 am on 6 December, the British and Irish delegates signed an agreement which satisfied neither side completely, but which most observers believed settled the Irish question for good. Almost at once, several leading Coalitionists moved to consolidate their position. On 8 December Sir George Younger stated that he had 'no idea how long the Coalition would last', but that some 'moderate, constitutional, almost Conservative party' would come out of it. Chamberlain added that the Coalition was 'a temporary state of things', and that there should be either a new party or a split in the Coalition. On 9 December the *Pall Mall Gazette*, owned by the Coalitionist Conservative M.P. Sir John Leigh, announced that Lloyd George would proclaim this new national party, 'composed of Conservatives, Unionists, and Coalition Liberals', at a meeting to be held in January 1922. The *Chronicle*, Lloyd George's personal newspaper, corrected this the next day, and said that the January meeting would be restricted to Coalition, or 'National', Liberals. Among other things, this exchange showed how confused government supporters were about the aims of their leaders.[14]

Lloyd George still hoped to capture much of the Liberal public which had moved towards Asquith since 1918, and he was not mistaken in his reliance on the Irish settlement to reverse the drift, for numerous Asquithians acknowledged that he had, in his own brutal and vacillating way, solved the Irish question. John Morley, though not an active Asquithian, carried much weight with Liberal internationalists; he told H. A. L. Fisher that he 'fully approved of LG's handling of Ireland—thinks it a wonderful effort of will'. E. M. Humphreys, one of Lloyd George's most bitter critics in Wales, said that the settlement was due to 'the skill, tenacity, and courage of the Prime Minister'. D. R. Daniel, a Liberal who had been disenchanted with Lloyd George for some years, wrote that 'Ulster has been a bit dished. It is a big triumph'. The only opponents of the Irish Treaty when it was presented at a special session of Parliament on 16 December were 58 Conservatives and Independent Conservatives, and two Coalition Liberals whose Liberalism had long been suspect. Virtually all the Conservative opposition came from Diehards and Ulstermen, and 206 other Conservatives, roughly four out of five, supported the treaty. Parliament then prorogued until January.[15]

Following this successful debate, Lord Birkenhead held a dinner for Chamberlain, Lloyd George, Churchill, Beaverbrook, Sir Laming Worthington-Evans, T. J. Macnamara, C. A. McCurdy, and Sir Archibald Salvidge : in other words, most of the top Coalition leaders except for Sir George Younger. Salvidge was surprised at Younger's absence, as he undoubtedly knew the Conservative machinery best. According to Salvidge, Lloyd George expected that the euphoria surrounding the Irish settlement would sweep him back into power if he held a snap election. There were two plans, one for a coupon election, as in 1918, and the second for a more limited electoral arrangement which would not necessarily imply resumption of the Coalition afterwards. Salvidge thought the ground should be laid, for instance by bringing Bonar Law back into the cabinet (his health had improved), so he could not lead a Conservative revolt. McCurdy and Lloyd George both spoke in favour of an election, but Chamberlain opposed one. Winston Churchill and Birkenhead remained quiet so as not to intimidate the others, and Lord Beaverbrook, for one, misunderstood their attitude, and attributed their silence to tacit opposition to Lloyd George's plan.[16]

After this dinner, Chamberlain described the conference to Younger, and asked his advice. Lloyd George, he said, 'professes not to have made up his mind,' but in fact was virtually decided. 'I am myself opposed' to an early election. Younger replied rapidly that he was indignant at the 'cynical way in which the P.M.'s advisers appear to regard the interests of their chief as paramount to any others'. In a second letter, Younger told Chamberlain that 'a procession of M.P.s would support him in his struggle against an early election. Younger has usually been considered the chief trouble-maker in this election scare, but this correspondence in Chamberlain's private papers shows that Younger was not striking out on an independent track, but merely carrying out Chamberlain's wishes and loyally consolidating support behind his leader.[17]

Chamberlain also requested the chief party agent, Sir Malcolm Fraser, to predict the result of a February 1922 election. Fraser replied that Lloyd George would get a majority, but would also

'split our party from top to toe'. He expected that at least 372
Coalitionists would be elected, taking allowance for too-hopeful
estimates. Even if 50 Diehards seceded, there would have been
322 Coalitionists, for an overall majority of 29 in a house of
615; and that would be counting all Asquithians, Labour, Diehards and Ulstermen as opponents of the Coalition. Fraser
doubted whether 'the feeling against the formation of a new
party would be as strong as the feeling against again going to
the country as a coalition'. While a new party was comprehensible, a coalition was nebulous.[18]

The Coalition Liberals supported an early election, and
McCurdy told Lloyd George that 'The cardinal question is,
where will our Tory friends be in a few months from now. I
think the movement among the Tories for a break away from
the Coalition will grow. If they find a live man to lead them it
might become a stampede'. According to McCurdy's sounding,
'today the great bulk of the Tories will I believe follow you. I do
not see how the position is likely to improve, but I do see how
it might rapidly become worse'. After a tour of Lancashire,
McCurdy said that all reasonable Liberals there supported an
early election, and that 'the opposition comes from the Conservative machine'. Sir William Sutherland, another of Lloyd George's
organisers, said that voters normally took little interest in foreign
affairs, but that this was an exceptional period because of the
obvious connection between foreign crises and domestic instability. Voters were therefore ready for an election to be fought
on those issues of foreign policy where Lloyd George was
strongest, such as the proposed settlements with Germany and
Russia, naval disarmament and the Irish Treaty.[19]

Younger accused Sutherland of leaking the election proposal
to the Press. On 1 January the *Sunday Times* and *Observer* both
mentioned it, as did the *Chronicle* on 3 January. The *Pall Mall
Gazette* of 4 January spoke of two 'wing' leaders, Chamberlain
and Churchill, with Lloyd George as co-ordinator. The *Manchester Guardian* stated that one factor supporting an early
election was that the Diehards opposed it, and it added that the
forthcoming 'National' Liberal congress would prepare the way
for such an election. The proposal as the *Manchester Guardian*
saw it was to have two parties with one programme in the
election, possibly with increased Coalition Liberal seats.[20]

Younger retaliated against what he regarded as a Liberal trick to outmanoeuvre his party, and said that if the Government called an early election, 'a number of Conservatives will decline to go to their constituencies as Coalitionists, and I shall most certainly be among that number'. The *Manchester Guardian* considered Younger's professed interest in lords reform as a blind to cover his annoyance with the well-publicised Coalition Liberal move to increase their share of seats. It expressed surprise that Younger spoke of his discontent so publicly, and said it was 'difficult to estimate the effect of the declaration'.[21]

On 5 January Younger told the Press that the election proposal was 'pure opportunism', and he sent a letter to all chairmen of constituency Conservative parties, excepting only Chamberlain's own local party. This letter contained several arguments against an election, stated that many Conservatives would run independently of the Coalition and concluded by saying that 'I believe you will agree that the foregoing views correctly interpret the feelings of our friends as a whole'. This letter too was published in the Press.[22]

The *Chronicle* described Younger's communications as 'an act of disloyalty to the Prime Minister', while the *Manchester Guardian* felt that Younger had been able to get away with his insolence only because of Lloyd George's absence at the Cannes Conference. McCurdy interpreted Younger's position as an attack on the make-up of the Coalition; he thought that Younger hoped to pressure Lloyd George into becoming a Conservative. Younger, said McCurdy, opposed the rapidly growing Coalition organisations, as they would allow Lloyd George 'to turn elsewhere than to the Unionist wing of the Coalition' for support. Lloyd George was ceasing to be a premier without a party and was becoming a premier with one, and this worried the Conservatives. McCurdy mentioned two proposals, an early election and fusion. An early election would cleave the extremists away from the Conservatives, but would make the majority more reliable. The general secretary of Lloyd George's 'National' Liberal Party agreed, saying that the influence of the Conservative central office on the local associations was waning, and that in a quick election the Conservative organisation would be at its most effective in preventing Conservatives from contesting Coalition Liberal seats. McCurdy also told Lloyd George that

Austen Chamberlain had definitely informed Lord Burnham, proprietor of the *Daily Telegraph*, that 'if an early election is held, he will retire from the Coalition'.[23]

Although McCurdy suspected Chamberlain, the latter was at that moment criticising Younger for the 'great trouble' he had caused in sending his letter to the constituency chairmen. Chamberlain said this had made dissolution inevitable, because the air would have to be cleared; the work for fusion, which was Chamberlain's goal, would best be achieved in a period of quiet, not in one of partisan strife. This correspondence showed once more how Chamberlain could be misunderstood. While he was denouncing Younger for acting too independently, McCurdy was describing him as 'in complete agreement with Younger'. Such misunderstandings were too frequent to be accidental, and resulted from Chamberlain's inability to state his case clearly.[24]

This quarrel over the date of the election aroused the Conservatives; so long as they had been able to delay decisions on future alliances, they had done so. The January crisis demonstrated that they would soon have to come off the fence and commit themselves for or against permanent coalition. Moreover the method by which Younger and McCurdy took their soundings indicated to both sides that there was more partisan discontent over Coalition policy than there really was. Younger's public discussions may have resulted from his absence from the preliminary discussions, and in fact it was surprising that he had not been invited when several minor figures such as Worthington-Evans and Macnamara had been. Another problem was that the supporters of an early election did not take Chamberlain's veto as final. Since he was the Conservative leader, his word should have carried more weight than it apparently did, with Lloyd George, Churchill and the other Coalition leaders at Birkenhead's dinner.

Another consequence of this January crisis, but one which could not have been foreseen, was that the best opportunity for an election slipped by. Lloyd George's foreign policy was checked later in 1922 by the failure of the Cannes and Genoa conferences, the outbreak of civil war in Ireland and finally the Chanak affair. This disappointing 'National' Liberal conference was also a setback, but it would probably have been more successful had an election been in the air. As it was, Lloyd George's apparent defeat on a partisan issue was one reason for the quiescence of the 'National' Liberals.

On 12 January the Cannes Conference ended on a sour note. After his famous game of golf (actually not a game at all, but a pose for photographers), Aristide Briand fell as French premier. Lloyd George had depended on him to assist in reconciliation with Germany, but his replacement, Raymond Poincaré, helped frustrate those policies, and thus indirectly helped cause the fall of Lloyd George. Lloyd George returned to a political crisis of his own, but tried to play it down by ridiculing the talk of an election. 'Who started it? I did not. I never started the idea,' he told *The Times*'s correspondent. He did not fight Younger openly, but he had problems with the Coalition Liberals.[25]

Edwin Montagu and H. A. L. Fisher both opposed the meeting which was intended to found the 'National' Liberal Party. Fisher recorded that at a meeting of Coalition Liberal ministers, 'we squash the National Liberal Party. We are Liberals'. Nonetheless the party came into being at a quiet conference of several hundred delegates from all over the country. The major speakers were Winston Churchill and Sir Gordon Hewart, the attorney-general. Hewart said that the Conservative Party contained many good Liberals, and that the two groups would probably stay together. However, to ensure fair distribution of seats, the Coalition Liberals should build up their organisation; this would also come in handy if the Coalition should end. The leader of the Coalition Liberal 'wing', Winston Churchill, denounced Labour's 'grotesque threats and outrageous fallacies'. He felt that the Liberals had finished their distinctive work, and that they should stop class aggression by working within the Coalition. None of the speeches generated much reaction from the delegates, and the congress dispersed, without a quarrel, but also without enthusiasm.[26]

The crisis in the Coalition continued when on 1 February Birkenhead spoke of 'grave decisions' and 'grave perils' which could only be countered if the Conservatives sided with other patriots. Younger on the other hand said there would be 'no new Coalition bargain'. This assurance did not satisfy Colonel Gretton, who told the Press that the Government was trying to merge existing Conservative groups with those of a new party. Gideon Murray, another Diehard, said that fusion would be 'a real disaster'. Gretton, Murray and thirty-three other Diehards met Austen Chamberlain and several other leading Coalition ministers. Gretton, who headed the group, said that the Government should be reconstituted without Lloyd George, 'the evil genius of the Coalition'. Chamberlain told the Diehards that he hoped for fusion, and the meeting broke up. Afterwards Gideon Murray told Chamberlain that he could replace Lloyd George as premier if he wished, but Chamberlain 'made an evasive reply and we parted'.[27]

A few days later, on 21 February, Chamberlain told the council of the National Unionist Association that the Government had the legal right to dissolve Parliament at any time, but that it should not pick a time merely because it would be politically opportune. The situation was unclear, with a vast number of uncommitted voters, and with new issues instead of those which had divided the two main parties before the war. Conservatives welcomed those from whom they were divided only by a few obsolete and irrelevant shibboleths. 'If they will not join our organisation, let them form their own', and co-operate with the Conservatives in the next election. For that election Lloyd George and he did not contemplate a joint manifesto, but an understanding similar to that of Joseph Chamberlain and Balfour, in which each side had some freedom so long as both agreed on the main points at issue. But under the Balfour-Joseph Chamberlain agreement, the Conservative leader had been premier, and the Conservatives probably read this speech as indicating Chamberlain's desire for that office. In addition, the speech indicated that Chamberlain had shifted away from his previous support of fusion.[28]

A day later, on 22 February, Sir George Younger stated that it was 'no longer essential that the Coalition as it at present exists should continue to exist after the next election'. He, like Chamberlain, hoped to follow the precedent set by Balfour and Joseph Chamberlain. The Lloyd George Government was a marriage, and there should be a divorce, but a divorce which 'would leave the parties extremely friendly'. The Conservatives would not turn the Coalition Liberals adrift, but would co-operate with them. On 24 February he added that he had never contemplated a second coupon election; but that after an election which the Conservatives would fight on their own policy, 'we

shall probably work on the group system, as they do in France.
The groups nearest to each other will form a kind of co-partnery
in order to form a government'. He did not anticipate antagonism
between the Conservatives and Coalition Liberals, but rather
that they would continue to work together in the national
interest. The *Liberal Magazine* described these suggestions as a
'cynical display of political hypocrisy'.[29]

Several prominent Coalitionists reacted strongly against
Younger's proposed divorce and subsequent living in political
sin. Birkenhead said there was 'not the slightest chance' to form
a Conservative majority, and that Younger was like a cabin boy
who decided to take over the ship in the midst of a storm. He
was even more suspicious 'when the cabin boy has announced
that he does not intend to make another voyage'.* Edwin
Montagu told Lord Reading that the Conservatives were 'getting
more and more restive', and that Chamberlain 'looks anxious
and worried, torn between loyalty to his party and loyalty to
the prime minister', while Churchill shifted from one position
to another. At a luncheon of Coalition Liberal leaders, F. E.
Guest and C. A. McCurdy both favoured an immediate dissolution, while Montagu supported resignation after finishing the
reform programme. Lloyd George was 'furious' about Younger's
letter to the Conservative chairmen, and said he was 'not going
to be bullied by a second-rate brewer'.[30]

At a dinner on 28 February Lloyd George told the Coalition
Liberal ministers that he had complained to Chamberlain about
Younger's indiscipline. It was 'necessary to find out what Younger
represents'. Lloyd George had offered to resign because he could
not go on. Lord Beaverbrook later described this threat of
resignation as 'possibly not serious and not even sincere', but
Countess Lloyd-George said that the premier kept office only to
carry through the Genoa Conference, which was to come in
April. Chamberlain replied at once that Lloyd George's resignation would be ruinous.[31]

Lloyd George's threat leaked to the Press, and on 1 March
the *Daily Telegraph* published full details. The *Daily News*
called it a direct challenge to the Conservatives, who would
have to give a new pledge of loyalty. The *Daily News* expected
them to give it: the Coalition Liberals would probably be the

* Younger had previously stated that he did not intend to seek re-election.

smallest group in the next Parliament, and would have to yield some offices to the Conservatives, so the Tories could wait until after the election before upsetting the existing arrangements.[32]

On 3 March Chamberlain dismissed the events of January and February as 'small bickering' and 'local jealousy'. He under-played too much, since, whatever their origin, the squabbles had clearly taken on considerable significance. Chamberlain said that Lloyd George should not be allowed to leave office. He then repeated, so he said, advice he had given on 21 February, and suggested that 'when we go to the country we go as a govern-ment'. This government would have an agreed programme. This speech puzzled Conservatives, as Chamberlain's views had seem-ingly shifted in two months from fusion, to a form of symbiotic non-alliance, to going to the country 'as a government'. Super-ficially at least, this last implied having a second coupon election.[33]

On 5 March Churchill said that the Coalition would transform itself into a 'strong, united, permanent national party'. Sir Philip Sassoon told Lloyd George that Churchill was trying to ingratiate himself with the Diehards, but if his speech was read in con-junction with Chamberlain's it would seem as if the two ministers had decided to maintain the Coalition on the same lines as before, if not on closer ones. On 7 March Balfour added to the im-pression when he referred to 'a great national party, to one of whose wings I belong'. This was very different from the position that Chamberlain had outlined on 21 February, when he had foreseen separate development of the Conservative and Coalition Liberal Parties.[34]

The *Daily News* was incredulous that Lloyd George should accept the assurances of Chamberlain and Balfour without similar assurances from the rank and file too. It said that the Tories were 'completely out of hand and all that is in doubt is whether the patient will live for a few weeks or a couple of months'. One important Conservative who was out of hand was Sir Alexander Leith, chairman of the council of the National Unionist Association. He told Chamberlain on 4 March that if the ministry went to the country as a coalition, it would contradict the Conservative leader's previous assurance that there would be no second coupon election. Chamberlain replied that he had not changed his position, but that Leith had misunderstood him.

Conservatives and Coalition Liberals were two parts of one great constitutional party, and movements for differentiation had risen only because of tactical differences, not because of different principles. A revised version of this correspondence was published on 10 March.[35]

On 9 March a political sensation transformed these discussions. Edwin Montagu, Coalition Liberal secretary of state for India, resigned because of his publication without cabinet approval of a telegram from the Indian Government criticising the cabinet for favouring Greek interests in Asia Minor and Constantinople. Chamberlain announced the resignation to the 'wild joy of the Diehards'. According to H. A. L. Fisher, two Diehards then said, 'Now we have got to get rid of these Liberals Shortt and Fisher'. Many regarded Montagu's fall as a personal setback for Lloyd George, though in reality Montagu's rash action had enabled the premier to eliminate a colleague whose Indian reforms had antagonised Conservative M.P.s. As early as 1920 Montagu had said that 'The British Empire is dead', and numerous Tories suspected that he was helping to bury it. Thus Montagu's resignation in one sense strengthened Lloyd George's position with the Conservatives. But although Montagu had gone, Lloyd George found difficulty in replacing him with a moderate Conservative who carried weight with both parties in his Coalition. He first asked Lord Derby, a Conservative free trader, but Derby refused. He then asked another Conservative free trader, the Duke of Devonshire, but the duke refused too. Finally Viscount Peel, a less prominent Conservative, accepted. The two refusals soon became public knowledge and made the Coalition seem a sinking ship.[36]

On 14 March over 200 Conservative M.P.s discussed the future of the Coalition. The Press reported that a motion defending the Coalition could not be adopted, but the meeting was more complex than the brief report indicated. Few Conservative M.P.s present knew who had organised it : in fact, the organisers had been two pro-Coalition backbenchers, P. J. Hannon and Edward Goulding, who had set it up on their own without consulting Chamberlain. Sir H. W. Chilcott, also a supporter of Chamberlain, felt that such unofficial meetings should cease, as they created confusion. C. A. McCurdy told Lloyd George that Diehards made up only about 40 of the more than 200 M.P.s present, but that they had been the only organised group. The Diehards had seized lists of Conservative M.P.s friendly to the Coalition and had torn them up. The Diehards 'were acting on a deliberate plan and the timidity of the chairman helped them'. McCurdy felt that 'this was nothing but the concentrated rowdyism of this old Tory gang', and was unrepresentative of the Conservative M.P.s at large. Sir William Sutherland said that the friendly Conservatives were 'very sick about this meeting', because they had not been organised to defend the Coalition viewpoint. The chairman had become timid 'and though the Diehards were a minority he did not put the resolutions to a vote. Those present tell me the Diehards would have been beaten easily'.[37]

Chamberlain told Chilcott that he did not normally interfere with private meetings of M.P.s, and said that 'I have myself refrained from calling a party meeting', because such a meeting was 'more likely to emphasise differences than to heal them'. Salvidge warned Chamberlain that it would be impossible to reconcile the Diehards to Lloyd George, or his policies, and that left alone, the Diehards would increase their strength. However Chamberlain 'was not prepared to have it recorded of him that he split the party which had been handed over to him as a united force'.[38]

Chamberlain's failure to face the Diehard rebellion squarely was the chief cause of his fall, for although he did not want to split his party, the Diehards had no such reservations. His delays merely gave the Diehards more time to organise, and as Sir William Sutherland observed, as long as the Conservative leaders refused to confront the dissidents, 'they detract[ed] from the Prime Minister's position and his power and [left] it open to every enemy'.[39]

On 18 March the Press announced that 33 more peers and 34 more M.P.s adhered to a manifesto the Diehards had published several weeks previously. This manifesto had demanded 'Conservative and Unionist principles', but otherwise it had been limited to a few vague statements against crime and high taxes. Sir Leslie Wilson, the chief Conservative whip, expected the Diehards to play themselves out; on the other hand McCurdy told Lloyd George that the position would improve only if the Conservative leaders preached coalition or fusion unreservedly.

Only one thing would alter the temper of the Conservatives,[40]

and that is the disappearance of their electoral majority. A general election which left the Conservative Party dependent upon allies would completely change the situation. The Diehards would no longer be listened to; Coalition would no longer be regarded as an unnecessary expedient.

On 5 April Sir William Joynson-Hicks proposed a motion of general non-confidence in the administration; this backfired because it required the Conservative M.P.s to commit themselves for or against the Coalition instead of letting them retain their semi-neutral position. The usual Diehard accusations that Lloyd George was befriending murderers alienated wavering M.P.s, especially when Chamberlain denounced the rebels openly. However he did not state his own position, but confined himself to personal attacks on Joynson-Hicks and his associates. After this debate, the domestic political crisis cooled briefly without being resolved, but Lloyd George's foreign policy took two serious knocks. These were the failure of the Genoa Conference, and the beginning of the Greek rout in Asia Minor. In the case of Genoa, the Russo-German agreement frustrated his hopes for a general peace settlement, and in the other case his ex-protégé sank miserably into defeat and revolution.

In January the *Manchester Guardian* had stated that Lloyd George would have two major achievements, the Irish Treaty and a fully representative congress at Genoa at which even Lenin might be present. If this reconciliation had succeeded it would have been one of the greatest triumphs of modern British statesmanship, and it would also have secured his position with the Conservatives, at least for a while. The Irish and naval agreements came off virtually as planned, but the Genoa meeting did not. The replacement of Briand by Poincaré made a Franco-British understanding precarious, let alone a Franco-German one. Poincaré's narrow views were partly responsible for the failure of this conference, but most of the blame lay with the Russians and Germany, who signed the Treaty of Rapallo almost as soon as the Genoa meetings opened. Superficially this treaty merely patched up differences between the two states, and the

Economist said that 'little exception has been taken to the terms'.*
Nevertheless the methods by which the Germans and Russians
had negotiated it alarmed the other countries, and the Genoa
meetings dispersed.[41]

On 16 June Sir George Younger told a Conservative conference that many critics had been unfair, as the difficulties of the
Government had been unparalleled. He agreed with Chamberlain that the Coalition must end, but felt that the Conservatives
could not secure a party majority and so must collaborate with
the Coalition Liberals. The *Liberal Magazine* commented that
this speech ended 'the battle of the Georges', but in reality the
battle was not over.[42]

Six days later, on 22 June, Sir Henry Wilson was murdered
on his London doorstep by two Sinn Feiners.† Wilson had been
elected for North Down in February and thereafter had been
prominent in Diehard protests. He had also been a military
adviser to the Government of Northern Ireland. Earlier in June
the Diehards had published a second manifesto, which had not
contained as many names as that of March, and Wilson's murder
revived their drooping fortunes.

The Diehard speakers maintained that Lloyd George had
handed the government of Southern Ireland over to weaklings
who had been able to get only a bare majority of 64 votes to 57
in favour of the Irish settlement. This debate showed the unease
of moderate Conservative M.P.s about Ireland, and also the
depths of the Diehard distrust of the premier. Colonel Gretton
asked if the government 'or so-called government of Mr.
[Michael] Collins has any authority to put down crime or
murder'. It was cruel to the Irish to hand them over to gunmen.
Ronald McNeill, one of the ablest Diehard speakers, accused the
Government of knowing nothing about Ireland. Collins was no
longer, 'outwardly at all events', running the murder gang, but
he was in charge of a government which let the gang kill as it

* Secret terms of the Treaty of Rapallo allowed the Germans to develop
weapons such as aeroplanes and poison gas which they had been forbidden
to do by the Treaty of Versailles. By the terms of Rapallo, the Germans were
to design and train in the use of such weapons in Russia in return for
technical assistance.

† Curiously, on the same day that Wilson was buried (26 June), the Law
of Property Act, 1922, was passed. This act had as one clause a specimen
will of a fictitious Henry Wilson. Cf. *Public General Acts* (1922) 294.

pleased.* McNeill did not want to turn the clock back, but 'sooner or later the reconquest of Ireland would be an unavoidable necessity'. McNeill had warned Sir Henry Wilson about the Sinn Fein danger, and Wilson had admitted his danger while saying 'but it would be much nicer to be shot by them than to shake hands with them'.

Gideon Murray said that 'as we all know, the government have not been above shaking hands with murderers', even though 'they themselves would not commit murder'. The arch-culprit, Lloyd George, he demanded,

> who shakes hands with murderers, the man who lunches with Bolshevist leaders who are double-dyed murderers, the man who by his follies and weakness and shiftiness has cost us Ireland and is breaking up the Empire—that is the man who ought to be thrown to the wolves.

The Diehard speeches counted much less than Bonar Law's ominous warning. He questioned the good faith of the Collins Government, and said that the Coalition had to do better for Ireland. 'If they do not, I will be against them, and I hope the House of Commons will also be against them.' Law had not previously shown his displeasure so clearly, and in this speech, he signified that he might rally opposition to the existing Conservative leaders. Only 78 M.P.s voted against the Government, while 344 supported it, including two Diehards and 95 non-Diehards who voted against Chamberlain at the Carlton Club Meeting in October. The pro-Coalitionists of October supported the Government by 67 to 4, showing that the pro-Coalition forces were solidifying, while the waverers were beginning to drift towards the Diehards, although three-quarters of them still backed Chamberlain.[43]

A debate on the sale of honours took place on 17 July, but it had far less impact on the Coalition than a conference of the Conservative leaders with some discontented junior ministers on 20 July. Amery wrote that several juniors were anxious about the future, but that Birkenhead proceeded in an 'astonishingly arrogant and offensive manner to lecture them for their silliness

---

* Sinn Fein terrorists murdered Collins on 22 August 1922.

and want of loyalty'. Chamberlain agreed with Amery's description, and said in a letter that Birkenhead had 'scolded and brow-
beat the juniors'. According to Amery, the meeting ended with
a few pontifical sentences from Chamberlain, 'and we dispersed,
most of the juniors spluttering with indignation'.[44]

The Parliament of 1919–22 wound up on 4 August with the
intention of reassembling on 14 November. However the 1922
election intervened, so that this was the last day that Lloyd
George or any other Liberal spoke in the commons as prime
minister. By an ironic quirk, the very last speech in this Parliament was a defence of Lloyd George's Greek policy by Sir
Donald Maclean, who had led the Independent Liberals until
Asquith's re-election in 1920. Maclean said that Lloyd George
was on the side of humanity in his defence of oppressed races
against persecution. Nonetheless Lloyd George's actions in the
Asia Minor dispute helped prepare his downfall.[45]

By a secret wartime treaty, Britain had promised Smyrna and
its hinterland in western Asia Minor to Italy. Later Lloyd George
had allocated it to Greece, ostensibly because the area was Greek-
speaking. Although this change could be justified on linguistic
grounds, it annoyed the Italians, who began helping the French
undermine British policy in the region. Curzon thought that the
French were consistently treacherous because they envied Britain's
position in the Moslem world; more likely, they suspected that
Lloyd George wanted a strong pro-British Greece to dominate
the north-eastern Mediterranean. In addition Lloyd George was
the most effective Allied opponent of large reparations from
Germany, and if the French could wreck one major aspect of
his foreign policy, they might gain leverage to change his reparations policy. In this they would have the support of the many
Conservatives who were both pro-Turkish and in favour of
higher reparations.[46]

So long as the Anglophile Venizelos was virtual ruler of
Greece, Lloyd George pursued a pro-Greek policy, but when
King Constantine returned to power in later 1920, Lloyd George
had less reason to believe that the Greek Government would
favour Britain, and British policy became less committed. In
July 1922 the French Government suggested that peace negotia-
tions start between the Greeks and Turks. At the time Greek and
Turkish forces were fairly evenly balanced in south-western Asia

Minor, though the Greek lines were overextended. The Greeks decided to retire from their forward position, but they still had designs on Constantinople, occupied by a weak Turkish régime under Franco-British control. Before consolidating his position in Smyrna, King Constantine diverted two divisions from Asia Minor towards Constantinople. This withdrawal seriously weakened the Greek lines.[47]

On 3 August the cabinet discussed what they termed 'the Greek menace to Constantinople', and decided to reinforce the British garrison there. Winston Churchill said 'it was useless to depend on the mere skeleton force' in the city, and a day later, Lloyd George told the Commons that if the Greeks attacked Constantinople, the British could not prevent them. This was simply a statement of obvious fact; but he added that the Turks should come to terms with the Greeks. In effect he told the Turks that the Greeks still had some cards to play. Instead the Turks took advantage of the weakened Greek lines on the Smyrna front, and routed the Greeks there. They then swept north towards the Straits and Constantinople.[48]

Kemal, the Turkish nationalist leader, had limited objectives, but if he was not opposed, his victorious army would have been tempted to expand beyond those objectives into European Greece. The British did not have enough men in the area to stop this, but they issued on 17 September a communiqué stating that British forces would prevent the Kemalists from crossing into Europe. It also called on the Dominions, the French and the Italians for help. It was supposed to cool the Turks off, and it did so. They did not cross into Europe in force, but the communiqué alarmed many in England who feared that Lloyd George was about to entangle them in another war. Even his secretary was 'horrified at the unwisdom of the message, conveying as it did the prospect of renewed warfare on a large scale'.[49]

The communiqué, though provocative, perhaps because it was provocative, made the situation in the Near East easier. Sir Harold Nicolson described it as a 'reckless and triumphant gesture' of which Lloyd George could be proud; but for contemporaries it was easier to see the recklessness than to see the triumph. There are times when the threat of force, or even the limited use of force, can avert a major war, and it is often difficult for outsiders to judge whether a statesman is taking a carefully calculated risk, or whether he is being reckless. In 1922 south-eastern Europe was nearly as unstable as it had been in 1914, and some would say it was even more unstable because of the increased hatreds caused by the war. A serious conflict in the area would have led to chaos, and if it spread northward, could have started another European war. The British Government could not stand by idly when it was possible to stop such a war. Yet this communiqué was widely regarded then and since as a major error.[50]

The Government had not prepared the public for its announcement, and few understood the extent of instablility in central and south-eastern Europe. This lack of preparation helps explain why the public interpreted the Greek rout as a deserved defeat for Lloyd George's aggressive policies. Labour leaders in particular opposed the Government strongly. J. R. Clynes condemned the Government for meddling in other countries, while to J. H. Thomas the communiqué was 'not only a profound blunder, but humiliation'.[51]

From the Government's viewpoint, Conservative want of enthusiasm was even more significant. J. E. Singleton, prospective Conservative candidate for Lancaster, said 'We want no war. We have had enough of it,' and Sir George Younger told Austen Chamberlain that 'I have never myself approved the P.M.'s policy of backing the Greeks'. The Turks, he said, 'fight in a gentlemanly way. . . . To compare a Turk with a Levantine Greek is to compare gold with dross.' Most other Conservative politicians who spoke on the subject admitted that the Government handled the actual Chanak crisis effectively, but they added that the crisis should never have arisen in the first place. The most important comment came from Bonar Law, in a letter published in *The Times* on 7 October. Law said that firm action had stopped the Turks from embroiling the Balkans in another war, but that 'we cannot alone act as the policeman of the world'. If France did not support Britain, Britain should imitate the United States, restricting its attention to its empire.[52]

Government policy towards Turkey changed frequently between 1915 and 1922, but the reasons for the changes were rarely explained to the public, so it was hardly surprising that the attitude of most politicians in mid-September was one of isolationism. J. M. Kenworthy, Asquithian M.P. for Hull Central, demanded to know why Britain should fight for Thrace : 'It is not as big as Yorkshire and not half as valuable.' F. H. Rose, Labour M.P. for Aberdeen North, said that 'there was not an interest in Asia Minor or in Europe that was worth to him a drop of blood from one of his countrymen'. Members of all parties opposed intervention in foreign problems, even if such interventions kept the peace. Clearly the road to Munich began in Chanak.[53]

Even before the Chanak crisis, Chamberlain had intimations of revolt. Lord Derby told him that many would support a Coalition Liberal, but that fewer would back a Lloyd Georgian. Chamberlain was surprised by this letter, and asked Derby to kept his grievances quiet. On 16 September, Sir George Younger, who was still trying to patch up the Coalition, told Chamberlain that Bonar Law would help if Lloyd George took a holiday; but he informed his leader that Law was not as inclined as he had been to efface himself.[54]

On 17 September the Coalition leaders met at Chequers to assess their position. Chamberlain told the others that the Conservative organisation expected the two Coalition allies to get a majority, but that it would not be secure unless the Conservatives were allowed to choose a premier from their own ranks. As usual he did not say enough :[55]

The whole of this I told frankly to the group at Chequers, only representing the feeling against LlG's premiership as the result of the natural desire of the largest section to have their own leader in the first place, and slurring over, tho' not wholly omitting, the purely personal aspect.

Since the 'purely personal aspect' was decisive, Chamberlain served his colleagues poorly by glossing it over. The other ministers present were more hopeful about the future, and decided to dissolve Parliament as soon as possible. On being informed of this decision, Younger was 'frankly appalled', and said that 'we shall split our party in twain'. Colonel Leslie Wilson was '*very* disturbed', and said that there was little chance that the Conservative organisation would approve of a second coupon election. He said in a later letter that he wished to dissociate

9 'You're next!'—Lloyd George as seen by David Low on the eve of the Carlton Club
meeting

himself publicly from the project. At this, Chamberlain spoke of his own 'infinite pain and regret' that Wilson should desert his leader. He felt his own usefulness was over, if his followers paid so little attention to his views. On 15 October he told Wilson that he would call a meeting at the Carlton Club of all Conservative M.P.s. This meeting, to be held on 19 October, would determine the party's policy.[56]

6

The Carlton Club Meeting

On 19 October 1922 a private meeting of Conservative M.P.s brought down one of the most powerful governments since the passage of the First Reform Bill. Much has been written about the Carlton Club Meeting, but few accounts have gone beyond reports of the speeches made at it. Nevertheless a vast amount of material for a detailed examination has been publicly available ever since 1922, and a study of this material leads one to revise some traditional views of the meeting. Among other things it shows that Stanley Baldwin played only a minor role; Baldwin's later prominence made his actions on 19 October seem more significant than they did at the time. A second thing which has usually been overestimated is the effect of Bonar Law's speech on the actual vote at the meeting. Bonar Law did not change the vote of many M.P.s, but he had a real importance which has generally been overlooked, in the brief election which the Carlton Club Meeting precipitated. This chapter examines the convergence of forces which resulted in the fall of the Coalition, and it also estimates how far the events at the Carlton Club Meeting itself toppled the Government.

13–18 October, 1922

On 13 October Austen Chamberlain publicly demanded main-tenance of the Coalition in face of the 'common foe', Labour. No question of principle divided Liberals and Conservatives, he said, and it would be 'criminal' to allow personal and party prejudices to sacrifice the interest of the country 'at a moment of national danger'. If those who sought to preserve social order were divided, Labour would win, and it would 'not be the moderates of the Labour Party who would prevail'.[1]

The next day, Lloyd George defended his Turkish policy. Most Conservative M.P.s had not taken a public stand either way, and Lloyd George wanted a greater commitment than this. He told his audience that if Britain had not stood firm over Chanak, the crisis could have led to a major war. After all the war of 1914–18 had started in the Balkans, and one could not achieve peace by a show of cowardice. The Turks were bloodthirsty and had massacred thousands of Greeks and Armenians; who wanted them to enter Europe? Lloyd George refused to utter 'the litany of the cynic, "Am I my brother's keeper?" '. However he did not foresee war, as the Turk was 'very amenable to persuasion'.[2]

Lloyd George's speech came when Curzon was negotiating with the Turks, and when the Turks themselves were becoming more concerned than ever about a Greek revival. After the Greek collapse in September, a revolution had deposed Constantine. The new Greek regime was on good terms with Lloyd George, and Kemal was apprehensive about possible British military aid to Greece. British politicians were worried too: Lord Beaverbrook thought Lloyd George wanted a war with Turkey to justify an election 'with a whopping majority for his leadership'. However British forces in Turkey amounted to only nine battalions (about 5,000 men), and reinforcements would take thirty-one days to reach Constantinople. In those thirty-one days the Turks could overrun the British positions, so Lloyd George could not afford to let the Turks know just how weak the British forces were, in case Kemal's wilder subordinates invaded European Greece. His dangerous bluff worked.[3]

Lloyd George may have hoped to provoke a crisis in the Conservative Party, so that it would say definitely whether it backed him or not. Viscount d'Abernon, who worked closely with the premier, said that he had often provoked incipient crises to get rid of them as soon as possible. It might even have been in Lloyd George's interest to be repudiated by the Conservatives. In March 1922 C. A. McCurdy had advised him to resign, thus forcing an election. McCurdy believed that the country would then realise that 'no party was strong enough to carry on government on party lines; that the traditional two-party system of England had broken down; and that the Coalition, so far from being an immoral or doubtful expedient, was a stark necessity.[4]

Whatever Lloyd George's motives had been, there was no noticeable wave towards him. G. R. Lane-Fox, Conservative M.P. for Barkston Ash, told Bonar Law that despite the blandishments of Lloyd George and Chamberlain, he remained opposed to another coupon election. Reginald Clarry, fighting the Newport by-election as a Diehard, ridiculed Lloyd George's 'amateurish diplomacy', and Colonel Gretton said that 'in the Near East, the Prime Minister and his friends had backed the wrong horse'. Arthur Henderson, also speaking in Newport, described Lloyd George's speech as 'positively dangerous'.[5]

Chamberlain's speech did not win much support either. Even Diehards such as Lord Salisbury felt that if the country was in such a state that the Bolsheviks were ready to take over, it was a strong case for purging the Government of Lloyd George. More significant opposition came from Sir Leslie Wilson and Sir George Younger. Even before Chamberlain spoke, Wilson opposed a second coupon election, and he believed that the Conservative conference would oppose one too. Other Conservative M.P.s who normally supported the Government also began to rebel. Sir Arthur Griffith-Boscawen 'could not support so barefaced an attempt to avoid consulting our official party organisation'. L. S. Amery decried the 'negative policy of anti-Socialism', but remained willing to follow Chamberlain. On 16 October he called a meeting, attended by seventeen Conservative ministers and under-secretaries. He wanted to postpone decisions on the future of the Coalition until after the election, but some of his colleagues wanted to depose Lloyd George at once. Chamberlain heard of the meeting and accused Amery of plotting his overthrow; Amery replied that, far from plotting, he had been trying to frame a compromise 'which would get us out of what most of us felt to be an impossible situation'.[6]

Amery's group met again on 17 October. Baldwin told it that nothing would make him serve again under Lloyd George; but others were less certain about booking a one-way ticket to the wilderness, and the meeting did not come to a definite conclusion. On 18 October Amery suggested to Leslie Wilson that the future should be decided by a party meeting held after the election. Wilson submitted this to Chamberlain, and later told Amery that Chamberlain had agreed to it.[7]

Also on 18 October Sir Samuel Hoare held a meeting of backbench Conservatives. Accounts of this meeting differ slightly. Lord Davidson wrote that about eighty M.P.s had been chosen 'both for their local ties and their standing in the country'. He said that two under-secretaries made passionate speeches and persuaded their colleagues to work for party independence. Contemporary newspaper reports said that forty M.P.s had been 'selected for their standing in the country, but without regard to their views' on the Coalition. Though the M.P.s supported independent action in the election, they did not rule out post-electoral co-operation with the Coalition Liberals. They asked Hoare, E. G. Pretyman, and G. R. Lane-Fox to persuade Bonar Law to take the party out of the Coalition, and they also framed the resolution which was subsequently passed at the Carlton Club Meeting.[8]

The same day, the executive of the National Union decided to call an emergency party conference for mid-November. This executive had many Diehards on it, but fewer supporters of the Coalition. On 18 October for the first time in 1922, acknowledged opponents of the Coalition made up the majority of those present. Several members of the executive who supported the Coalition, such as Sir F. B. Mildmay, Sir William Bull and Sir Laming Worthington-Evans, were absent. The executive voted 'unanimously' (Salvidge abstained) to adjourn for one day, to see what happened at the Carlton Club. Even if the M.P.s supported the Coalition, then the November conference might repudiate it.[9]

On the eighteenth many Conservative politicians visited Bonar Law, trying to persuade him to condemn the Coalition. He had no intention of supporting the Coalition openly, but there was a strong possibility that he would remain aloof. However, 'partly at the insistence of his own children', he decided to appear at the meeting. According to Sir George Younger, Law had made up his mind to attend on 18 October, but on the morning of the nineteenth Younger found[10]

Bonar sitting in an armchair in front of the fire in his carpet slippers. 'Aren't you ready to start?' I said. 'No,' he replied, 'I'm not coming'. 'But you *promised* to come,' I said, 'and you can't change your mind like that. The whole future of the

Party depends on your coming and getting us out of the Coalition. Where are your boots? Let's get them on.' His boots were on the other side of the room, and I brought them across and helped him to put them on, and without any further protest he came down to the meeting with me.

19 October, 1922

A meeting of M.P.s was relatively favourable fighting ground for the Coalition leaders, who expected that a Labour victory in the Newport by-election would drive wavering Conservative M.P.s towards the Coalition. Few anti-Coalitionists expected to beat Chamberlain and Lloyd George : Baldwin anticipated defeat and talked of leaving politics altogether. J. R. P. Newman, M.P. for Finchley, also opposed the Coalition, 'but he had not thought they would win'. G. E. W. Bowyer, M.P. for Buckingham and an opponent of the Coalition, was 'shocked' by the victory of his own side. The biographer of the Diehard Sir William Joynson-Hicks said that the result 'startled everybody'. The Diehard *Morning Post* belittled the meeting before it was held, and suggested that the decision to hold it had been made by someone 'less honest and more cunning that the right hon. member for West Birmingham'.* On 18 October the *Birmingham Post* discussed the effect of a large majority, or a moderate one, for the Coalition. It did not even consider an adverse majority and predicted a big victory for Chamberlain. The *Glasgow Herald* of the same date said the defeat of the Coalition was 'not seriously apprehended'. Thus most observers expected the Conservative M.P.s to back the Coalition. This probably explains the tradition that the result was caused by last-minute factors such as the Newport by-election or the speeches of Baldwin and Bonar Law.[11]

At least eleven Conservative M.P.s were absent from the country at the time of the meeting, on government business. None was known to support the Coalition. An official delegation to Brazil comprised six M.P.s, all Conservative. Two, Sir Douglas Newton and Sir Phillip Richardson, had repudiated the Coalition in by-elections early in 1922. A third, Sir Philip Pilditch, had weathered three Diehard storms in his constituency, and by

* i.e., Austen Chamberlain.

September 1922 he had agreed to stand as 'a Conservative pure and simple'. A fourth, A. C. Morrison-Bell, was a Diehard.[12]

Another Conservative M.P., Earl Winterton, had opposed extended coalition in January 1922; he was in India on government business for the period of the Carlton Club Meeting. Sir R. Park Goff had voted against the Government forty-seven times; he was in Constantinople during October, on government business. F. Willey had announced his opposition to prolonged coalition in early 1922; in October he was in the United States presenting a memorial to Edmund Burke on behalf of the Government. Sir C. A. M. Barlow, another known opponent of continued Coalition, was in Geneva at this time, representing the Government at the League of Nations.[13]

The Conservative ministers also pruned the list of those attending the meeting by excluding three Diehards who sat as Independent Conservatives: they were Sir Thomas Polson, J. M. M. Erskine, and M. F. Sueter. Lord Robert Cecil, also an Independent Conservative though not a Diehard, was not invited either, and Lord Hugh Cecil was not asked until strong pressure had been applied.[14]

The absence of these fifteen men made no difference to the result of the Carlton Club Meeting, since the eventual majority against the Coalition was 101. However Chamberlain and his colleagues appeared to be using underhand methods to keep power; to be sure of victory, Chamberlain should have excluded all the known Diehards. Then he might at least have achieved the result he desired.

The meeting began at 11 am on Thursday 19 October. At least 286 Conservative M.P.s were present in the large upstairs smoking room-library of the Carlton Club. The room had been cleared for the occasion, and provided with a small platform for the party leaders. The Diehards arrived early and sat as a separate group, so they could console each other. They expected Chamberlain to announce a compromise which would preserve the Coalition under his leadership. They had decided not to speak, as they had learned from their experience at the 1921 party conference, when Diehard speeches had alienated many delegates. However they deputed Lord Hugh Cecil to put their case if it became absolutely necessary.[15]

Another early arrival was Oliver Locker-Lampson, Chamber-

lain's parliamentary private secretary. He carried two glasses of
'an amber-coloured fluid', which he placed on the mantelpiece
behind the leaders' platform. Bonar Law then arrived and sat in
the body of the meeting. Chamberlain and Birkenhead came
later, accompanied by shouts of 'Judas' and 'traitor'. Chamberlain looked pale and upset, and put his tumbler of fluid behind
his chair. Birkenhead, who was 'as usual, quite unmoved', took
'a perfect sensible attitude' to his tumbler.[16]

Sir Winston Churchill once said of Austen Chamberlain that
'he always played the game and always lost it'; and to the
extent that he stood by his colleagues, the description was
accurate. But what game was he playing in 1922? Neither his
colleagues nor his followers could be sure. Before the Carlton
Club Meeting, he had told Lloyd George that 'he must not
suppose from the line I was going to take at the Carlton Club
that I was in any way committed to an indefinite support of his
Prime Ministership'.

Again, on the morning of the meeting, he had told Leslie
Wilson that 'If I carried the meeting with me, I should summon
another meeting of members after the election to consider and
decide upon the position of the party'.[17]

Chamberlain did not tell these things to the assembled M.P.s;
but since he had little personal contact with most of them, he
should have realised that they were unlikely to comprehend his
position unless he outlined it clearly. He told the meeting that
there would be a regular election, without coupons, but that the
Conservatives should co-operate completely with the Coalition
Liberals. He added that this would leave the Conservatives under
a heavy obligation to their Liberal allies. Chamberlain did not
require each Coalition candidate to be bound to the Government
as it existed : each candidate 'should stand under his own party
name, and should retain his party loyalty unimpaired'. However
the cabinet would go to the country as a Coalition, and would
be reconstructed afterwards. He did not mention his reservations
about Lloyd George, and might have carried the meeting if he
had done so. Nor did he make it clear how far the obligations to
the Coalition Liberals would extend, or whether the parties
would fuse in the next Parliament. He did say, rightly, that he
was bound to the M.P.s only, implying that he would not act at
the behest of the party conference. The conference was respon-

sible only to the militant members of the Conservative Party, while the M.P.s were responsible to the entire electorate.[18]

Chamberlain may have felt that an open statement about his views of Lloyd George's premiership would alienate Liberal voters; as it was, he alienated the Conservatives. Amery felt he had gone back on his promise that there would be a final decision on the Coalition after the election. Viscount Windsor, M.P. for Ludlow, told his constituents that 'as soon as Mr Chamberlain made his speech', he realised that his leader 'held out no real hope of breaking away' from Lloyd George. Lord Hemingford said that Chamberlain's 'uncompromising and somewhat aggressive attitude' surprised many M.P.s 'and even before Bonar Law's speech, tended to make us support the break up'.[19]

Stanley Baldwin followed Chamberlain and made a brief speech in which he described Lloyd George as a 'dynamic force' which could disrupt the Conservative Party, just as it had disrupted the Liberals.

> I should like to give you just one illustration to show what I mean by the disintegrating influence of a dynamic force. Take Mr. Chamberlain and myself. He is prepared to go into the wilderness if he should be compelled to forsake the Prime Minister, and I am prepared to go into the wilderness if I should be compelled to stay with him.

At the time, Baldwin was a minor minister, barely in the second rank of Conservative leaders, and Chamberlain was the elected leader of the party. The logical conclusion of Baldwin's speech was that if Baldwin or any other Conservative repudiated any party leader, then the party leader should go rather than the critic. The same argument could have been used against Baldwin himself, during his own leadership. Baldwin did not say why or how Lloyd George was a divisive force, and he did not criticise any of Lloyd George's policies or plans. However it was not Baldwin's logic, but his emotional reaction against Lloyd George which pleased his audience.

E. G. Pretyman then called on the Conservative Party to contest the election on its own. He wanted local Conservative parties to have the right to support or oppose Coalition Liberals as they wished. He defended Lloyd George, and then moved 'That this meeting of Conservative members of the House of

Commons declares its opinion that the Conservative Party, whilst willing to co-operate with the Coalition Liberals, fights the election as an independent party, with its own leader and its own programme'.

G. R. Lane-Fox, seconding this resolution, said that the M.P.s could not pretend to be independents when in fact they supported the Coalition. He also denied that there was 'any desire to have proscription or exclusion of those with whom they had been working. If he could be of any assistance he would be only too willing to speak to the constituents of the Coalition Liberals'. Following Lane-Fox, F. B. Mildmay, one of Chamberlain's strongest adherents, said he agreed with Pretyman and Lane-Fox, and that he believed Chamberlain agreed with them too. A Diehard, Sir Henry Craik, interjected that he would not abate any of his principles.

During the proceedings Bonar Law looked 'very nervous and unhappy, apparently not having made up his mind what line he was going to take'. He began his speech 'almost inaudibly', according to Sir William Joynson-Hicks. Chamberlain later said 'he had never heard Bonar make a worse speech'. Law told the M.P.s that he had come reluctantly to the conclusion that it was time to leave the Coalition.

> Let me say at once of what I am afraid. I am an opportunist. I am not influenced as much as Sir Henry Craik is by the difference of principle. There are things that are vital. On that there can be no comment. But life is a compromise, and if I had been in Mr. Chamberlain's position I think it is almost certain that I would have differed with a large section of our own party, apart altogether from other sections working with him. But I say this: I saw with perfect equanimity the smashing of the Liberal Party; it did not disturb me a bit. As to Mr. Lloyd George, whoever else may speak with disrespect of him I never will. We may differ from him, and during the whole course of my cooperation with him I could see quite plainly that the time might come when we would differ; but that difference will never make me think that he did not render a service to this country in the war for which the country can never sufficiently thank him [applause]. Mr. Lloyd George cannot look on the Unionist Party with the same sort of

feeling I have. In the nature of the case, although I am sure
he does not deliberately try to do it (I am quite sure of that),
if it were broken I do not think it would break his heart
[laughter] just as the breaking of a little part of [the Liberal
Party] did not disturb me.

The passage just quoted was suppressed from the public report
of the Carlton Club Meeting. Sir Malcolm Fraser, Sir George
Younger and Sir Leslie Wilson told Bonar Law that 'the average
reader who is apt to be stupid might misinterpret your avowal
of being an opportunist and also your reference to not being
influenced by the difference of principle'. In addition, they said,
the passage might create greater tension in constituencies where
the Conservatives were trying to get Coalition Liberal support.[20]

Lord Balfour, who followed Law, saw the matter as a question
of honour. He rejected Baldwin's suggestion that Lloyd George
would destroy the Conservatives. This implied that Lloyd George
was trying to force Liberal measures on Conservative M.P.s; but
if anything, the modification of views had been on Lloyd
George's part. He considered the motion to say that if a Conservative candidate needed Liberal votes, he could announce
support for the Coalition; but that if other Conservatives felt
they did not need outside help, they could say they opposed
coalition. Balfour labelled Pretyman's motion dishonourable.
Balfour was noted for carefully hedged statements rather than
plain remarks of this sort, but his accusations of disloyalty and
dishonour did little good to Chamberlain's cause, and made
future reconciliation more difficult.

Leslie Wilson said that while private M.P.s could run as non-
Coalition Conservatives, he, as chief whip, could not. His constituents would ask whether there would be a Conservative
premier if the Conservatives got a majority. He could not tell
from Chamberlain's statement what he should answer. Chamberlain later wrote to him:[21]

It is, I suppose, the first occasion on which the Chief Whip
has thought it necessary, or indeed consistent with the extremely confidential personal relationship which exists between
him and the Leader, that he should work and speak against
his Leader at such a gathering. I hope you will find yourself

in sufficient agreement with Bonar Law to make it unnecessary for you to repeat so unfortunate a precedent.

Chamberlain could have accepted the resolution as it stood. This would have been only a minor concession on his part, but it would have appeased moderate Conservatives who opposed indefinite prolongation of an undefined alliance, but who recognised the need for co-operation with the Coalition Liberals. He would have satisfied many had he done no more than assure his followers that he would maintain a separate Conservative organisation after the election. J. F. Hope, a supporter of the Coalition, proposed adjourning the meeting to give the leaders time to frame a compromise, but Chamberlain pressed for 'a decisive conclusion' at once.

Some M.P.s thought they were voting for Chamberlain, when they were actually voting against him. Sir William Lane-Mitchell and Sir Alexander Richardson both told P. J. Ford that they thought Pretyman's motion 'was substantially in agreement with your views'. Ford told Chamberlain that he was right to force the issue, but that 'about 50 votes were cast under an entire misapprehension'. Ford's estimate of 50 may have been exaggerated, but some M.P.s were obviously confused. Moreover Chamberlain allowed his opponents to pass a moderate resolution which obtained far more support than a straightforward condemnation of the Coalition would have done. Lord Hugh Cecil wanted the meeting to denounce Lloyd George by name, but no other speaker supported him except another Diehard. If Chamberlain had been more conciliatory, he could have carried the meeting. Instead he challenged his opponents to a fight, the purpose of which was unclear. In doing so, he voluntarily assumed the position of an extremist, and let his opponents take that of moderates. This was a reversal of their real positions, and pointed out strikingly his deficiencies as leader.[22]

The voting was not secret, but on cards marked with the name of the M.P.s to whom they were issued. Some ballots may have been mixed up or marked inaccurately, but the party leaders knew the opinions of the rest. Austen Chamberlain's papers contain a list marked with their votes: this list is reproduced in Appendix I of this book. Many M.P.s told their constituents how they had voted, and in nearly all cases their statements agreed with Chamberlain's list. A hundred and eighty-seven voted for Pretyman's resolution, while only 86 voted against it. There were also at least a dozen abstentions. Chamberlain resigned almost at once.

It has often been stated that the intervention of Bonar Law and Baldwin turned the tide against the Coalition at this meeting. Even on the face of it, this seems unlikely, and it is certainly difficult to reconcile with the view that there was a widespread rebellion against the Coalition by constituency parties and M.P.s. Probably the reason why people considered the speeches of Bonar Law and Baldwin as decisive is that, until the meeting began, few had expected Chamberlain to lose. However according to the M.P.s, the speeches at the Carlton Club merely confirmed opinions already held by a large majority of themselves.

Appendix I examines the attitude before and at the 19 October meeting of all 380 Conservative M.P.s. It has not been possible to trace the developing opinions of 80 of those who voted against the Coalition, either because they did not speak in public on the subject, or because their speeches were ambiguous. An over-whelming majority of the remaining 107 who did discuss the Coalition made up their minds before the meeting. Excluding the two M.P.s who, according to P. J. Ford, thought they were supporting the Coalition when in fact they were voting against it, there were 33 Diehards and 72 other M.P.s in this group. Only one, Edward Manville, M.P. for Coventry, said unequivo-cally that he decided to reject the Coalition as a result of events at the Carlton Club. Seven more M.P.s in the group may also have decided only at the last moment, though the evidence for this is very flimsy in some cases. Five other M.P.s did not say definitely before the meeting that they would oppose the Coalition, but they all faced independent Conservative opposition in their constituencies, and this, rather than the speeches of Bonar Law and Baldwin, was probably the deciding factor with them. Yet another M.P., Viscount Ednam, had renounced the Coalition in a 1921 by-election, and he too likely had decided his position before the meeting.[23]

Therefore, of the 105 M.P.s examined, only 8 probably made up their minds at the meeting. Another 5 who had not previously repudiated the Coalition in public likely voted against it because of constituency pressure. The remaining 92 stated before the meeting that they would contest the 1922 election independently of the Coalition. Even if all the Diehards are left out of the calculation, there were 59 who made up their minds before the meeting, and only 8 who decided at it. The inescapable conclusion is that, while the Carlton Club Meeting was spectacular, it was in reality little more than a collective acknowledgement by the Conservative M.P.s of views they had previously expressed on separate public platforms. The handful of Conservative M.P.s who came out for party independence after having been on the fence made only a slight difference to the result. The anti-Coalition majority would still have been two to one against Chamberlain, if he had chosen to regard it as such. Lord Beaverbrook compared the Carlton Club to a bull-ring, and Bonar Law to a matador. The Coalition-bull was in the ring, 'but no matador, no killing of the bull'. Bonar Law denied this, and attributed his success to the deep-seated determination to end the Coalition of the local Conservative parties. It is doubtful whether Law himself made any inquiry into Conservative feeling in the constituencies. The available evidence, from a study of Conservative activity in practically every constituency in 1922, indicates that the Diehard revolt was unimportant. However, there was widespread dissatisfaction with the Coalition, and even more with Lloyd George personally. Nobody seemed to know Chamberlain's ultimate aims, or if he had any. In the absence of a straightforward and comprehensible lead from him, many Conservative M.P.s preferred to appease a handful of Diehards, who would at least vote Conservative, than to obtain half-hearted support from an ill-defined Coalition.[24]

Except in a few unusual cases, the revolt was limited to the M.P.s and the Diehard groups. Nearly all the M.P.s who rebelled had the support of their local parties; but the M.P.s who backed the Coalition also had such support. In some seats with retiring M.P.s, the local parties put pressure on the prospective candidates to drop the Coalition, but the prospective candidates could not vote at the Carlton Club Meeting. Apart from a few seats, the M.P.s were not forced into rebellion by their local parties, and it seems that most of them rebelled to retain electoral popularity and freedom of action. They did not know whether open support of the Coalition would help them in the forthcoming election, but they knew it would drive away some

Diehards. At the same time, most of them felt they could retain ties with their Coalition Liberal allies even if they ran independently of the Coalition. It is apparent from the analysis of the vote at the Carlton Club Meeting that the result was not in question; but the analysis was not available to the M.P.s, and few thought a revolt would succeed. The rebels therefore thought they were in the fortunate position of being able to dissociate themselves from the Lloyd George Coalition without weakening what they regarded as the only probable alternative to a Labour government. They did not reject the general idea of coalition, though they did not want to be tied firmly to the existing one. Since Chamberlain himself did not want an indefinite Lloyd George Premiership, it was unfortunate for him that he did not communicate his feelings to his followers.

Only a handful of M.P.s wanted their party to retain its purity by keeping out of all coalitions, and even the Diehards were divided on the question. Many Conservative M.P.s resented the relative freedom of the Coalition Liberals to support or oppose the Government, and they did not want to be the only party to lose popularity. A show of independence would help them in their constituencies, and having made statements of their independence, the M.P.s could not retract without losing face. In the summer of 1922 Chamberlain had told G. K. Cockerill, M.P. for Reigate, that the Conservatives would fight the forthcoming election separately from the Coalition Liberals, and that they would have their own programme and their own leaders. Cockerill wrote to Chamberlain, 'I therefore asked your permission to make an announcement to that effect in my constituency, where I was speaking that afternoon. You said I could do so, and I did so.' Cockerill felt Chamberlain had misled him and voted against the Coalition at the Carlton Club Meeting.[25]

The vote at the Carlton Club did not reject future coalitions; it just stated the claim of the Conservatives to form a government on their own if they got a majority. In some respects the vote made the formation of future coalitions easier, since the Conservative candidates seemed more willing to accept Lloyd George once they had given him a rebuke and had shown him the limits to his power. In the 1922 election, many Conservative candidates who had previously opposed Lloyd George and his Government strongly kept quiet, or even spoke in favour of the Coalition's record.

It would be misleading to say that the vote at the Carlton Club Meeting was without significance : its immediate result was the fall of the Government and its replacement by a Conservative one. Few informed observers expected the new Government to last beyond the election in unchanged form, but its existence was one of the few certain factors in the election, and thus the mere fact of its existence influenced the results.

It would also be erroneous to maintain that Bonar Law's influence was unimportant, though as this chapter has shown, his presence did not change the votes of many M.P.s at the meeting. The true importance of Bonar Law was that he led his party capably through an election where it would have been easy to make serious blunders. Bonar Law's moderation was a noticeable contrast to the activities of his chief opponents. Many perplexed voters consequently preferred him to his rivals, and this preference was instrumental in giving the Conservatives their majority.

7

The Uncertain Trumpet: political confusion in early November 1922

For if the trumpet give forth an uncertain sound,
who shall prepare himself to the battle?
I Corinthians, xiv 8

Most general elections in recent years have been contests between two parties for control of the commons, and they have been conducted along fairly clear lines established prior to the campaigns themselves. The psephological interest in these elections has concerned the question of which party would win, and it has been assumed that someone would win. It has also been a foregone conclusion that no election would make a fundamenatl difference to the political structure of the country, and that the parties would be the same ones after the election as before it. In 1922 there was a race, but nobody knew precisely which parties were opposing each other, as the party alliances varied from place to place. As the *Manchester Guardian* said, 'never perhaps has a general election been held where the issues were less clear and the electors received less guidance.' J. L. Garvin, editor of the *Observer*, said he would be 'surprised at nothing; anything may happen', and The *Nation* described the campaign as 'a state of confusion unknown in any former election. The old party lines are gone'.[1]

Much of this confusion resulted from the large number of uncertain factors in the election. Elections generally have but one major unknown factor, that is, the victor; but in 1922 there were further uncertainties concerning party leadership and policies, the extent of and danger from the rise of Labour, and most important, the alignment of parties in the next Parliament. As the election results showed, the three main parties had roughly equal support. Many politicians expected this, but they did not know which way the votes would be distributed from one constituency to another. Party alignments could develop in several ways, depending on that distribution : a Conservative majority would have produced a period of stability tending to polarise politics between a one-party government and a largely Labour opposition. If the Conservatives failed to win a majority, the Liberals might have allied with either Labour or the Conservatives, or any of the three parties might have formed a minority government. In the 1923 election, no party gained a majority, but the range of possibilities was more limited than it had been in 1922 : by 1923, in contrast with the previous year, there was a single Labour leader; the Liberals were reunited, on the surface at any rate; and the Conservative leaders who had deposed Lloyd George were relatively entrenched. Their party had governed alone for the first time in decades, and it knew it could win an election. This increased Conservative self-confidence, the lack of which had underlain Conservative co-operation with the Liberals before the Carlton Club Meeting. The results of the 1922 election were important in producing these changes, and consequently in determining the future course of British politics. As this chapter indicates, the Carlton Club Meeting did not reduce political confusion; rather it heightened uncertainty, and delayed solution of several important matters until after the declaration of the poll.

No party had unquestioned leadership in 1922 : a quarter of the ex-premier's followers called themselves Liberals without prefix. Sir Alfred Mond, Lloyd George's minister of health, did this in Swansea; J. E. B. Seely stood as a 'non-party man' in Ilkeston, while another former Lloyd George Liberal campaigned as 'plain Jim Walton, of Don Valley division'. Many other Lloyd Georgians hardly mentioned their leader, and the group could not be regarded as a band of loyalists. The attitude of many Independent Liberals to Asquith was also doubtful, and so many Liberal candidates wavered between the two Liberal leaders that it was difficult to gauge the effect of the election on their party. As it was, twenty-eight successful Liberals could not be counted definitely in one faction or the other. The remaining Liberal M.P.s were divided almost evenly, as each faction elected just over forty; and this meant that the electors gave no clear indication as to which Liberal leader had more support.* [2]

The Conservative Party temporarily shelved the question of leadership during the 1922 election. Hardly any Conservative candidates openly rejected Bonar Law, though a few did so. These Conservative rebels and half-hearted supporters were unlikely to depose Bonar Law even if he failed to get a clear majority, because his stature among Conservatives was too great for this. However a parliamentary deadlock would have confirmed the predictions of Austen Chamberlain, Birkenhead and their associates, and it would have strengthened their position in post-election cabinet shuffles, especially in relation to last-minute seceders from the Coalition such as Baldwin and Curzon.

There was no leader of the Labour Party, and the 1922 election demonstrated that the party needed more than a temporary house leader such as J. R. Clynes. It was often difficult during the election to determine what the official Labour policy was on issues such as capital levy, since one Labour speaker often said one thing, while another contradicted him. The Labour Party was more solid, and problems of leadership less significant than in the other parties, but a strong leader would have been able to present a more coherent programme than the collection of semi-official spokesmen did during the 1922 campaign. Many candidates ridiculed the absence of a Labour leader. The prefix-less Liberal in the Newport by-election just before the general election said that at least he had to choose between only two leaders, while in the Labour Party 'there were so many that he could take his choice of half a dozen or more'. After the election, the Labour M.P.s picked Ramsay MacDonald as leader by a margin of five votes over J. R. Clynes, with the Scottish Labour M.P.s supporting MacDonald strongly. In 1922, the proportion of Labour M.P.s from Scotland was 20.4 per cent compared

* Prefixless Liberal candidates in the 1922 election are listed in Appendix II.

with 16.9 per cent in 1918 and 17.8 per cent in 1923. While the difference may seem slight, it was sufficient to give Mac-Donald his narrow majority over Clynes.[3]

Perhaps the most apposite comment on the confusion of leadership in all the parties was Sir John Simon's[4]

All the political prophets were searching the horoscope of Mr. Lloyd George, calculating fortunes, estimating influences. Which party was he going to attempt to lead? Was he going to lead the Conservative Party or the Liberal Party, or perhaps, the Labour Party [laughter, and a loud voice, 'I don't think!']. Which party was he going to split? And even more insoluble conundrums.

So long as the question of leadership was unsettled, the parties had difficulty in outlining their policies precisely. In the beginning of October the issues of politics seemed fairly clear. Labour stood for some form of socialism, while the Coalition opposed it; the Asquithian Liberals opposed the Coalition from a party viewpoint, but not because of a fundamental divergence of principles. The fall of the Coalition destroyed the basis of the Asquithian criticism, and the 1922 election came before the new Government made many serious mistakes for either group of Liberals to criticise. Moreover, compared with Lloyd George's ministry, the new cabinet had relatively few prominent figures for the Liberals or Labour to attack. The views of the new ministers on many subjects were not widely known; even the accusation that they were Diehard views meant little, since the Diehards seemed to have few common sentiments of much political relevance, except dislike of Lloyd George and devotion to what so many of them called 'the workman's glass of beer'.[5]

The election of 1922 was characterised by a systematic effort by the leaders of all three non-socialist parties to present as few policies as possible. A meeting of Bonar Law's leading supporters decided on 20 October to fight the election on the issue of 'a change in government'. This meeting eliminated contentious proposals from the Conservative manifesto, and in his first speech as Conservative leader, Bonar Law remarked, 'This is not the occasion for making a declaration of policy'. Lloyd George retorted, "I have no slogan', and Asquith, who made no major speech in the first eleven days of the four-week campaign, condemned the new Government without making a single specific criticism, his sole argument being that it was another coalition. Years before, Disraeli had said that a Conservative government was Tory men and Whig measures. Apparently Bonar Law's Government was Tory men and no measures, and the position of Law's opponents was scarcely clearer.[6]

Although the Conservatives tried to avoid new issues, the other parties might have stirred up old ones. It was in the Conservative interest to campaign on the basis of a blank slate, for some old issues such as Ireland, lords reform and Welsh Disestablishment were unfavourable ground for them. The war and activities of Lloyd George were more favourable for the Conservatives, but they avoided them too.

Ireland had been for years one of the most important factors in British politics, and it had been the most important single issue from 1919 until the Carlton Club Meeting. Yet it played virtually no part in the election campaign, and in an eighty-page description of the election, published by the Conservatives, Ireland merited only one page; and it merely quoted some innocuous speeches by Bonar Law. Another major issue from the Conservative standpoint had been reform of the house of lords. In fact Sir George Younger and other Conservatives had used the supposed urgency for lords reform as an excuse to prevent the proposed January 1922 election. In the actual election campaign, very few candidates discussed lords reform, even those who had supported it most strongly in January. A third issue prominent in pre-war politics had been religion, especially church schools and Welsh Disestablishment. Almost no Conservative candidate mentioned these in the 1922 election, and the extent to which religion had gone out of politics as an overt issue could be seen from the reply of Admiral Sir Guy Gaunt, Conservative candidate in Buckrose, to a heckler:

What is your opinion of the disestablishment of the Welsh Church. This, I must say, was a facer. I did not even know there was a Welsh Church. On the spur of the moment, I should have been inclined to say that a good healthy bomb was the best way of disestablishing it.

However he thought better of this and replied, 'I implore you, sir, not to mix religion with politics'.[7]

The origins of the war, and the heritage of bitterness caused by conscription played a slightly larger part in this election than Ireland, lords reform or religion, but again, only a few Conservatives mentioned them. Most Asquithian Liberals also avoided issues predating 1918, and Labour candidates generally stuck to post-war topics as well.

The most remarkable change in issues in this short election was the rapid disappearance of Lloyd George from the centre of the political stage. He had been the symbol of his Government in a way that few premiers had been up to that time, or have been since; but in the election campaign after his fall, few politicians except strong Asquithians spent much time denouncing him. Candidates of other parties or groups had little to gain by adopting a strong position for or against him, since he was so controversial that his opponents were likely to lose the votes of his supporters, and vice versa. Public interest in Lloyd George remained high, but it centred on what influence he would exert on political alignments after the election.

The removal of Lloyd George as a major campaign issue destroyed the Asquithian campaign strategy, which had concentrated on personal criticism of him. The Liberal publication department had issued thirty-three leaflets between January and October 1922, thirteen of which had dealt mainly or wholly with Lloyd George. Only one pamphlet had mentioned the Labour or Conservative Parties, and Asquithian attempts to identify the new Government with the old did not persuade many, since the new ministers were clearly on bad terms, temporarily at least, with the Lloyd Georgians. Thus the Asquithian campaign had been directed against one man, and by election day that man was not in office.

We have seen that most issues predating the election were not often mentioned. Many of them were irrelevant in the post-war years, but even relevant ones such as tariff reform were deliberately avoided. This created a vacuum in which a topic injected into the campaign seemed more significant than perhaps it really was. One example of this was Bonar Law's suggestion of amalgamating the ministry of pensions with other government agencies, thus saving the salary of a minister and a few civil servants. This modest suggestion became a major issue for a while, when opposition spokesmen insinuated that Law was trying to cut pensions. However the supposed threat from Labour soon displaced discussions of the pensions ministry.

In the time of the Coalition, the Red scare had been only one of many issues, and while the Diehards for example had feared and disliked Labour, they had often disliked the Coalition even more. The Diehards were probably the strongest opponents of Labour in 1922, but because they had fixed their eyes on deposing Lloyd George, they had risked underplaying what to them was the Labour menace. The fall of the Coalition and the removal of most issues of day-to-day disagreement between themselves and other Conservatives let the Diehards concentrate their crusading energies against socialism. This was particularly noticeable among Diehards who had campaigned in the Newport by-election immediately prior to the Carlton Club Meeting. De Fonblanque Pennefather, a Liverpool Diehard M.P., had said during the by-election that the chief threat from Labour was that it would bring prohibition: he had drawn a parallel between the Labour candidate's mascot, a cat, and 'Pussyfoot' Johnson, an American Prohibitionist. Lord Salisbury, the leading Diehard, had said that the country had few Bolsheviks, that he did not distrust Labour, and that the working class had 'good sense'. Sir Reginald 'Blinker' Hall had told a Newport audience that the country had nothing to fear from Labour but incompetence. The fall of Lloyd George transformed their speeches: Pennefather and Salisbury said during the general election that Labour would cut the social services and send the country into an economic tailspin, while Hall spoke of 'the Labour-Socialist and Communist menace'. This movement of the Diehards to join in the general Conservative campaign against Labour tended to simplify the lines of political discussion. On the other hand it meant that even the Diehards acknowledged the need in certain cases for supporting Liberals against Labour. In turn this meant that the general idea of coalition would have a wider base of support in the Conservative Party than previously.[8]

Divisions between Conservatives and Coalition Liberals remained unclear however as local parties made arrangements which often conflicted with arrangements in nearby constituencies. In general the 'nationalisation' of politics in the past century has made local factors less and less significant. This nationalisation of issues did not appear fully-blown at any particular date, but by the beginning of this century, general elections were more national than local, and since then local influences have shrunk even further. However in 1922 national and local issues interacted in a complex and confusing manner : the political scene resembled a landscape by Seurat, with many individual segments which made up a coherent picture when glimpsed at a distance, but which exhibited considerable variation from neighbouring segments when examined close up.

Before the development of mass political organisations, local factors often dominated elections; since the emergence of the modern party system, national issues and alignments have prevailed. In 1922 several national issues such as socialism and free trade remained influential in many constituencies, and the party leaders issued manifestos and made speaking tours of the country. Nevertheless local factors were also very important in this election. Local political groups decided what the party alignments would be in their constituencies, and they often did so on the basis of variable factors such as the personalities of the candidates. The nominees of a given party frequently pursued different and even contradictory policies; this meant that party alignments varied considerably from one constituency to another. Some candidates rejected all advances from other parties, while other candidates acted as mini-coalitions in themselves, building up fragile local alliances. To some extent the election of 1922 resembled a present-day general election less than it resembled a large number of by-elections, as it was a collection of numerous local campaigns (overridden in some cases by national issues), in which the only real category was the individual. This may be described as electoral nominalism. Several other elections of the 1920s also showed this tendency to fragmentation, but the election of 1922 was far more complicated than they were, and it is not going too far to describe it as the most complex of this century. Merely listing the types of contest in 1922 indicates the complexity.

During this election, many local parties supported candidates of other parties to prevent the election of even less desirable candidates. Instances of men receiving two nominations were common, and there were even some who received three. For instance in Kinross and West Perth, James Gardiner first received the Lloyd George Liberal nomination. He then offered

Table 5 Types of contest in 1922

Type of contest	Number of seats involved
Con.-Asq. Lib.-Labour	115
Con.-Labour	108
Con.-Asq. Lib.	65
L.G. Lib.-Labour	45
Con.-Prefixless Lib.-Labour	34
L.G. Lib.-Asq. Lib.-Labour	20
Con.-Prefixless Lib.	19
Con.-Asq. Lib.-L.G. Lib.-Labour	12
Con.-L.G. Lib.-Labour	11
Prefixless Lib.-Labour	11
L.G. Lib.-Asq. Lib.	11
Contested 2-member seats (11 types of contest)	24
Contested universities (5 types of contest)	8
51 other types of contest	75
Uncontested	57
Total 78 types of contest + uncontested	615

Bonar Law general support, and got the Conservative nomination, upon which he announced that he was a prefixless Liberal. This obtained him the Asquithian nomination, and, having been nominated by all three parties with an organisation in the constituency, he was unopposed. Sometimes candidates received support in exchange for pledges, and sometimes they got it without strings attached. In Leeds the Conservatives backed three Lloyd George Liberals who stated outright that they opposed Bonar Law. One of the three said he had not even been approached by the Conservatives. On the other hand, when the Conservatives asked for the views of Walter Forrest, the former Coalition Liberal M.P. for Pontefract, he said he 'could not say whether he should support Mr Lloyd George, Mr Bonar Law, or Mr Asquith, or any other leader, until he had seen their programmes'. Forrest had been relatively popular with the Pontefract Conservatives, and later in the 1920s he was one of the most right-wing Liberal M.P.s. However in 1922 the Conservatives decided:[9]

The man who did not know by then whom he was going to

follow was no use to the Conservatives of Pontefract or to the people of England. . . . Nobody would have hesitated to support Mr. Forrest if he had said he would be a Unionist [i.e. Conservative], but they could not afford to wait.

Because it was uncertain what the overall national party alignments would be after the 1922 election, there was no national pattern of co-operation or conflict between the Conservatives and Lloyd George Liberals. In Scotland, Lancashire and many large boroughs, there was general co-operation, while in Wales and East Anglia, almost as many seats had conflicts as had co-operation. Altogether the Conservatives and Lloyd George Liberals co-operated in 160 seats and conflicted in 55.* The remaining 400 seats did not have official arrangements between the local parties. Co-operation was most extensive in the multi-membered boroughs than elsewhere. It might be assumed that this was simply because Labour was strongest in such places, but this was not so, as Labour conducted some of its most vigorous campaigns in the mining constituencies of South Wales, West Yorkshire and Durham. In those places the Lloyd Georgians and Conservatives co-operated in 10 seats and conflicted in 6. In the boroughs outside London with more than one member, there was co-operation between the wings of the old Coalition in 68 seats, and conflict in only 13. The much higher degree of co-operation in the large boroughs cannot be explained solely by reference to the Labour threat, significant though that threat often was. The influence of the local party organisations was important, particularly where a regional or county organisation dominated a number of local parties. The Conservative organisation officially recognised the supremacy of the local groups in this matter when Sir George Younger notified each constituency chairman :[10]

No pact of any kind exists [between Conservatives and Coalition Liberals].

The situation was clearly explained by Mr. Bonar Law in his speech at Glasgow. The local Unionist executives are left in perfect freedom to select such candidates as they please, and where it is decided locally to run a Unionist candidate,

* Appendix II lists all Liberals in 1922 with Conservative support, and vice versa.

the Central Office will accept the local decision and will officially support their candidate.

When, however, arrangements are made locally where both sides agree not to oppose each other in particular seats, the Central Office will accept that arrangement.

The 'arrangements' could not properly be compared to those of the Conservatives and Liberal Unionists before 1914, nor of the National Government after 1931. The earlier and later arrangements represented nationwide movements in favour of particular policies or particular governments, while the 1922 deals were local matters which often conflicted with deals in neighbouring constituencies. This often led to difficulties. At that time, many people had two votes, in different constituencies for which they had different qualifications. Thus a Conservative voter in Leeds West was recommended to support the Lloyd George Liberal to keep Labour out, while in the contiguous seat of Leeds Central, the same elector, if he had a business vote, was recommended to vote for a Diehard who was trying to unseat a Lloyd Georgian faced with Labour competition. The Lloyd George Liberal in Don Valley had Conservative support, while another Lloyd Georgian in Doncaster, a constituency almost wholly surrounded by Don Valley, had Conservative opposition. To complicate this further, the Lloyd George Liberal organisation in Don Valley was identical with the Doncaster Conservative organisation. The Lloyd George Liberals in Hackney North were also in a perplexing position, for the leading Lloyd Georgians there supported both the Conservative and Asquithian candidates.[11]

This confusing election campaign opened with the general expectation that there would not be a majority government in the following Parliament, and the conduct of the parties during the campaign did not exclude the possibility of indefinite coalition. L. S. Amery, a perceptive observer, said that two things have led to the two-party system, chance and the notion that there can be only two positions on a political subject. However he said that 'the decisive and continuing influence has been the fact that a governing team with a majority in Parliament can normally only be replaced by another team capable of securing an alternative majority'.[12]

If no party had won a clear majority in 1922, a situation
different from that described by Amery would have developed.
Coalitions have proved successful in many countries, in Scandi-
navia, and in post-1945 Germany and Austria, and similar
coalitions could have worked in Britain after 1922. The minority
Parliaments of 1924 and of 1929–31 failed to produce real
coalitions, but by then party lines had become so firmly redrawn
that fusion or alliance of parties was far more difficult. The only
major problem in forming a coalition after November 1922 was
that personal bitterness would have made certain specific combinations hard to form. However it should be noted that the
Liberals were reunited from late 1923 to mid-1926, even though
their leaders continued to have reservations about each other;
and if the Asquithian and Lloyd George factions could work
together, it was even more likely that the former Coalitionists
could have done so.

Amery suggested that in the past there have been two teams
which have replaced each other in government. This was not
so between 1915 and 1922. In those years, there was but one
team, from which some dropped out as others came in. Even
the change of government in October 1922 was not a complete
break, since all but two of Bonar Law's cabinet had been in at
least one of the Coalitions from 1915 to 1922, and ten of them
had been in Lloyd George's Government right up to the Carlton
Club Meeting. The two completely new ministers were the
Marquess of Salisbury, lord president of the council, and Lord
Novar, secretary of state for Scotland. At the time Lord Novar
was still a Liberal. Bonar Law clearly wished to smooth the
transition from one government to the next, and just before the
Carlton Club Meeting, he asked Sir Archibald Salvidge, 'Do
you think that I or Curzon imagine we can rule the country
with the sort of people that will be left after the break tomorrow?
I must have Austen and F.E. back at the first opportunity'. A
week later Lord Peel, Law's secretary of state for India, wrote
to Lord Reading, the viceroy of India:[13]

No one of course can prophesy the outcome of the election,
and it may well be that some other form of cooperation or
combination may be essential to obtain a parliamentary
majority. But the Conservative Party, having obtained its own

leader, and secured its own independence, would, if it failed to obtain a majority at the polls, no doubt be in a more chastened mood and perhaps it would carry on the King's Government in conjunction with some others.

Reckonings of this sort have one major defect: they do not consider the backbench M.P.s, who had just deposed their leaders, ostensibly because the leaders had tried to maintain a coalition. If the backbenchers had not changed their views, speculation about further coalition would have been unrealistic. However the following examination of a representative sample of Conservative backbenchers shows that at the very time when anti-Coalitionist sentiments had apparently triumphed, most Conservative M.P.s anticipated renewed coalition.

The M.P.s examined were chosen only from those who had voted at the Carlton Club Meeting. Four were Diehards, 14 moderate and anti-Coalitionists and 7 pro-Coalitionists. These proportions were virtually the same as in the parliamentary Conservative Party as a whole. The M.P.s were:

Pro-Coalition	Anti-Coalition, but not Diehard	Diehard
E. Gardner (Windsor)	T. Bennett (Sevenoaks)	W. Ashley (New Forest)
E. Gray (Accrington)	H. Betterton (Rushcliffe)	R. Hall (Liverpool-West Derby)
H. Hope (West Stirlingshire)	D. Brown (Hexham)	C. James (Bromley)
T. Inskip (Bristol Central)	P. Dawson (Lewisham West)	J. Marriott (Oxford)
W. Preston (Stepney)	C. Erskine-Bolst (Hackney South)	
W. Raeburn (Dumbartonshire)	E. Fitzroy (Daventry)	
K. Wood (Woolwich West)	K. Frazer (Harborough)	
	J. Gould (Cardiff Central)	
	D. Hacking (Chorley)	
	A. Loyd (Abingdon)	
	H. Morrison (Salisbury)	
	J. Newman (Finchley)	
	R. Terrell (Henley)	
	G. White (Southport)	

This analysis considers first the M.P.s who had supported the previous Coalition, then those who had voted against it. According to *The Times* of 25 October 1922, 'almost half' the supporters of Chamberlain on 19 October soon seceded to Bonar Law. If *The Times*'s estimate was accurate, it would have confirmed the general view that, no matter how divided the Conservatives have been before elections, they have almost invariably closed ranks behind their leaders in actual election campaigns. This may have been so in other elections, but it was only partly true in 1922. Even the one M.P. mentioned by name in *The Times*'s report was dubious proof. The M.P. concerned, T. W. H. Inskip, had voted for the Coalition, but had then become Bonar Law's solicitor-general. However even though he was in Bonar Law's Government, Inskip accepted a series of conditions proposed by some of his Liberal constituents. Among other things, these conditions required him to oppose lords reform and tariffs, but the most important requirement was that he should 'cooperate with Mr. Austen Chamberlain and other Conservatives in any measures which they may deem advisable to take jointly with Mr. Lloyd George and the National Liberals'. Inskip was no exception to the general rule that the M.P.s who had voted for the Coalition at the Carlton Club Meeting favoured renewed coalition if Bonar Law failed to get a majority. Sir Walter Preston, also in our sample, 'was rather proud' of supporting the Coalition; and Kingsley Wood said that he would follow Bonar Law, but that he was prepared to co-operate 'with men actuated by similar views of an anti-Socialist and constitutionalist nature'. The remaining four pro-Coalitionists in the sample were Hope, Raeburn, Gray and Gardner. Hope and Raeburn both openly called for renewed coalition; Gray had been at the Carlton Club Meeting, but was not listed by Chamberlain as having voted. He may have been a teller for Chamberlain, though, since when he knew the result of the meeting, he publicly denounced the 'intrigue and personal ambition' of the anti-Coalitionists. During the election he often praised Lloyd George, but refused to support Bonar Law until Law revealed his programme. On the other hand Ernest Gardner, M.P. for Windsor, had voted for the Coalition, then had gone over fully to Bonar Law; but as he was retiring from politics in 1922, his views were practically irrelevant. Yet

Gardener was the only one of the seven pro-Coalition M.P.s in this sample who gave Bonar Law much reason for comfort.[14]

A large majority of the M.P.s had rejected the Coalition, but it remained to be seen whether this had been a reaction against Austen Chamberlain and the particular structure of the previous Government, or whether it represented a deeper antagonism to coalitions in general. The anti-Coalitionists in this sample mostly expected some new combination to emerge from the chaos of the election campaign. The opinions of three M.P.s in the sample cannot be stated precisely : they were T. J. Bennett, A. T. Lloyd and G. D. White. Each had voted against the Government at the Carlton Club Meeting, but there was little indication in their election speeches of their attitude to post-election alliances. Two M.P.s in the sample definitely rejected any form of coalition : they were R. Terrell, who had broken away from the Coalition in May 1922, and the Diehard J. A. R. Marriott. If Marriott, Terrell and the three doubtful M.P.s are counted together, then at most 5 of the 18 anti-Coalitionists of 19 October remain opposed to coalition. The other 13 supported one, even though they had voted against Chamberlain.[15]

Two M.P.s of the thirteen implied during the election campaign that they had voted for the Coalition on 19 October, when they had actually voted against it. H. B. Betterton was in this position, as was C. Erskine-Bolst. Erskine-Bolst did not even stand as a Conservative in the election, but as a Constitutionalist with Lloyd George Liberal support.[16]

Two more of the thirteen M.P. had wavered before the Carlton Club Meeting, but had then voted against the Coalition. Both subsequently reverted to mild support of coalition. They were Douglas Hacking and E. A. Fitzroy. After the Carlton Club Meeting, Hacking told his constituents that the Coalition had created 'a wonderful world position', but that it had been best to break away, to preserve Conservative unity. Nonetheless he would favour continued joint action with the Lloyd George Liberals. Fitzroy had apparently voted against Chamberlain on 19 October to forestall Diehard attacks in his constituency. In July 1922 he had labelled proposals for an independent Conservative Party as 'a disaster', and he had called on the Diehards to 'join the Coalition to keep the Socialists out'. He had made no public criticism of the Government between July and October, although he had voted against it at the Carlton Club. During the election, he remarked several times that the Conservatives and Liberals should co-operate after the fashion of the Conservatives and Liberal Unionists in the 1890s.[17]

The remaining nine M.P.s in this sample had opposed the Coalition for some time before 19 October, and all had voted against it. Yet each was willing to support future coalitions if Bonar Law did not get a majority. They were D. Clifton Brown, Sir Philip Dawson, Sir Keith Frazer, J. C. Gould, Hugh Morrison, and J. R. P. Newman, none of whom was a Diehard; and three Diehards, Wilfred Ashley, Sir Reginald Hall and Cuthbert James.

D. C. Brown thought that 'a coalition may be necessary', while J. C. Gould believed that the Carlton Club decision indicated 'no permanent split', but rather an internal rearrangement. J. R. P. Newman, who had been one of the strongest non-Diehard opponents of the Coalition before 19 October, said that 'supposing, as was likely, that neither party had a clear majority over the other groups combined, then something had to happen'. He suggested that the parties would form new combinations. The fault of the old coalition, he said, was that it had been electoral as well as parliamentary. M.P.s who had wished to chasten it had been unable to do so, since that would have involved a breach of faith with their constituents. He wanted a freer hand from his constituents in the next Parliament so he could support or oppose any coalition, depending on its specific actions. Dawson, Frazer and Morrison substantially agreed with these views.[18]

Of all the Conservative M.P.s, the Diehards had been the most opposed to the Lloyd George Coalition; yet three of the four Diehards in this sample were willing to support a new coalition if the Conservatives did not win a majority. The position of Wilfrid Ashley was the most curious. On 16 October Ashley had written to the Diehard paper, the *Morning Post*, that 'even if Labour did come to power, many voters say openly that they do not regard Mr. Clynes as a greater danger than the Prime Minister'. He said that at least Clynes was sincere in his socialism, while Lloyd George might betray anything. Ashley had spoken and voted against the Coalition at the Carlton Club Meeting, but on the very day of the meeting he told the Press that 'although there might be a certain number of Tories elected, that did not mean they were prevented from co-operating afterwards with Labour and the Liberals'.[19]

It is unlikely that many Conservative M.P.s shared Ashley's idea of co-operating with Labour, but Cuthbert James, another Diehard, 'when asked if he would give his support to Mr. Bonar Law if the latter should decide to join Mr. Lloyd George, replied, "Yes, certainly".' [20]

Another Diehard, Sir Reginald Hall, stated : [21]

> In the event of the Conservative Party being returned by an insufficient majority to carry on the government of the country, I am prepared to support my leader in any steps he may deem necessary to take to cooperate with any other party to form a stable government.

To conclude, in the sample of 25 Conservative M.P.s who had been at the Carlton Club Meeting, only two definitely rejected coalition for the future, while three more took ambiguous positions.* One pro-Coalitionist also took an ambiguous position, but he was retiring. The remaining 19 all stated clearly that they would support some form of coalition if their party did not get a majority, and most of them expected that that would be the case. In effect they were saying that they would take the whole cake if they could, but that if not, they would take only part of it. However even the realisation that they might not be able to take it all was a change from the view many of them had held previously.

The majority behind an anti-socialist combination after the 1922 election would probably not have been much different from a majority behind a purely Conservative government : each would have attracted most Conservatives, although a bipartisan coalition might have alienated a few Diehards. This survey of Conservative M.P.s has indicated that even some Diehards, perhaps most of them, would have backed a new anti-socialist coalition. Such a coalition might have been based on fusion of the Conservatives with some of the Liberals, or perhaps only on

---

* Even Neville Chamberlain, for some time a personal enemy of Lloyd George, hedged his bets. During the election he exhibited an Indian Red chrysanthemum at a Birmingham flower show. He named the flower 'Lloyd George'. *Bristol Evening News* (8 November 1922).

close affiliation. At any rate there were several possibilities, each of which had some support in the election campaign. Not least of these possibilities was that the Conservatives and Lloyd George Liberals would agree to share major policy decisions. Whatever those decisions had been, such an outcome would have preserved a much larger role for the Liberals in the 1920s than they eventually had. In this chapter we have seen that policy and leadership were confused in each party in this election. We have also seen that party alignments varied considerably from one area of the country to another, and sometimes from one part of a city to another. The Conservative M.P.s were uncertain of their party's future and the sample of twenty-five of them showed that most were willing to contemplate a revised version of the Coalition which they had brought down on 19 October. However, if the election yielded a straightforward Conservative majority, the talk of coalition would have been meaningless. Thus it is necessary to consider briefly in this chapter the closeness of the election, and more extensively in the next chapter, how the Conservatives came to win their party majority.

In 1922 Bonar Law got a substantial majority in terms of seats, 77 if all independent Conservative victors are counted. Yet this was one of the closest elections on record : each of the three main parties got approximately a third of the vote, and no fewer than 103 M.P.s, a sixth of the total, had majorities of under 1000 votes. Conservatives won 38 of these contests. In each of these constituencies a turnover of 500 votes would have changed the result. In addition, a further 38 M.P.s had majorities between 1001 and 1500. Since the introduction of universal suffrage in 1918, only the 1923 election has approached this number of close fights, as Table 6 indicates.

Table 6   Number of M.P.s with majorities under 1000*

1918	54	1931	21	1955	42
1922	103	1935	48	1959	43
1923	123	1945	50	1964	40
1924	65	1950	45	1966	46
1929	68	1951	44	1970	48

* The 1918 figure excludes six seats in Southern Ireland.

In the very close contests, the events of the campaign probably determined the winners : even if the campaign influenced only a few hundred voters in each seat, it is clear from Table 5 (see p. 143) that this was sufficient to affect the distribution of seats decisively. The combined Conservative pluralities in their 30 closest seats came to only 7475 : thus if 3738 voters (half plus one of 7475) in these 30 constituencies had voted for the second runners, Bonar Law would have lost his effective majority in Parliament, and would have been dependent on the Lloyd Georgians and Chamberlainites. Even relatively minor influences would have caused such a change, but in 1922 a fortunate series of chances favoured Bonar Law in almost every way.

One such chance was the continuing Liberal quarrel. In 1923 the Liberals patched up their differences immediately before the election. In 1922 a delay of even a few months might have given the Liberals time to effect a token reconciliation, but the election came on them too quickly for this. It is impossible to determine precisely how many Liberal voters turned away from their party's factional squabbles to side with the Tories, but the results in the two-member constituencies are illuminating. Four of these seats had Asquithian, Lloyd Georgian, Conservative and Labour candidates in 1922. The overall figures, excluding votes shared with Labour were :

Straight votes		Split votes	
Conservative only	35,021	Con.-L.G. Liberal	72,047
L.G. Liberal only	10,158	Con.-Asq. Liberal	6,264
Asq. Liberal only	18,002	L.G. Liq.-Asq. Lib.	16,167

The Asquithian votes divided as follows : 44.5 per cent straight Asquithian, 40.0 per cent shared with the Lloyd Georgians and 15.5 per cent shared with Conservatives. That is, just over one Asquithian in seven helped the Conservatives rather than Liberals of the rival faction. In these four constituencies, the factional division was worth more than 1000 votes to the Conservatives; even if such support was worth only 500 votes to each Conservative candidate elsewhere, it was more than enough to push the Conservative cart over the electoral hill.[22]

Events of the election campaign itself (described in the next chapter) also helped the Conservatives improve their insecure position. Most studies of electoral behaviour suggest that habit is a powerful force in elections; but in 1922 electoral inertia was less important than usual, because it was the first election for many voters. In 1918 79 seats had been uncontested (excluding Southern Ireland), and only 53.8 per cent of those eligible had actually turned out. In 1922 only 57 seats were uncontested, and the turn-out was higher, 72.7 per cent. Moreover, confused though it was, the election of 1922 was more partisan than that of 1918, which had been to some extent a plebiscite on Lloyd George. The voters enfranchised in 1918, but who had not voted then, may have been influenced in their political choice by class, religion and other factors, but they did not have the additional influence which acts on most voters today, habits. This alone made the election unpredictable, and it also underlined the importance of the 1922 election in setting future voting patterns. Voting habits may be broken, but it is easier to establish new habits where there have been none previously than it is to break existing ones. The fact that many voters cast their first ballot in an election where numerous passing influences favoured the Conservatives gave the Conservatives a long-term advantage they might not otherwise have had. Thus the election campaign of 1922 not only produced a majority of seats for the Conservatives, thus fixing future party alignments; it also had a far-reaching effect on voting patterns.

8

The General Election of 1922

The election of 1922 fell into two distinct halves: until nomination day, the parties recovered from the shock of the Carlton Club Meeting, but a possible debate over the fall of the old Coalition failed to develop. The electors had a brief period of repose after the tumult of the Lloyd George years, but in the second half of the campaign new issues appeared which knocked many voters out of their complacency. It can be argued that both the period of quiet confusion and that of revived strife were necessary to produce a Conservative majority in this election; the first showed the voters the contrast with the unsettled days of the Coalition, and the second made them realise how precarious was their newly acquired peace.

Lloyd George resigned three hours after the Carlton Club Meeting, and then returned to Downing Street to discuss the future with the other ex-ministers. Sir Alfred Mond advised him to come out as a Liberal, and H. A. L. Fisher recorded in his diary that the other Coalition Liberal ex-ministers agreed. Lloyd George had a previous engagement to speak at Leeds on 21 October, but as Fisher noted, the ex-premier was 'rather doubtful whether to speak—if so what to say'. Nevertheless Fisher prepared some notes for him.[1]

The next day Lloyd George left St Pancras Station as 'a free man. The burden is off my shoulders. My sword is in my hand.' His train stopped at several points on the way to Leeds, all but one of which either had elected some Lloyd George Liberals in 1918, or were to do so in 1922. During his tour on 20 October he moved from a modified acceptance of the situation at Bedford, in which he did not denounce those who had deposed him, to an appeal at Wellingborough for support against 'a mere party game'. Still further on his way, at Sheffield, he protested that Tory hotheads 'have thrown the gauntlet into the ring, and I mean to pick it up and to go on fighting the old battle for a steady, but progressive England'.[2]

These speeches lasted only a few minutes each, and Lloyd George probably composed them on the spur of the moment, to please his enthusiastic audiences. This would explain his progressively more critical attitude to the Carlton Club Meeting, and it would also account for his retreat at Leeds the next day. In his speech there on 21 October Lloyd George offered a few uninspiring comments on his record and on Bonar Law, who, he said, was 'honest up to the verge of simplicity'. As for his own plans, 'I will do nothing mean, nothing petty'. Fisher, who drafted the speech, thought it very good, but other observers considered it 'curiously uncombative', and *The Times* commented that Lloyd George had evidently lost the sword he had been brandishing the day before. After this débâcle, Lloyd George had little impact in the campaign. Sir Alfred Mond told him later that 'Wales cannot understand its leader not leading', but Lloyd George had already taken one strong partisan position and had then failed to follow it through, so a second reversal would have cost him what credibility he still retained.[3]

The explanation for the ex-premier's reversal at Leeds was fairly simple. Before the war he had been noted for aggressive speeches which may have been distorted, but which had been convincing because of their vigorous presentation. His comparative docility in this election was not due to age, since he was forceful in attack afterwards. He was tired in 1922 after six years as premier, but the main reason why he failed to stick to his initial aggressiveness was his desire to maintain good relations with the Conservative backbenchers who were his most likely future allies.

On 20 October, while Lloyd George was blundering on his way to Leeds, the rebel Conservative chiefs pondered their course of action. They decided to avoid partisan controversy wherever possible. In particular they hoped to keep tariffs out of the election. L. S. Amery, a noted tariff reformer, wrote the relevant section of the Conservative manifesto: it did not mention tariffs at all. The four most prominent Conservatives in the prospective cabinet were Bonar Law and Lords Curzon, Derby and Salisbury. Both Derby and Salisbury were free traders, and even if he had wanted to do so, Law did not have the self-confidence to stand without them; nor could he afford to alienate the Liberal voters on whom he counted for his majority. Therefore, even though Amery hoped that a non-committal platform would leave the door open for tariffs, Bonar Law stated explicitly that they would not be introduced before another election.[4]

On 21 October Lord Derby appealed to the Lancashire Conservatives to stand by the Lloyd George Liberals in the county. It would be 'churlish' to split the moderate vote, letting Labour win. The Coalition was ended, he said, 'but co-operation remains'. The Lancashire Conservatives followed this advice and did not oppose any Lloyd Georgians, except one who was attacking the Conservative-held seat of Salford West. Also on 21 October the Conservative headquarters in London revealed that it had advised the Scottish Tories to continue electoral pacts with the Lloyd George Liberals as if nothing had happened at the Carlton Club. The ex-premier found it difficult to pose as the injured party when his supposed detractors failed to detract.[5]

On Monday 23 October the Conservative politicians held two important meetings. A dinner for Austen Chamberlain attracted forty-six M.P.s, a little more than half the number who had voted for continued Coalition only four days previously. Three M.P.s at this dinner, Sir R. B. Chadwick, H. Foreman and Sir William Rutherford, had voted against Chamberlain, and two more, N. Grattan Doyle and W. E. Horne, had not voted either way. However there was no net shift towards Chamberlain, as some of his other supporters at the Carlton Club Meeting drifted to Bonar Law. Balfour, the chief speaker at the dinner, said that Lloyd George had not used his position to further Liberal aims at the expense of Conservative goals. On the contrary, during the entire period of coalition, there had not been 'at any moment any difference of opinion on any party issue'. He was scandalised that the Conservatives could tell Lloyd George :[6]

'You have led us so well and so gallantly, you have done incalculable service not merely to the Coalition Government but to the country [loud cheers]. We have no difference of

opinion with you in the present, we do not foresee any differences of opinion with you in the future, but we find that
the party machine has had enough of you, and we ask you
to leave.' Who is going to play that rôle? For what reward,
for what consideration is any man going to degrade himself
[burst of prolonged cheers] to the point that he would give
such a message to such a man? [renewed cheers]. It is simply
a question of how gentlemen would behave in certain circumstances.

The Coalition dinner was colourful, but it was not the focus
of attention that day. A few hours before, at the Hotel Cecil,
Curzon, seconded by Baldwin, had nominated Bonar Law for
the Conservative leadership. Curzon told his audience that the
seven lean years of subservience to Lloyd George were over.
Foreshadowing the Conservative strategy, Curzon told the 152
peers, 67 candidates and 220 M.P.s that Bonar Law's policy
would be 'sobriety rather than fireworks. Stability will be his
watchword, not sensation'.

In his first speech after his resumption of the Conservative
leadership, Bonar Law said that Lloyd George had done much
for the country, but that he had no right to a lifetime premiership. Even if the new Government was no better than its
predecessor, it was at least, he said, a change and a fresh start.
Lloyd George had described him as 'honest but simple' : if the
testimonial was deserved, 'I can ask no better'. It had been
impossible to maintain the Coalition because pressure within the
Conservative movement had grown so great. He refused to
state his policy, although he said specifically that he would not
advance the Diehards to office merely because they had been
the first to oppose the Coalition. After this speech he went to
Buckingham Palace to be made prime minister.[7]

The Conservatives rallied quickly to the new Government,
but some pro-Coalitionists of 19 October turned to Bonar Law
without repudiating Chamberlain, while at the same time
numerous former opponents of the Lloyd George regime
announced their readiness to back renewed Coalition. The
general attitude seemed to be that whoever won the election
would have their support. No important regional Conservative
group rejected the Government, but some hedged. For instance

the Scottish Conservatives decided at a conference to follow Bonar Law so long as he left undisturbed their electoral truce with the Lloyd Georgians. On the other side the Conservative Coalitionists did not oppose a single ordinary Conservative critic of the former Government. The so-called 'Lloyd George Conservative' in Bournemouth was soon unmasked as a Liberal, and in Paddington North, a bona fide Conservative Coalitionist withdrew from a contest against the anti-Coalition M.P. as soon as a 'Radical' (i.e. Liberal) candidate appeared.[8]

The formation of the Conservative Government gave the party leaders more prestige inside their organisation, and this made it easier for them to arrange co-operation between their party and the Lloyd George Liberals. After 19 October dissident Conservatives had often felt that they had little to lose by breaking local electoral truces. Now they might jeopardise the unstable net work of alliances which bolstered their long-sought Conservative regime. Sometimes, especially where they had nominated candidates prior to the Carlton Club Meeting, they were still willing to take such risks, but elsewhere, as in Lancashire and Scotland, they held back.

From the election of Bonar Law as Conservative leader on 23 October until 2 November, political issues seemed scarce. The entire election campaign after 23 October lasted only three weeks, and it is unusual for politicians to remain silent in such a short election. However not only politicians, but the Press, tended to avoid issues. Even newspapers which might have been expected to give full coverage to the election did not do so : the *Chronicle*, Lloyd George's own journal, like many others, paid almost as much attention to the attempted poisoning of the chief inspector of Scotland Yard with a box of chocolates, and to the remarriage of the Kaiser.

The dullness of the early campaign was caused partly by the continued presence in London of many Conservative candidates, who were busy re-establishing their party machinery; and partly by the confusion about which parties would nominate candidates in each constituency. Another influence moderating the partisanship of non-socialist politicians was the simultaneous campaign for the borough councils. A Labour government at Westminster seemed only a future possibility, but many places had already experienced Labour rule at a local level, and in 1922 the local

Conservative and Liberal parties often formed alliances to defeat these local Labour governments. The anti-Labour combinations were generally successful, and it might be said that in the midst of the 1922 election, numerous local politicians were anticipating that of 1924, using cries of 'Poplarism' in place of a 'red letter'.

The term 'Poplarism' derived from the social welfare policies of certain Labour-controlled boards of guardians in east London. In the early 1920s local authorities were responsible for more aspects of welfare than at present, and in the absence of a national scheme for paying relief, ratepayers in areas of high unemployment paid much higher taxes than those in areas of moderate or low unemployment. In 1922 the portion of persons on relief varied from 2.8 per cent in the western district of London to 9.8 per cent in the eastern; nationally it ranged from 1.3 per cent in Halifax to 13.2 per cent in Sheffield. To help their unemployed, and also to draw attention to flaws in the relief system, the Poplar board of guardians made large payments for which they had insufficient funds. The Labour boards of guardians in Stepney and Bethnal Green followed their example. The voters apparently preferred 'Poplarism' to orthodox welfare administration, for in the 1922 London borough council elections, Labour lost only 24 of its 102 seats in boroughs practising Poplarism (23.5 per cent), compared with a loss of 302 out of 486 seats (62.1 per cent) in the other boroughs. Nevertheless 'Poplarism' gave Labour a bad reputation in financial circles, and even some Labour reformers such as Beatrice Webb condemned it. Thus it became a major issue bringing together Liberals and Conservatives in the local elections. In many places these pacts in the local elections carried over into or reinforced co-operation in the Parliamentary elections held less than two weeks later.[9]

In most parts of the country, Liberals and Conservatives combined against Labour in the local elections; but even where the parties themselves did not do this, the voters often did it on their own. For example in Worcester the Liberals and Labour each nominated one candidate in two two-member wards, against two Conservatives; but despite this Liberal-Labour co-operation, the Liberal voters apparently split 2 to 1 in favour of the Conservatives in one ward, and 3 to 2 in the other. The results, excluding

voters who 'plumped' for one candidate or who voted for two
Conservatives, were:

	St Peter's ward	St Nicholas ward
Lib.-Lab.	235	43
Lib.-Con.	412	65
Lab.-Con.	92	82

These figures show that even in a place where Liberals and
Labour attempted to co-operate, the Liberal voters were recalci-
trant. In any case Worcester was exceptional, and elsewhere
co-operation of Liberals and Conservatives was the norm. The
overall effect of this Liberal-Conservative co-operation was, as
one might have expected, a serious loss for Labour, so far as the
number of seats won and lost was concerned. Few voting figures
were published, but those which were indicated little or no shift
from Labour since the previous local elections in 1919. Nevertheless most national newspapers saw the local elections as a
disaster for Labour.[10]

The most important thing about these local elections was their
timing. The results were not known until 2 November, and in
many places, 3 November; as nomination day for the general
election was 4 November, this left only one day for local parties
to rearrange or break municipal political pacts. Also, while the
local elections had been in progress, the national politicians had
tended to keep silent.

Thus until nomination day, the election campaign was relatively quiet: even reactions to the Carlton Club Meeting had
been muted. However in the second half of the election new
factors transformed it into a more lively conflict of individuals
and factions. These new influences were: a series of attacks by
Birkenhead and Churchill on the Conservatives who had deposed
them; a renewal of the Turkish crisis; and the emergence of
Labour as the main opposition party, with a platform of its own,
including a levy on capital. Each of these factors confirmed the
drift of floating voters towards the new Government, and there
was no significant countervailing current to check that drift.

In British elections, personal quarrels have generally been veneered with criticisms of policy if the feuds have been along partisan lines; but in 1922 several personal clashes in early November added zest to what had been up to then a comparatively uninteresting campaign. It was natural for the ex-ministers of the Coalition to resent their overthrow, but it was surprising that some of them yielded to their passions in public, for they could only lose by inflaming ordinary Conservatives against them. In his biography of Balfour, A. K. Young reprinted an account of a Coalitionist dinner at the end of October 1922 :[11]

They agreed that Law was an ambitious man and that even to be Prime Minister for three weeks would mean much to him. Birkenhead was bitter about Curzon. When Curzon and he had parted after Winston's dinner, before the Carlton Club Meeting, Curzon's last words had been, 'I'm game', and then he wrote a letter reflecting on the presence there of Lord Birkenhead and Nunk [Balfour]. Lloyd George was very unrestrained about Curzon. Nunk pleaded he was clever. 'No,' said Lloyd George, 'and really, he is so weak.' . . .

They had a very low opinion of Amery. They asserted that Amery was the son of a Salonika Jew named Hinri or something like that. Was it libellous to call him a Jew? Can it be libel to call a man one of a nation that has produced Jesus Christ and Philip Sassoon, asked Lord Birkenhead?

Lloyd George and Austen Chamberlain made only an occasional thrust against Bonar Law, for they anticipated working with him later on; but Churchill and Birkenhead were less restrained. In the case of Churchill, the blasts emerged from his hospital bed, where he was recovering from appendicitis. Lloyd George managed to tone down some of these bedside missives, but others reached the Press substantially unaltered. On 31 October he denounced the new first lord of the admiralty, L. S. Amery, who, he said was a spendthrift, not a penny-pincher like himself. Amery, not one given to self-abasement, retorted that the ex-ministers were paying their tributes to each other's intellect, and bemoaning the fate of a nation deprived of such stars and left to wander in 'the dim illumination afforded by second-class brains'.

Now, he said, there was an even more sensational picture, 'from the brush of that well-known painter, Mr. Winston Churchill'. Churchill he described 'how the late government of economists, led by no less a super-economist than himself, were just about to bring home the rich harvest of economies to the people when the whole applecart was upset by that obstinate Mr. Amery'. Amery said he had never opposed naval economy in his talks with Churchill, and their only disputes had been over the length of the speeches Churchill made to his subordinates.[12]

After Amery's rebuttal, Churchill was silent for a few days, and then attacked a more sensitive and less cautious ex-colleague, Lord Curzon. On 8 November Curzon remarked that he had not known of the cabinet's manifesto of 17 September 1922, which had called on the Dominions to aid Britain in the Chanak crisis. In a letter to *The Times* of 10 November Churchill pointed out that Curzon had been absent from the cabinet meeting where the manifesto had been discussed because he had been too diffident to spend a night in his London house when it had not been prepared for his presence. However both Churchill and Lloyd George had notified him of the matter by telephone and telegraph.* Regarding the fall of the Coalition, Churchill said Curzon's attitude had undergone 'a sudden and nimble change' at the last minute. He had 'secured his position in the new Administration, and is able to present himself blandly and evenly brazenly as an enlightened and far-seeing critic, detached from, and superior to' his ex-colleagues.[13]

Curzon replied the same day that Churchill's comments were 'characterised by copious inaccuracy and no small malevolence'. He denied receiving sufficient information on the Chanak crisis, and said he had had none about the manifesto until he had read it in the Sunday papers. As for his support of the Coalition, as soon as he had read Lloyd George's Manchester speech, he had told Chamberlain that he could not countenance a second coupon election. Churchill replied further that Curzon's remarks did not deny the fact that his 'extraordinary somersault in the nick of

* Telephone messages did not always reach Curzon. In September 1920 his secretary had telephoned him at his country house, whereupon Curzon had told the secretary never to call him on the telephone except in case of emergency, because he had to walk too far to reach the telephone, which was in a distant part of the house. Cf. Ronaldshay, *Curzon*, III 72.

time' had enabled him to emerge prosperously. Curzon did not follow this up, in public at any rate.[14]

Another Coalition crusader was Lord Birkenhead, who beginning on 1 November made about one denunciation a day; a wide variety of fellow Conservatives were his targets. He began with a catechism of Sir Leslie Wilson, who was contesting Westminster-St George's against the Diehard J. M. M. Erskine. Wilson denied Birkenhead's accusations of last-minute ratting, but on 13 November Birkenhead publicly endorsed Erskine. 'Although I do not agree with all your views,' he said, 'I strongly advise my neighbours and friends to vote for you. You, at least, have neither fled from a constituency nor abandoned a leader.' * Aided by this, and also by the publicity he received in a successful lawsuit against Wilson's followers, Erskine won the seat by 3500 votes.[15]

Birkenhead next attacked Sir George Younger, 'a great wirepuller', who, having burnt the Tory Party boats in the direction of Lloyd George, was searching for 'a new line of rafts somewhere else'. Younger preferred to drop six Conservative leaders rather than a few Diehards, and he might soon turn against Bonar Law as he had done with Chamberlain. The replies of both Wilson and Younger were mild, but Younger, for one, was enraged. He told Lord Derby that 'FE has done his party no good by the attitude he has taken in his speeches. . . . I hope you will give it him in the neck when you answer the attack he made upon yourself'. This referred to Birkenhead's inexplicable denunciation of Derby.[16]

On 21 October Lord Derby had called on the Lancashire Conservatives to co-operate fully with the Lloyd George Liberals. Ten days later, Birkenhead condemned Derby for urging the Lloyd Georgians to desert their leader. When Derby pointed out his errors, Birkenhead did not retract, but instead challenged Derby to repeat his statements in the House of Lords. This reversed the usual procedure, and implied that Birkenhead was afraid to debate the subject in a place where he would be liable to a lawsuit. These personal attacks, some of which were almost baseless, probably antagonised uncommitted voters, and they certainly

---

* Wilson had given up his old constituency, Reading, in order to contest Westminster.

made the two ex-ministers' chances in future governments less likely.[17]

Most followers of Lloyd George did not attack the new regime as directly as Churchill and Birkenhead. The two ex-ministers damaged their own cause in the election, and also made the possibilities of renewed coalition afterwards less likely, at least if such a coalition were to include themselves. Neither Birkenhead nor Churchill was fully accepted in Conservative circles for some years, even though they were in Conservative Government later in the 1920s.

Birkenhead and the other former ministers gave Bonar Law several openings to display debating skill. For instance Birkenhead said he contemplated the new Government much as Wellington had looked on the raw recruits in Spain in 1809, 'I do not know whether they will frighten the French, but by God they frighten me'. Law pointed out that these troops later defeated the Old Guard at Waterloo. Again, when Lloyd George described himself as an angel of peace, Bonar Law asked why such an angel needed the sword he had brandished on his way to Leeds. At other points too, he turned the rhetoric of Lloyd George and Birkenhead on the authors, in a mild fashion which aroused little antagonism. While this was perhaps a minor point, it defused the Coalitionists' claim that they had a monopoly of brains.[18]

The personal quarrels of the new and old ministers affected individual fortunes, rather than the election as a whole. However the renewed Turkish crisis influenced the entire campaign. In the Chanak affair of September some Conservative M.P.s had rejected the Coalition, and a few more had left after Lloyd George's anti-Turkish speech of 13 October. Practically all accounts of the Turkish question end there, without referring to the forgotten crisis of the first two weeks of November 1922. This second crisis died down rapidly and had few obvious consequences, but its electoral influence probably outweighed that of the far-better-known Chanak affair.

In early November the Allies were preparing to negotiate with Turkey at Lausanne : but there were two Turkish governments, one at Constantinople, ruled by the Sultan, and another at Angora (Ankara) led by Mustapha Kemal. It was the latter regime which had defeated the Greeks and which had threatened the British at Chanak. The sultan's authority was confined to Constantinople, where he relied on British, French and Italian soldiers to maintain his 'worthless and invertebrate regime', as Curzon called it. But both it and the Angora Government were to attend the Lausanne Conference, despite the fact that one was a mere shadow. Kemal's Government rejected proposals that the sultan should share in the honours of victory, because there was a chance that unless the sultan was completely disgraced in the eyes of the Turkish people, the Allies might use him in further struggles with Angora.[19]

Reports in British newspapers on 2 November told of denunciations of the sultan by Ismet Pasha, the Turkish nationalist delegate to Lausanne; the reports also mentioned Kemal's repudiation of the Mudania Agreement, which he had signed less than a month before. The agreement allowed Britain to maintain a series of neutral zones, to safeguard the Straits, until the conference was over. On 3 November the Kemalist representative in Paris informed Poincaré that Angora did not recognise treaties made by the sultan since 16 March 1920; he added that the Kemalists claimed the right to nominate the caliph. The sultan's authority was dual, religious and political, the religious part being his caliphate; so it appeared that the Kemalists were preparing to depose him. On 5 November the Kemalists seized Constantinople. In the neutral zones they marched up to the barbed wire entanglements of the British, and though they only made faces at the British, it seemed that they might soon show less restraint. Few shots were fired, but two of them killed British soldiers.[20]

Turkish demands increased daily. At one point the Nationalists called for more territory, and also for an indemnity of £240 million. Perhaps the Turks were merely stating their maximum demands before the Lausanne Conference in order to obtain what they really wanted, but whatever their purpose, they alarmed British leader-writers. The *Chronicle* called the situation 'extremely critical', while *The Times* believed it was as dangerous a crisis 'as any since November 11, 1918'. The *Manchester Guardian* said it 'must be a sad shock' to those innocent enough to suppose that the removal of Lloyd George would cause all the lions of international politics to turn into doves of peace. The Government felt the presence of danger too, and requested all cabinet ministers connected with war to stay in London during the crisis.[21]

From 9 to 14 November newspaper reports were alarming and contradictory. On 11 November for example *The Times* mentioned rumours of Anglo-French co-operation and conflict in the same issue. The British cabinet was also uncertain : when Briand had been French premier, a serious clash between Britain and France had been improbable, because Briand had realised that French security in Western Europe depended in the end on British goodwill. Poincaré, his successor, was less perceptive. According to Clemenceau, Briand knew nothing and understood everything, while Poincaré knew everything but understood nothing. Poincaré deserved his nickname of 'clenched fist' (*poing-carré*) : he stood for a strict, legalistic interpretation of French rights in Europe, regardless of the ill-will this attitude created. J. L. Garvin felt that Poincaré's 'pomposity and dogmatism make him hard to deal with'; and Curzon added that Poincaré was jealous of Lloyd George's personal ascendancy over the international conferences after 1918, and that this coloured his whole attitude to Britain. Curzon described Poincaré to the cabinet as 'a clever, hard, rigid, metallic lawyer' with an 'explosive temper'. It remained to be seen how far he would compromise with Britain in this crisis, if at all.[22]

On 7 November Poincaré informed the British ambassador in Paris that he agreed to the proclamation of a state of siege in Constantinople if it were necessary, but he felt it was 'premature' to consider the consequences if the proclamation did not stop the Turks. The British forces were insufficient to contain the Turks, and although the French had two divisions at Marseilles, eight days' sailing time from Turkey, a British force this size could get to Constantinople only after a delay of thirty-one days. Consequently the French attitude was decisive. Poincaré eventually agreed to discuss the Turkish problem with Curzon and Mussolini (who had just taken power in Italy) before the Lausanne Conference. Perhaps Poincaré was more co-operative than usual because Lloyd George had left office; or he may have hoped to pacify the British in advance of his projected occupation of the Ruhr, which took place two months later. Whatever his reason, the new Conservative Government could claim that it had resolved one problem left by Lloyd George, that is, relations with France.[23]

However communications with Constantinople were delayed by an accident to the cable, and the Turks evidently hindered repairs. The newspapers received some garbled accounts from the East about Poincaré's instructions to the French commander, and *The Times* said it had never been so difficult to determine what the French wanted. Right up to the end of the election, the Press published conflicting descriptions of French motives. On polling day, 15 November, most of the conflicts had been reconciled in public, but by then the crisis had already influenced British politics. In any case what had come up so quickly could rise again later, and the solution, such as it was, was unclear even on election day.[24]

Practically all the politicians who discussed the Turkish affair called for national unity behind the new Government; even some of Lloyd George's followers edged towards the new Government on this issue. One was Sir Hamar Greenwood, who told his Sunderland electorate that he would 'support the government in dealing faithfully with the Turk'. In this case, Greenwood had Conservative opposition, and the simplest way for the electors to follow Greenwood's own lead in supporting the Government would have been to vote Conservative. Asquithian, and even Labour politicians also praised the new Government's handling of the crisis, as of course did many Conservatives. Curzon told a meeting of London Conservatives that 'the pretensions of the Nationalist Turks could not be tolerated : they were an affront to the Allies and a challenge to Europe'. J. W. Hills, the new financial secretary to the treasury, described the position as 'menacing', while Cuthbert James, a Diehard, told his constituents in Bromley that 'terrible things' might happen in Constantinople 'in the next few days, or even hours'. Lloyd George, he said, deserved credit for getting Britain out of the Chanak crisis safely, but Britain did not want to wage a holy war. Many other Conservative candidates said similar things.[25]

Perhaps events in Turkey influenced few voters, but in 1922 only a few were necessary to give the Conservatives a clear majority. The crisis gave the Government something to say, and more important, something to do. Until this point in the campaign the Government had been unable to demonstrate the difference between its policy and that of the Coalition. Its handling of Turkey marked a clear distinction : while the new regime stood for peace and for solidarity with France, the old one had apparently stood for war, without allies if necessary. Thus the new Government refuted dramatically the allegation that it was just a revised coalition.

The personal attacks on Bonar Law's ministers helped the Government win public approval, and the Turkish crisis probably gave Conservative candidates the edge in many close fights. However the chief issue of the last two weeks of the election campaign was the capital levy. The Labour Party had previously fought as an ally of the Liberals, or else it had engaged in missionary activity for socialist theories; it had not made an issue of its own the main debating point of an election. In 1922 there was reason to believe that the Labour programme, especially the capital levy, would attract much support from non-socialists. During and after the war there had been a widespread demand for taxation of war profits; such a tax would relieve income-tax payers, who were then paying no less than 6s in the £ (the standard rate in 1970 was 8s 3d). Czechoslovakia had taxed accumulated wealth without damaging its economy severely, and some Labour M.P.s used this as a model for their own plans. In fact the Czech example was misleading, for the capital levy there took place at a time of inflation, and it reduced the money supply to manageable proportions. In 1922 Britain had just gone through a period of severe deflation, and needed a greater, not smaller, money supply. A second major difference was that in Czechoslovakia, much of the levy fell on German and Magyar landowners, whose opposition to it naturally counted less than if the levy had hurt the Czechs most.[26]

Not only Labour, but politicians of all parties had supported the idea of a levy, at least until 1920. Stanley Baldwin's donation of 20 per cent of his fortune to the treasury was a form of voluntary levy, but few followed his example, and most politicians who favoured the levy argued that it should be compulsory. Asquith, in his election address of January 1920 had proposed investigating whether it was possible 'to make a Levy upon Capital in order to extinguish part of the War Debt'. E. Hilton Young, Coalition Liberal M.P. for Norwich, wrote in 1920 that 'a Capital Levy promises to provide a pathway to the state of content and mutual confidence' needed for industrial peace. Less than a year later, Lloyd George made Young financial secretary to the treasury, and presumably he would not have done so if Young's views had diverged markedly from his own. In 1917 Bonar Law had also argued for a capital levy, saying that 'It would be better both for the wealthy classes and for the country to have this Levy on capital and reduce the burden of the National Debt'. When some of his followers labelled the proposal confiscatory, he told the commons that 'there is nothing of confiscation if such a thing were done'.[27]

Proposals for a capital levy had come before the commons several times after 1918. In May 1919 a Liberal motion for a levy got 23 Liberal votes out of 89 cast; 9 Coalition Liberal ministers who had been present had not voted. A similar motion by Labour in June 1920 got 19 Asquithian, 13 Coalition Liberal, 47 Labour and 5 Conservative votes, and a commons committee reported in May 1920 that a capital levy would be useful and 'is practicable in an administrative sense'. By 1920 then the idea of a capital levy had received support from many leading politicians, Labour leaders and economists. Non-socialists found it unattractive, but they also found high interest payments unattractive.[28]

Labour was the first, and only, party to endorse the capital levy officially; it did so in a pamphlet by F. W. Pethick-Lawrence, which argued that a levy would cut taxes for those earning less than £1200 a year, by eliminating interest payments on war debts. Pethick-Lawrence said that payment could be made in government bonds, shares in railways, mines, land and the like. The state would become part-owner of many enterprises, especially in businesses whose capital was frozen. Labour economists rejected arguments that a levy would cause forced sales of goods, thus reducing prices, and consequently reducing the yield of the levy. They pointed to Austria, where the Dorotheum (the state pawnshop) had accepted payment in kind for part of the levy there.[29]

Although the capital levy had wide backing up to 1920, it did not figure largely in political discussions during the two subsequent years, and non-Labour politicians mostly dropped it. Much of the war wealth had disappeared during the deflation of 1921–2 anyway, and Labour politicians had turned to Irish and industrial questions. If Labour had carried out a more intensive and sustained campaign, it might have profited more than it did from reintroduction of the levy in the midst of the 1922 election. As it was, anti-Labour spokesmen misrepresented the Labour policy; if this opposition had appeared a few months before, it would have lost much of its effect by election day.

The capital levy scare was not a Conservative 'roorback'* like the 'red letter' of 1924, or the postal savings scare of 1931. On the contrary Labour politicians introduced and garbled it, thus leaving the way open for Liberal and Conservative criticism. The Labour manifesto, which appeared on 25 October, mentioned a graduated levy on fortunes over £5000. This stirred little interest, which indicates that Labour had done a poor job of creating interest in the issue before the election. Nevertheless the Labour leaders refused to drop their plan, and on 2 November *The Times* reported Arthur Henderson as saying that a levy would reduce taxes by cutting into the swollen coffers of profiteers. J. R. Clynes on the other hand wrote in *The Times* two days later that Labour was 'not wedded' to the levy, but that it was the best policy available. In the same issue J. H. Thomas also said he favoured a levy if it worked, but that he did not regard it as a fetish. Both men cited Bonar Law's remarks in favour of a levy in 1917.[30]

During the election the Conservatives published the fourteenth edition of their speakers' handbook, *The Campaign Guide, 1922.* It described the levy as 'an impossible position' which would cause 'such a collapse in trade as would lead in turn to an agitation powerful enough to destroy the Government which made the proposal'. After the fall of the Coalition, Conservatives were quiet on the issue, but they could not let Labour speakers quote Bonar Law's old speeches without making some reply. Bonar Law clarified his position on 4 November, when he denied that he had favoured a levy after 1917, though he had thought one feasible in that year. A levy in 1922 would be harmful, and he felt that Labour stood for both a levy and high income taxes. This was the signal for a nationwide Conservative blast against the levy. Lord Robert Cecil said it would be as bad as a levy on intellect; Lord Ullswater, speaker of the commons until 1921, said it would lead to an economic catastrophe; Lord Derby said

* The *Oxford English Dictionary* defines a 'roorback' as 'a false report or slander invented for political purposes'.

it would cause all capital to flee the country, as had happened in Switzerland when a levy had been proposed there.[31]

About this time, the Conservatives published a pamphlet which became known as 'The Clutching Hand'. It showed a hand with fingers ready to grasp a small house and garden, a bicycle and a bundle of pound notes. Above this was written 'What you have the "Labour" Party wants'; below, 'They'll search your pockets'. This pamphlet stated that Labour would seize everything from anyone worth more than £1000, since Labour really aimed at 'the ultimate extinction of wealth'. It was 'not "Labour" Party v. other political parties. It is "Labour" Party v. your pockets'. The pamphlet said that the lower limit of the levy was to be £1000, but as the Conservative central office knew,* the limit actually proposed was £5000, so the pamphlet was misinformed or misleading, or both.[32]

In 1922 there was no public opinion poll to gauge the ebb and flow of public views, but some clues may be found by examining editorials and letters to the editor of various newspapers. These formed only a very rough guide, but it was noticeable that in newspapers in all parts of the country, if letters dealt with national issues, they mostly discussed the capital levy; almost invariable, they were unfavourable. For instance *The Times* published numerous anti-levy letters, but only one (from A. A. Milne, author of *Winnie the Pooh*) supporting it.

In the last days of the election, many Conservatives and some Liberals fostered the idea that numerous Labour candidates opposed their party over the levy. There is little evidence that Labour was seriously divided on the issue, though a few such as Clynes and Thomas had reservations. However the party had not briefed most Labour candidates fully about the levy, and as few of them had much training in economics, the introduction of what seemed a revolutionary measure played into their opponents' hands. It was ironic that Labour itself raised the issue and stimulated further discussion when the other parties had ignored it; Labour had only itself to blame when the capital levy backfired. Another effect of the levy issue was to drive wandering Liberals into the Conservative camp. Few possessors of capital were likely to vote Labour, but middle-class Liberals might well

* *Gleanings and Memoranda*, the official Conservative journal of record, gave the correct figures in its October and December issues.

have been influenced to vote Conservative in this election by the 'wasted vote' argument.

When the election was nearing its halfway mark, the lines dividing the three non-socialist groups were imprecise. The campaign to that point had neither helped nor harmed the Government much, and some alliance after the election seemed probable. Events of the second half of the campaign strongly favoured the Government : the Turkish crisis, the reaction to attacks on the new ministers, and the capital levy all helped Bonar Law at the expense of his non-socialist rivals, and they probably provided that slight edge which was essential to Conservatives in close seats. While no opinion poll was taken in this election, many editors discerned a shift of floating voters towards the Conservatives as the election campaign proceeded The *Spectator* put the turning-point at the beginning of November, and other journals tended to agree. Several newspapers made detailed predictions at several points in the election, and these almost all showed shifts towards the Conservatives. Certainly such predictions were little more than guesswork in many cases, but they did show that editors regarded the events of the election as a bonus to the Conservatives. Two typical predictions were those given in the *Northern Daily Chronicle* and the *Aberdeen Daily Journal.* On 27 October the *Northampton Daily Chronicle* predicted that the Conservatives would get 300 seats; on the eve of the poll, they predicted 340 Conservative seats, which was a moderate working majority. Similarly the *Aberdeen Daily Journal* raised its estimate of Conservative strength from 275 on 26 October to 330 at the end of October. Studies of some recent elections have suggested that only a small proportion of the electorate has changed its mind during the course of the campaigns. However these recent elections have been conducted in a fairly stable political situation, where the party lines and policies were clear before the campaigns started. In 1922 the number of people who made their choice during the election was greater. For one thing, half the electors had never voted before; for another, numerous lifelong Liberals and Conservatives had to reconsider their position where their party was not running a candidate. This factor assumed considerable importance in 1922, since no party nominated candidates for more than two-thirds of the constituencies. Nominations did not close until 4 November, which gave committed partisans without a candidate of their own only eleven days to decide which alternative party to back. Thus the events of the last two weeks of the election very probably made the difference between a majority for Bonar Law and an unpredictable Parliament of minorities.[33]

9

Lloyd George and Welsh
Politics after 1918

Just as the election of 1922 was a turning-point for British
politics, so it was a watershed for Wales and for Lloyd George,
who had dominated Welsh politics for many years. If the Conservatives had not obtained a majority in 1922, they would have
had the option of approaching either Asquith or Lloyd George
for support; but part of Lloyd George's bargaining power and
prestige rested on his predominant position in Wales. Even without strong Welsh support, Lloyd George would have been a
significant force in British politics, but without a Welsh stronghold, he was less likely to return to office quickly. Yet even
before his fall, much of Wales had started to drift from him.
The results of the 1922 election confirmed this drift. In 1918
nearly every successful candidate in Wales had run under his
banner, or at least had not opposed him openly. In 1922 the
Lloyd George Liberals took only 7 of the 36 Welsh seats,* and
although he remained by far the most important Welsh political
figure, the ex-premier was unable to use Wales as Joseph Chamberlain had used Birmingham, as a base for wielding national
power. Forty years later K. O. Morgan wrote of him that 'even
in his own country, he may be a prophet without honour'.[1]

This chapter considers the impact of the peacetime Coalition
on Wales and shows the effect of the politics of the period on the
future of Lloyd George and his Welsh followers. It also considers
the Labour absorption of Welsh nationalism; these two themes

* Including the University of Wales constituency.

coincide in a study of the 1922 election in Carnarvon, a rural seat Labour gained in 1922. As Welsh Liberalism declined, few nationalists joined distinctly Welsh political parties; instead Labour came to dominate the political wing of Welsh nationalism. This was not merely because of natural Labour predominance in the mining seats : during the decades following the 1922 election, Labour continued to improve its position in all types of Welsh constituency, agricultural, coastal, as well as mining and industrial. Many seats Labour won, particularly after 1945, were the sort which in England turned to the Conservatives. Cardiganshire and Merioneth were two examples of this. Even in the Conservative victory of 1970, Labour won nearly every Welsh seat, whatever its social composition.

At first glance, Labour might seem an unsuitable vehicle for Welsh nationalism, as most of its leaders were Scottish or English, and they were not as involved in Welsh cultural life as many notable Liberals had been. Some Welsh nationalists hesitated about joining Labour for this very reason. The correspondence between Beriah Evans and E. T. John, Welsh nationalists who left the Liberals after 1918, is revealing in this context. After the nomination of Ramsay MacDonald as Labour candidate for Aberavon, Evans wrote John that Welsh Labour men were 'so angered with the foisting upon them of an alien extremist like Ramsay MacDonald, that steps are already being taken to secure an Independent Nationalist of the old "Lib-Lab" type'. Despite this, both Evans and John migrated to Labour, along with many other Welsh nationalists. No Welsh nationalist was elected as such until a by-election in 1966, and even then, Labour regained the seat in the 1970 general election. This failure of Welsh nationalism to take an effective political form stands as one of the more significant long-term results of the 1922 election.[2]

One explanation for this development is that some things which united the Welsh also tied them to England. The Welsh language was a barrier between the two peoples, but fewer than half the inhabitants of Wales spoke it. In any case the main thrust of Welsh nationalism had been religious, and Welsh nonconformists were literally ultramontane, in that they looked beyond the hills of Wales for assistance from the English nonconformists. Only one major nonconformist sect originated in Wales, the Calvinistic Methodists; the two-thirds of Welsh nonconformists who belonged to the Baptist, Congregationalist, Wesleyan and other denominations were allied to their larger England parent groups. The Liberation Society, which campaigned for Disestablishment of the Anglican Church, was founded in England by Englishmen, though it came to the forefront of Welsh political-religious activities. Irish and Welsh nationalism differed clearly on this point, because while religion tended to separate the Irish and English, it held the Welsh and some of the English together.

Another influence tying the Welsh to England before 1914 was their adherence to the Liberal Party. Originally this had been based in part on Liberal support for Disestablishment and related matters, but the political ties soon assumed an importance of their own, and Welsh Liberal M.P.s sometimes refrained from pushing Welsh claims in case such claims split their party. Fewer than a third of the Welsh Liberal M.P.s supported an 1869 motion for Disestablishment, and in the 1880s Tom Ellis, then the leading Welsh politician, opposed the formation of a distinct Welsh group, lest it fragment the Liberals. In 1892 J. Bryn Roberts, a prominent Welsh M.P., fought against a motion for Welsh Home Rule, as he thought it would injure Liberal unity.[3]

After 1918 the old allegiance of Wales to the Liberals was not as unquestioned as it had been. Lloyd George's flirtation with the Conservatives and the cleavage inside the Welsh Liberal organisation helped blur party loyalties, while the attainment of the political goal of Welsh nonconformity by the Disestablishment Act of 1920 made it less imperative to remain united behind the Liberal Party.* However habits and social differences remained which helped prevent the Conservatives from picking up much ground, and many old-style Welsh radicals turned to Labour. The ties Labour formed grew stronger during the 1920s, surviving even the débâcle of 1931. In that election, Labour sank in England from 226 to 29, but in Wales it held 16 of its 26 seats, and added to them in nearly every election up to 1966.

* A Disestablishment Act had been passed in 1912, which would have become law in 1914 under the provisions of the Parliament Act; when the war came, Asquith's Government suspended operation of the bill for a year. In 1915 it continued the suspension until six months after the war. Lloyd George's Government later revised the provisions of Disestablishment, giving the Anglican Church more generous endowments, and the act came into force in 1920.

Welsh nationalism was again tied to a mainly English political party, and the newly established loyalties to Labour made it more difficult for individual Welsh nationalists to strike out on their own. Economic reasons were not the only basis for this association with Labour, especially in rural constituencies. In England agricultural seats voting Labour almost invariably had high proportions of farm labourers, but in Wales Labour gains came where smallholdings predominated; an instance of the latter was Carnarvon, which voted Labour in 1922, even though it had the lowest proportion of labourers per farm of any constituency in England or Wales.[4]

Relative prosperity also dampened Welsh demands for autonomy before the war. Wales was not rich, but unlike Ireland it was not on the poverty line. On the one occasion in the late nineteenth century when Wales had serious economic problems (the 1870s), there was a demand for Home Rule, but when prosperity returned, this agitation declined. The English did not regard Wales as they did Ireland, as a rebellious area which an enemy might use as an invasion base. The population figures alone comforted Englishmen: in the eighteenth century Wales had only a tenth the population of Ireland. During the nineteenth century the Irish population declined while that of Wales grew moderately, but English attitudes to the two places had become set by then, and the leniency resulting from this English lack of concern kept Welsh grievances from becoming too great.

Finally, though small in both area and population, Wales had three distinct regions, and this worked against movements for autonomy. The anglicized southern coast was the only part of Wales where the Conservatives had much strength. Cardiff, Swansea and Newport, the only major cities in Wales, were all in this region. The South Wales mining district was more Welsh-speaking, but its economic system set it apart from other sections of the principality. The third region, consisting of nearly all the land area, was the so-called typical Wales of small farms, non-conformist chapels and rural radicalism. In the interwar years, the coastal region had 8 seats, the mining district 16, and rural Wales 11. Quite often, one Welsh region, such as the mining district, had more in common in some respects with similar English regions than with the rest of Wales; these divergent aims and attitudes, while not the only problem of Welsh nationalists, did prevent complete understanding.

This analysis has considered why Welsh nationalism took so long to develop into a strong political force of its own. Many influences bound Wales to England, and Welshmen generally felt they could achieve their goals by co-operating with the English. Welsh leaders rarely considered themselves traitors when they succeeded in the wider British field, as Tom Ellis had done to a limited degree in the 1890s, and as Lloyd George did after 1906.

Although Home Rule was not the only issue in Welsh politics, nor even the main one, there was a widespread consciousness of a Welsh identity based on language and social differences. These influences lay behind the electoral trends in Wales which differed markedly from those in other parts of Britain. In the 1920s the Conservatives fared no better in Wales than before the war, and sometimes they did worse. Much of this could be attributed to the Welsh social structure, in which there was a gulf separating the anglicized landowning and upper professional Conservatives on the one side, and less prosperous and less established Liberals and Labour on the other. This gulf was demonstrable among the political leadership, as the following analysis shows, but it probably extended to lower echelons too.

No social survey was taken in Wales in the 1920s, but in 1921 the first edition of *Who's Who in Wales* appeared. It contained information on 20,000 leading Welshmen, and unlike most such publications it listed their religion and politics. It is possible by using this book to draw a profile of Welsh society at that time. Those chosen for inclusion in any *Who's Who* are not necessarily typical of the population as a whole, but this volume reached much farther down in society than most, as it included one Welsh male voter in 30. This was eleven times the proportion of the English *Who's Who* of the same date, which had about 35,000 entries for a much larger population. The Welsh book then was more than a sample of the Welsh political elite : it was that elite. Most of the biographies were incomplete, but 994 gave sufficient information for our purposes. The 994 included 472 Liberals, 436 Conservatives and 86 Labour men. Labour was under-represented because in 1920–1 it was just rising to prominence, but even so the Labour sample was a useful guide.

The first distinction to be made between the parties was in religion. No fewer than 92.7 per cent of the Conservatives who stated a religion were Anglicans, compared with only 14.5 per cent of Labour and 8.7 per cent of Liberals. Religion was not the only major influence in Welsh politics, but it separated the Liberal and Conservative Parties, and thus influenced many political developments.

Table 7   Religion and politics in Wales, 1920

Denomination	Conservative	Liberal	Labour
Anglican	358	34	8
Nonconformist	14	347	47
Other, or vague	15	11	—
Not stated	50	85	29

Another distinction between the parties was their record of war work. About half the supporters of each party had done some war service, either military or civilian, but Conservatives far outnumbered both Liberals and Labour combined in the military category. Only four Labour supporters listed had any military experience, and all four were exceptional. One had served in the Boer War, another had commanded a labour battalion behind the lines, a third had been a Liberal candidate until the end of the war and the fourth was an independent Labour M.P. who left the party in 1920.

Table 8   War service and politics in Wales, 1920

Type of service	Conservative	Liberal	Labour
Military	111	41	4
Civilian	124	137	34
Total with war service	235	178	38
No war service	201	294	48

The education of the Conservatives also differed considerably from that of both Liberals and Labour : of the Conservatives who listed their education, 48.0 per cent had gone to English public schools, compared with only 13.1 per cent of Liberals and 10.6 per cent of Labour. Those with a Welsh education were 35.0 per cent of Conservatives, 67.9 per cent of Liberals and 80.9 per cent of Labour. There was also a noticeable difference in the occupations of the supporters of the three parties.

Table 9   Occupation and politics in Wales, 1920

Occupation	Conservative	Liberal	Labour
Anglican clergy	19	2	—
Regular military officer	57	2	—
Landowner or related occupation	47	28	—
Engineer, architect, surveyor	21	4	—
Doctor, dentist	27	9	4
Legal profession	59	48	4
Newspaper proprietor, journalist	14	13	3
Teacher or academic	11	52	4
Nonconformist minister	—	54	4
Other professional	14	9	6
Merchant	13	64	—
Other businessman	83	79	2
Working class	1	6	47
Other occupations	5	5	2
Not stated	65	96	8

This table can be summarised as follows :

Party	Agriculture, military, Anglican clergy, doctor or engineer	Nonconformist minister, merchant, or teacher
Conservative	171 (46.1%)	24 (6.5%)
Liberal	46 (9.7%)	170 (45.2%)
Labour	6 (7.7%)	8 (10.0%)

This examination of *Who's Who in Wales* shows that the Conservatives were distinct in several important ways from both Liberals and Labour. Thus it was not surprising that seceders from Liberalism turned to Labour in Wales, even if they had middle-class or agricultural occupations which in England would have inclined them towards the Conservatives. This helped explain Labour victories in rural seats such as Anglesey, Cardigan, Carnarvon and Merioneth.

The Liberal position in Wales was weaker than in 1914 for many reasons, one of which was the gradual shift from an agrarian to an industrial society. Lloyd George failed to adjust to this change, and continued to regard land reform as the foundation of radicalism even in the cities. He argued that landlordism was the root of social evils in both town and country; such arguments were unconvincing to town workers, who took to the Labour programme more easily. This social change was accentuated by the 1918 redistribution : before the war, the mining districts of Wales had had 9 seats and the rural districts 19, but after 1918 there were 16 mining seats and only 11 rural ones. However ideological confusion was not the only reason why Welshmen turned from Lloyd George. In the years after the war his appeasement of the Welsh Anglicans and his association with the Conservatives made him increasingly unpopular with Welsh nationalists as well as with industrial workers.

From his earliest days in politics, Lloyd George had had enemies who disliked seeing an acquaintance rising far beyond his origins. These men had worked with the premier despite their personal dislike of him. Similarly many Conservative M.P.s between 1918 and 1922 despised or feared Lloyd George, but felt they had little choice but to support him. It is a cliché to say that politicians court disaster when they mistakenly regard themselves as indispensable. It is more to the point in this case to say that Lloyd George fell because both he and those who backed him unwillingly knew he *was* indispensable, and that their pride tempted his reluctant followers to depose him as soon as they dared. Both Wales and the nation at large suffered for this during the interwar years; but England at least had mediocre successors to take his place, while Wales had no other political leaders of stature.

There was no national figure who could act as the premier's

Welsh lieutenant: his M.P.s after 1918 were mostly servile towards him, and did not offer friendly but constructive criticism. Sir Alfred Mond was his most forceful Welsh Liberal supporter, but Mond was an outsider, and not the ideal spokesman for Welsh interests. Chapter 1 has shown that Lloyd George's failure to ingratiate himself with the backbench M.P.s weakened his position after the first retirement of Bonar Law. Similarly, just as he failed to cultivate the M.P.s in Westminster, so Lloyd George did not cultivate the comparatively insignficant people who dominated Welsh constituency politics. He tried to keep his lines of communication open, but because he was burdened with the premiership at a time of almost unprecedented government activity, he relied on assistants and on the Welsh M.P.s. This proved insufficient and he could not rely on personal contacts with a small group of leaders to control all the local parties. As it was, he retained the support of the most prominent Welsh politicians, but lost that of numerous minor figures. Some evidence of this came after the 1922 election, when the tiny Asquithian organisation in Wales debated reunion with the much larger Lloyd George group. The papers of J. Bryn Roberts contain a complete list of the executive of the Asquithian group, and of the attitude of each member to reunion. Altogether there were 36 members of this executive. The 14 who were known well enough to be listed in *Who's Who in Wales* favoured reunion by 10 to 4, while the 22 who were not so listed divided 17 to 5 against reunion under any circumstances.[5]

Lloyd George offended these background figures partly because he ignored them, and party because his views on several Welsh topics were as easygoing as his attitude to luxuries, money and women. Many convinced Welsh nationalists felt that only Welsh concerns were important, and they often failed to realise the significance of wider political problems. As Lloyd George did not fit into their own small world, they considered him a renegade. Moreover they judged him by his friends and associates, many of whom were on the make, or distinct in some obvious way from ordinary Welsh Liberals. Also Archbishop Edwards and other Anglicans seemed closer to him, despite his former role as nonconformist chieftain, than did most nonconformists. The Archbishop even gave him communion, and many of his most prominent followers were churchmen. Lord St Davids, an Anglican, was chairman of Lloyd George's Welsh National Liberal Federation, while M. L. Vaughan-Davies, C. E. Breese, T. H. Parry, and Sir Evan Jones, all Anglicans, sat for the nonconformist strongholds of Cardigan, Carnarvon, Flint and Pembroke. All but Breese had been elected before the war, but their close association with Lloyd George during and after it indicated to some that the prime minister was leaving his origins behind.

Although he appeared to be drifting away from his Welsh roots, Lloyd George still regarded Wales almost as a personal fief, much as Joseph Chamberlain had done with Birmingham: according to Lord Riddell, 'LG frequently refers to Chamberlain's career and compares it to his own'. Lloyd George went so far as to make Venizelos a patron of the National Eisteddfodd, presumably because of his friendship with the Greek prime minister rather than for his contribution to Celtic culture. But Wales was no Birmingham. For one thing, Birmingham had fewer than 100,000 voters before 1914, while after the war Wales had over 1,000,000. Wales was also spread out over thirteen counties, the problems of which were more varied than those of one large but fairly compact city. Wales had three regions, and Lloyd George was familiar only with the rural nonconformist seats north of Glamorgan; the coastal and mining districts of the South did not follow him after 1918. Another difference between the positions of Chamberlain and Lloyd George was that Chamberlain had had fewer official responsibilities, and thus more time to maintain his political fences. Lloyd George still counted on Wales, yet after 1914 he acted as a national leader rather than as a Welsh one.[6]

The election of 1918 was fought on national, not Welsh issues. This disguised the fact that Lloyd George had been losing his grip on Welsh nationalism since the beginning of the war. There was no coherent opposition to him in his homeland during this election : Conservatives and many Labour men supported him, or at least remained neutral. Two Liberal M.P.s later drifted towards Asquith, but in 1918 neither campaigned openly as Asquithians. Lloyd George kept at least nominal control of nearly all the local Liberal associations, though this often meant little more than the nominal Asquithian control of English Liberal associations, since these groups met rarely between elections, if at all. The lack of organised opposition to Lloyd George within the Liberal Party left dissatisfied Liberals and Welsh nationalists with only Labour as an alternative. This was especially so after the passage of Disestablishment in 1920. E. Morgan Humphreys, editor of *Y Genedl*, practically the only Asquithian paper in Wales, commented that 'for more than a generation disestablishment has been the dividing question in Wales, not only in politics but also in religious and even in social life. Now it is gone, and there is sure to be, for a time, a vacuum which may well be filled by—well, who knows?' A year later, in 1921, Humphreys said that 'he would be a bold man who would prophesy anything about the future of Welsh nationalism today. We are between two periods. The literary revival of the beginning of the century has died down. . . . The next national awakening may take a political form.' However it was not to take the form of a specifically Welsh nationalist party.[7]

The changing attitude of some Welsh Liberals to Lloyd George can be seen graphically in the manuscripts of Beriah Evans and D. R. Daniel. They had organised Lloyd George's first election campaign in 1890, and had worked with him for many years. Both drifted away from him gradually after he became chancellor of the exchequer, and by the middle of the war both Evans and Daniel were unenthusiastic about their old colleague.

Beriah Evans was a teacher turned journalist. In addition to his literary work, Evans translated political material into Welsh for the Lloyd Georgians, Asquithians and Labour. In 1920 Welsh literary groups held a banquet, chaired by Lloyd George, which honoured Evans for his work for the Welsh language; at the time, Lloyd George was trying to win Evans to his side. However Evans did only what Lloyd George paid him to do, as the premier had made a slighting remark about him shortly after the 1906 election, and Evans had never forgiven him. Probably Lloyd George had forgotten the incident without realising that he had humiliated his old acquaintance. This was one more example of Lloyd George's disregard for the feelings of men he criticised.[8]

Evans did not hide his feelings from his frequent correspondent, E. T. John, Liberal M.P. for East Denbigh. The John Papers contain many letters from Evans denouncing Lloyd George, and as some of these letters predate the war, it is clear that the coming of the war merely gave Evans an excuse to bring his longstanding dislike into the open. He quoted with gusto such comments as 'The seductive eloquence of Mr. Lloyd George has been commandeered as apologist-in-chief for a smelling sentimentality masquerading as patriotism'. As for postponement of disestablishment, Evans thought it 'an exalted act of patriotism for Mr. Lloyd George to make a private treaty behind the backs of the Welsh Members'.[9]

Evans finally joined the Labour Party, along with John, but in their correspondence neither mentioned standard Labour concerns such as nationalisation; instead their letters considered mainly Welsh nationalism and the evil deeds of Lloyd George. At the same time, neither sympathised with the Asquithians, who according to Evans did not represent Welsh concerns. The quarrel of the two Liberal leaders led to an emphasis on personal matters of the sort which drove Evans to Labour. This suggests that in at least one case, a united Liberal Party could have held a supporter, and Evans' views are especially interesting in view of his long association with Lloyd George.[10]

D. R. Daniel, secretary of the Welsh Church Commission, knew Lloyd George more closely than did Beriah Evans. He regarded Lloyd George as to some extent the victim of circumstances. Perhaps because he lived in London and saw politicians of all shades, he had somewhat wider horizons than Evans, and he saw some of Lloyd George's redeeming qualities as well as his failings. Even so, his letters and diaries show that he had a great many reservations about the premier.

Daniel kept a diary in English, and in addition wrote a manuscript biography of Lloyd George in Welsh, which he never published. Daniel began this document in 1909 and added to it during the war. In this generally sympathetic account of Lloyd George, Daniel did not disguise his own feelings, such as his anti-Semitism. The personal and unreserved nature of the manuscript suggest that Daniel did not intend to publish it as it stood.

According to Daniel, Lloyd George 'went like a half-crazed bear with some dark-skinned Jew'; Daniel disliked the 'dresser of Jews, the Isaacs, the Samuels, and the Montagues, hook-nosed and swarthy, together with their wives in splendid clothes. To me it was they who had wounded this idol of the Welsh nation. It is these who throughout the ages have destroyed more than

one saviour'. The Jews, he thought, hoped to use Lloyd George
to get honours and titles. To do this, they tempted him with
luxuries 'on an oriental scale'; and as well, 'some Jewish women,
while they are still young, are beautiful and at all times cunning'.
Mrs Lloyd George was vulnerable too, because of her 'indisput-
able love of money'.[11]

Daniel was affronted by Lloyd George's non-puritanical ways;
curiously he did not believe the widespread stories of Lloyd
George's goatlike sexual activities, which according to Lloyd
George's son were his 'only form of recreation'. Daniel described
these rumours as 'worthless and contemptible gossip', though he
also said:[12]

> I remember G telling me years back that it was while with the
> army* around Conway Marshes that he——for the first time!
> I do not know about a second time. Fortunately as he has told
> me many times he got away from that slippery path. . . . I
> wonder how many young Welshmen stray to perverse ways in
> the armies.

The context of this remark indicates that Lloyd George con-
fessed some youthful sexual indiscretion, but what variety is
uncertain because of Daniel's reticence about naming it even in
his private writings. Daniel was more openly critical of Lloyd
George's other lax ways, his obvious love of luxuries and his
indiscreet financial dealings. 'The best clothes, the best food and
the most comfortable and luxurious furniture were his ambition
every time, and his weakness was that he did not show enough
sense of delicacy when accepting favours.' Lloyd George preferred London to Wales, 'the noise, the theatres and the res-
taurants. While his tongue worshipped Welsh Puritanism, he
was always in his roistering days akin to Charles II'. According
to Daniel, his undoing came when he accepted gifts and granted
favours in return: after the Marconi scandal he lacked the moral
position in the Liberal Party which would have enabled him to
leave the cabinet in August 1914 and to lead an antiwar movement. He had compromised himself too greatly, and for the
moment had put himself in Asquith's pocket. This interpretation
is disputable, but it shows that Daniel, a pacifist, was willing to

---

* In his youth, Lloyd George had been in the militia.

find excuses for continuing his friendship with Lloyd George
even during the war.[13]

Daniel was more affected by the postponement of Disestablishment than by Lloyd George's support of the war. He said that
when Lloyd George spoke in favour of postponement, he 'broke
the binding link between himself and his own nation'. He 'called
this great question of his country, the question of religious liberty,
a petty sectarian squabble'. From that day, wrote Daniel, 'I
heard scepticism on the part of his old followers and friends on
every side. This walks like an insect blight through Wales'. Daniel
ceased defending Lloyd George's views on the war, and a few
months later, while speaking to Lloyd George, said, 'We have
worn Belgium proudly on our sleeve, yet first and foremost in
falsehood and dishonesty'. Even so, Daniel still respected Lloyd
George's slick methods of foiling attackers. In November 1917
he saw the premier in a corner, but felt that 'the Welsh pole-cat
will turn in his skin and bite the slow ponderous Anglo-Saxon
as usual'. Daniel detested Lloyd George's war programme, and
thought the 1918 election 'a medley of trickery and dishonesty'.
He also felt that Lloyd George's Irish policy was disgusting, as
was his repeal of the land duties of 1909. By March 1922 he
thought that the Coalition wagon was 'creaking very much
these days—looks like the end of the unholy alliance. It is the
biggest piece of organised hypocrisy of the last hundred years'.
Nonetheless he confided to his diary that 'I cannot forget the old
times and old lies', and when the Coalition ended, Daniel hoped
that his fall would bring Lloyd George to earth 'from the heights
where he was held by an immoral and utterly dishonest political
combination'.[14]

These two views of Lloyd George, held by Evans and Daniel,
represented both sides of Welsh Liberalism, the one rejecting
Lloyd George without taking up Asquith, and the other regretting Lloyd George's policies, while still hoping in 1922 that he
could be regained for the Welsh cause. Both men had seen, even
before the war, that Lloyd George's views were broader than
their own, but their disenchantment reached a high pitch just
before his dismissal. This reaction against the most famous Welsh-
man of his day was not restricted to industrial areas where
Labour was advancing in any case; it spread through all levels
of Welsh opinion.

In 1918 the Liberals won 20 of the 36 Welsh seats, while Labour won 9. Only one Labour candidate won against a Coalition Liberal. This was not as overwhelming a Liberal victory as in 1906, when Liberals and Labour had taken every seat, but it was a strong endorsement of Lloyd George. No out-and-out Asquithian won a seat in Wales, though H. Haydn Jones (Merioneth) and David Davies (Montgomery) tended to side with the Asquithians. Otherwise the election in Wales, as in other parts of the country, was a favourable plebiscite on Lloyd George; but his position eroded quickly.

When Lloyd George became prime minister, the Welsh National Liberal Federation broke away from Asquith, but the federation apparently had more organisers than organised, and although nearly all the constituency Liberal parties in Wales backed the premier, many of them were as inactive as they had been before the war. According to E. M. Humphreys, a generation had grown up knowing little of Liberal principles: 'No meetings have been held in those districts for many years.' Especially in safe seats, Liberalism had been taken for granted, meetings had been infrequent, and party membership small. For instance the pre-war records of the Aberdare Liberal club show a steadily declining membership, though total club income rose because of increased revenue from billiards and refreshments. In Aberdare the Conservatives normally polled less than a quarter of the votes. However the I.L.P. was more active there than in most other parts of Wales, and one might have expected the Liberals to organise more effectively to counter this, but the records show a consistent decline. In 1921 the *Liberal Magazine* said, 'there are few active and well-organised Liberal associations in the thirteen counties of Wales'. The magazine turned a blind eye to the situation in many English Liberal associations which were also inactive; however it supported Asquith, as did most English local parties.[15]

In Wales Lloyd George merely maintained the existing inactivity during 1919 and most of 1920. His backers controlled the local parties, moribund though they often were, and an upsurge of activity might serve to focus opposition to him. This situation could change if the Liberal M.P.s died, retired or seceded to Asquith, but there seemed little chance in 1920 that this would happen on an extensive scale. Eventually Lloyd

George convened his federation in October 1920, and, in retalia-
tion for the expulsion of his followers from the Scottish and
English Liberal organisations, he expelled the Asquithians from
the Welsh party. To preserve themselves from 'the Moloch of
political opportunism', the Asquithians founded a group styling
itself the 'Welsh Liberal Federation'. Lloyd George called it 'a
clique of misfits'; his views could be dismissed by the Asquithians,
but Beriah Evans's opinion could not be ignored so easily, as
Evans had at first hoped that the new federation would help
bring Lloyd George down. He soon described it as 'an awful
fraud and frost'. The Asquithian newspaper *Y Genedl* was, he
felt, 'very feeble', and Asquith's personal stock was, 'and will
continue to be, at a discount throughout Wales'.[16]

The Asquithian federation never got off the ground, and even
strong Independent Liberals such as E. M. Humphreys soon
wondered why it did not meet, and why no Welsh M.P. joined
it. The federation did not carry many local parties with it, but,
according to E. M. Humphreys, this did not matter, because
'if a Liberal Association decides to support the Coalition it ceases
to be a Liberal association, and Liberals no longer owe any
respect to its decisions'. In other words the Asquithians felt they
could interfere with the autonomy of local Liberal associations,
even though this was one of their greatest criticisms of Lloyd
George. Humphreys nevertheless thought it important to claim
that several associations supported the Asquithian federation; he
included in one of his lists even Lloyd George's own local party,
which was far from divided. The Welsh Asquithian organisation
came to little, and by 1923 they had to cut expenditure by
eliminating one secretary, 'otherwise we shall come to a sudden
and ignominious end'. They also made their weakness apparent
in the Cardiganshire by-election of 1921. Their defeat in this
campaign marked the real end of Asquithian hopes in Wales,
and the start of the shift to Labour.[17]

The Cardiganshire by-election resulted from Lloyd George's
wish to put Ernest Evans in the commons as his main Welsh
organiser, in place of M. L. Vaughan-Davies, who had sat for
Cardiganshire since 1895. During 1919 the Press rumoured that
Lloyd George would arrange a peerage for Vaughan-Davies if
the latter enabled Evans to get the Liberal nomination. The
executive of the Cardiganshire Liberal Association frustrated this

by informing all its branches that it would not tolerate a Coalition Liberal replacement for Vaughan-Davies; but the executive had not consulted the association about this, and many members opposed this action. In June 1920, during the elections to the association executive, 'there were ample signs of friction', even according to the Asquithians. The new executive shelved the order forbidding a Coalition Liberal candidate, and Vaughan-Davies figured in the 1921 New Year's Honours List as Baron Ystwyth. Several men tried to get the nomination, chief of whom were Ernest Evans and W. Llewellyn Williams. According to the *Manchester Guardian* correspondent, Evans had a 'very amiable and winning personality', while Williams was 'a stern and unbending Liberal'. Williams was a leading Welsh nationalist, and a strong critic of Lloyd George. He had been M.P. for Carmarthen Boroughs from 1906 to 1918, and had opposed Lloyd George in the Maurice debate of 1918. His entry into the by-election as a staunch Asquithian was the first major test of Lloyd George's popularity in Wales after the war.[18]

The Cardiganshire Liberal executive was evenly divided between Asquithians and Lloyd Georgians, with the former perhaps in a slight majority. The executive required all candidates to accept the party nominee, to use the secretary of the association as election agent, and to state whether they were Coalitionists or 'free and independent Liberals'. Four of the five candidates rejected one or more of these conditions, and only Llewellyn Williams accepted all three. He had previously organised several village Liberal clubs in his favour, so he stood the best chance of getting the nomination, and could only hurt himself by refusing to stand by the party choice.[19]

The nomination meeting was rowdy, with clamorous booing and fist fights. At one point the chairman shouted at the delegates, 'Why in the world can't you behave yourselves? You are like a pack of animals'. Evans made a brief speech, then Williams repudiated Lloyd George, who had betrayed Wales by 'virtually re-endowing the church'. The association backed him by 206 votes to 127 for Evans. The *Manchester Guardian* attributed this partly to Lloyd George's attempt to force Evans on a local association noted for its independent views.[20]

Evans decided to run as a Coalition Liberal; but it was interesting that the Asquithians had also decided to run even if they had lost. E. M. Humphreys wrote that if Evans had been nominated, the Asquithians would 'break away, form a new association, and proceed at once to select a candidate'. As it was, Evans had the odium of creating the party split.[21]

Evans had substantial backing outside the local association : Sir William Robertson Nicholl, editor of the *British Weekly*, and a leading nonconformist, supported him, as did Lord Ystwyth, the former M.P., and the local Conservatives. Lloyd George did not speak in the by-election, but his wife did on many occasions. Evans kept fairly quiet, and at least did not alienate voters. On the other hand Williams's provocative speeches led to several riots. He denounced Lloyd George's 'pinchbeck Caesarism', his 'mean, petty, spiteful tyranny' and his system of sordid espionage'. After one of these speeches, a mob broke into his hall, smashed all the windows and hustled his supporters on to the street. 'A noisy crowd, chiefly composed of youths and students' broke up another meeting, while at yet another a Lloyd Georgian threw a stone which caught Ernest Brown, Liberal candidate for Salisbury, on the head.[22]

Perhaps individual candidates may rarely be worth more than 500 votes, but Williams seems to have been worth about 2000 to his opponents, since Evans won by 14,111 to 10,521. In the 1922 general election, Williams was not a candidate, and Evans won by only 12,825 to 12,310 over a new Asquithian. Nevertheless this by-election was more significant than the figures indicated. During the campaign numerous academic and literary figures adhered to Williams, as did the political organiser of the South Wales Miners' Federation. Labour did not win Cardiganshire until 1966, but the bitterness this by-election left in literary and nationalist circles undermined the Liberal hold on the Welsh intelligentsia. In 1923 Hopkin Morris, Asquithian candidate for Cardigan, and Ellis Davies, leader of the Welsh Liberal Federation, said that 'every Liberal who is worth his salt will very shortly be constrained to come into full association with the Labour Party in Wales'. The same year an independent Labour candidate won the University of Wales constituency. The intellectual revolt against the Liberals did not take effect immediately, but it was an important factor in the long-term swing in rural parts of Wales from Liberalism to Labour.[23]

In 1918 Labour had won only a single seat in rural Wales,

Anglesey, where Sir Owen Thomas had campaigned as an independent supporter of Labour. In 1922 Labour doubled its Welsh representation, but still had only one rural seat there, this time Carnarvon. Though the Labour candidate ran on the usual Labour platform, his margin of victory came from Asquithian seceders and disgruntled Welsh nationalists rather than from the normal Labour strength in the constituency. The 1918 and 1922 campaigns in Carnarvon revealed much about the major trends in Welsh politics at this turning-point.

The county of Carnarvonshire had two constituencies, Carnarvon District, an amalgamation of nine small boroughs which Lloyd George held, and Carnarvon. Carnarvon was a mixed agricultural and mining seat, with 29.1 per cent of its male population engaged in mining and 21.7 per cent in agriculture. Other important characteristics of the constituency were its high proportion of Welsh-speakers (75 per cent) and nonconformists (42.5 per cent in the religious census of 1905).

Before 1918 the county had had three seats, Carnarvon District, and two county divisions, Arfon and Eifion. In deference to Lloyd George, Carnarvon District was retained with small changes, though the other six districts of boroughs in Wales were suppressed. The merger of Arfon and Eifion created a political problem, as the M.P. for Eifion, Ellis W. Davies, was an enemy of Lloyd George, who among other things had accused Lloyd George's son of taking a safe job behind the lines in the war. Lloyd George supported C. E. Breese, a politically inexperienced Portmadoc solicitor, and son of Lloyd George's first employer. Some friends of Davies took advantage of the 1918 redistribution to declare that the old Arfon and Eifion associations were defunct. They set up a new association, and to give it an aura of reality, they chose their members from the people who had been delegates to the two old associations in December 1910. The Asquithians chose only a few delegates, all of them known to back Davies, and not surprisingly this 'association' nominated Davies.[24]

The village Liberal clubs of the constituency paid little attention to Davies' nomination, and elected new delegates. Three men sought this nomination, Davies, Breese and R. T. Jones, who was general secretary of the North Wales Quarrymen's Union. Although Jones was the Labour candidate, he received almost as many votes as Davies. Breese defeated both for the Liberal nomination, and won the election with 10,488 votes to 8,145 for Jones and 4,937 for Davies.[25]

The Asquithians maintained their association, but few if any village clubs joined it. In December 1921 the Lloyd Georgians staged a coup, and captured control of the association. The Asquithians in London said that Carnarvon Independents must form a new group at once, or they would 'either gravitate into their skins or gravitate towards Labour'. However their organisation collapsed, and only twenty-four attended an abortive nomination meeting in 1922. The Asquithians then tried to persuade Breese to renounce coalition, but he refused, saying that there would be another coalition within three months. Nonetheless he described himself as a prefixless Liberal, to win some Asquithian support. His campaign in 1922 was a colourless defence of the Coalition record, and persuaded few uncommitted voters.[26]

On the other hand R. T. Jones, the Labour candidate, offered a brand of mild radicalism which appealed to many Liberals. Indeed he had tried to get the Liberal nomination in 1918, and when he had been rejected, had stood as a Labour supporter of Lloyd George. Jones was, after Lloyd George, one of the most prominent men in North Wales. Unlike Breese, an Anglican who could not speak Welsh, Jones was a Welsh-speaking nonconformist. He had personally enrolled six thousand in his quarrymen's union and had been active in settling some important mining strikes in the constituency. He was also a popular speaker on temperance. In the 1922 election he did not oppose Lloyd George, and in fact condemned the Conservatives for deposing 'our countryman'. He had no Asquithian rival in this election to siphon off opposition votes, and he made a conscious effort to win the Asquithians over. For instance he opposed immediate nationalisation of mines and railways, though he favoured gradual nationalisation. His main appeal was personal : he thought the quarrymen should be represented in Parliament. Ellis Davies and his associates supported Jones during the campaign. This campaign was mild in comparison with most other straight fights between Lloyd Georgians and Labour, and there was no pre-election scare. This helped Jones prevent polarisation of the electorate over socialism, and he won most of the 1918

Asquithian vote. Breese's percentage rose from 44.5 per cent to 46.9 per cent, but that of Jones went from 34.6 per cent to 53.1 per cent. Some of Jones's increase came from a general shift towards Labour after 1918, but even more came from Asquithians who refused to support an ex-Coalitionist.[27]

This election started the Labour advance into what had previously been one of the chief Liberal strongholds, and it is noteworthy that it happened in Lloyd George's home county. After 1922 Labour advanced deliberately but surely: it lost Carnarvon in 1923 but regained it in 1929, along with several other rural Welsh seats. After the Second World War Labour improved its position in nearly every election, so that by 1966 it held 32 of the 36 Welsh constituencies. At the same time it held the Welsh nationalist vote to an insignificant fraction. Much of the explanation for this lay in the period 1918–22, when, as in Carnarvon, the bitter Liberal factional struggle enabled Labour to play the role of *tertius gaudens*. A more immediate result of the election in Carnarvon was that it discredited Lloyd George's position as master of Wales. His reputation could have withstood the loss of mining seats in Glamorgan and Monmouthshire, but his failure to hold what had been one of his safest seats dramatically weakened his hope to act in future as the Welsh Joseph Chamberlain.

10

The Victory
of the Second Eleven

Table 10   Results of the 1922 election

Party	Seats	Votes	% of votes	
Conservative	327	5,281,555	36.7	
Ind. Conservative	13	222,410	1.5	38.5
Other Conservative	3	38,109	0.3	
Labour	142	4,237,769		29.4
Asquithian Liberal	41	2,098,732	14.6	
Ll.G. Liberal	47	1,320,935	9.2	29.1
Prefixless Liberal	28	763,315	5.3	
Irish Nat./Sinn Fein	2	102,667		0.7
Constitutionalist	4	48,748		0.3
Communist/'Ind. Labour'	1	38,134		0.3
Others	6	241,258		1.7

One of the most striking things about the 1922 election was that such a confused campaign had clear and lasting significance to each major party. Four independents and Constitutionalists were in effect Liberals, three more were Conservatives and one was Labour. Thus the operating strength of the parties was Conservatives 346, Labour 143 and Liberals 120. This gave the Conservatives a working majority of 77. Labour solidified its position as the official Opposition, and the Conservative opponents of the old Coalition kept office. While the Conservatives had just a third of the votes, their majority of seats helped determine the electoral future of Britain. Also the election pushed Stanley Baldwin and Neville Chamberlain to prominence, as both owed their rapid promotion in 1923 to the fact that numerous Conservatives better known than they were, were out of office when Bonar Law retired in May. The Liberals, in contrast with the other two parties, received a setback, for they remained divided over leadership. While the election helped settle the question of leadership in the Conservative and Labour Parties, it accentuated the Liberal difficulties, and hence hastened the party's decline. This chapter considers the effect of the 1922 crisis on the development of the three parties, and also examines briefly the change in political attitudes during 1923 which made coalitions less likely than they had been before the election.

During 1923 both Labour and Conservatives often acted as if the election of 1922 had been just another incident in the continuing transformation of British politics from the pre-war Liberal-Conservative rivalry to the post-war Labour-Conservative polarisation. In addition Labour and Conservative leaders tended to be less accommodating to Liberals seeking alliances than they had been during the 1922 election campaign, when they had anticipated a Parliament of minorities. Yet on examination, one can see that the results of the 1922 election distorted public opinion. The Conservatives won a majority of seats with only 38 per cent of the vote, the lowest percentage obtained by any majority government during this century; and though Labour formed the official Opposition, it had almost the same number of votes as the combined Liberal factions. However each party acted independently of the Liberals, since for the time being there was no need for coalition.

In 1922 the parliamentary Labour Party moved from being a weak trade union group to an effective force with a more dynamic leadership and a broader base in Parliament than previously. Between 1918 and 1922 the Labour M.P.s had outnumbered the Asquithians, but they had not emerged clearly as an alternative government, partly because of ineffective leadership, and partly because their position as the official Opposition had seemed to be the artificial result of temporary Liberal divisions: counted together, the two Liberal groups had had more than twice as many M.P.s as Labour, and if they had linked forces, they, rather than Labour, would have been the obvious alternative to the Conservatives. After the election, Labour had twenty-three more M.P.s than the Liberals, and Liberal factional differences left Labour effectively unchallenged as the official Opposition. Yet Labour's position was less substantial than it appeared.

Labour won only slightly more votes than the Liberals (29.4 per cent as compared with 29.1 per cent); but if the independents who supported the Liberals and Labour were counted, then the Liberals had a few more votes than Labour. In addition, if the Liberals had not run conflicting candidates, they would have won four seats which went Conservative and ten which went Labour; in each seat, the combined Liberal poll was higher than that of the winner. Counting the independents, the Liberals won 120 seats, but by patching up their differences, the Liberals would have made this Liberals 134 and Labour 133. This would have been quite separate from any gains in votes the Liberals would have made if they had stood together, and had offered a genuine alternative to the Conservatives. A one-seat lead over Labour would have been only a moral victory, but moral victories are important.[1]

Another way in which Labour strength was weaker than it seemed was that the party's percentage poll did not rise uniformly. In many seats it actually receded, which indicates that Labour's drawing-power was more limited than it appears in retrospect, with the knowledge that Labour formed the Government only a year later. The overall Labour poll rose from 22.2 per cent in 1918 to 29.4 per cent in 1922, but this shift was much more marked in some areas than in others. Mining districts, and the slums of Glasgow, London and Sheffield had almost all the high swings to Labour, and 64 of the 82 Labour gains. These areas were only a small proportion of the constituencies in the country, and elsewhere Labour gains were more limited. In the 603 territorial seats in Great Britain and Northern Ireland, Labour increased its support in 235, or 37 per cent of the total. It also intervened in 83 seats it had not contested in 1918, but its strength in most of these seats was minimal. The Labour vote declined in 85 seats, the party withdrew in 64 and it did not contest either the 1918 or 1922 elections in a further 135, so that its support was either miniscule or declining in 284 seats, that is, in more seats than it was increasing. On the whole Labour was not on the crest of a tidal wave in 1922, except in certain areas. The distribution of its votes showed that it had far to go before it could hope to win a majority.

More important to Labour than its 7.2 per cent increase in votes was the change in the character of the parliamentary party, which became less obviously trade unionist than before the election. A Liberal journal, the *Nation*, put the number of middle-class Labour M.P.s at 54, just over a third of the total of 142 (or 143 counting the Prohibitionist supporter of Labour from Dundee). Some longtime Labour supporters may have agreed with F. H. Rose, M.P. for Aberdeen North, who 'would willingly swop all the super-intellectual middle-class cranks who have so magnanimously climbed on our backs', but others realised that the presence of middle-class M.P.s helped dispel the notion that Labour was interested only in trade union questions. The selection of Ramsay MacDonald as leader added to this impression of a broader-based Labour Party. Winston Churchill later described MacDonald as 'the boneless wonder'. Perhaps he was boneless, but he was certainly a wonder in comparison with J. R. Clynes, who had been a mouthpiece for the unions rather than leader of an independent party. MacDonald's own intellectual contributions were small, but the fact that he had written several tracts on social policy gave him a stature which Clynes lacked, and he was personally much more appealing as well. Taken together, the new middle-class Labour M.P.s and the new leader helped create the impression that the Labour Party was no longer a mere outgrowth of a special interest group, but was becoming a truly national party.[2]

Labour's new position as the official Opposition, and its national pretensions, made relations between it and the Liberals more strained. If anything those relations became more confused, because while Labour had officially stood apart from the Liberals in the election, the two parties had in fact conflicted in only half the seats. Both before and during the election, numerous Labour politicians had considered limited pacts with the Liberals, and if the Liberals had co-ordinated their efforts after the election, they might have extended this co-operation to more seats. One difficulty was that the conflict between the Liberal factions distracted them from what should have been a major effort to make a deal with Labour.

The difficulties in the way of a Liberal-Labour pact were greater than they had been when Ramsay MacDonald had made an electoral bargain in 1903 covering a few dozen seats. In 1922 there were, in addition to the I.L.P. as in 1903, numerous Communist groups and hundreds of local Labour parties, which could frustrate alliances which had the support of the national party. Even where Labour did support the Liberals in 1922, there was sometimes dissension in local Labour ranks, as in Torquay and Birkenhead East. On the other hand it was not unusual to find Liberal and Labour candidates in neighbouring constituencies running parallel campaigns: thus the Labour candidate in Leicester East and the Liberal in Leicester South co-operated unofficially, but they did not acknowledge their joint candidacies openly. Occasionally local Labour groups went even further. In Hanley some members of the I.L.P. backed the Asquithian, a social reformer who had supported conscientious objectors in the war and who had backed land reform, against the official right-wing Labour candidate. In most parts of the country there was a fair amount of Labour support for pacts with the Liberals, but there was no national co-operation between the parties. Even Labour leaders who favoured co-operation generally confined it to semi-private support, and agreed with the chairman of the Penrith and Cockermouth Labour Party that there should be an alliance, but that the action of many Liberal leaders 'seems to have made the confidence which must be the basis of all alliances impossible'. He did not refer solely to the Lloyd George Liberals, but to the party as a whole, since it had not developed a coherent policy towards Labour or the Conservatives. Labour was still feeling its way about the changed electoral position after 1922. The secretary of the Manchester Liberal Federation had written in 1921 that when Labour came closer to a majority, with perhaps 300 seats, 'its frame of mind would become more reasonable'. But Labour was not even near a majority of seats or votes in the 1922 election, and it had to have time to adjust, and to demarcate electoral zones of activity with the Liberals. Such time was not available.[3]

In addition to having insufficient time to prepare pacts, the Asquithian leaders were ambivalent towards the Labour Party.

One might have supposed that the top Asquithians would have developed a strategy on this topic between 1918 and 1923, but it was difficult to determine the official Asquithian view of the subject after the 1922 election. Asquith himself professed to be 'not in the least alarmed by the Red Spectre', and Sir John Simon, hardly a socialist or even moderately left-wing, said, 'I do not believe that we ought to treat Labour as the common enemy'. Conversely, the *Liberal Magazine*, the official Asquithian journal, said that 'under socialism, individual freedom would practically disappear', and that 'the Labour Party is a morbid political coalition held together by insincerity'. The relation of the Asquithians to Labour resembled that of the Lloyd Georgians to the Conservatives in their inability to choose between Liberal reunion and electoral pacts with other parties. The indecisiveness of the 1922 election, so far as the Liberals were concerned, maintained this beyond the campaign itself.[4]

From December 1922 to November 1923 there were 15 contested by-elections.* Asquithians and Labour conflicted in 9; in the other 6, the Liberals gave Labour a free run in 3 and Labour gave the Liberals a free run in 2. In Tiverton, the only other contest, the Labour Party disavowed the independent Labour candidate, who had been the official Labour candidate in 1922. The Labour vote there dropped from 1,457 to 495, which was just sufficient to shift the seat from the Conservatives to the Liberals. Balacing this, the Liberals had straight fights with Labour in Whitechapel and Morpeth, each of which had had Conservative candidates in 1922. More significant than either contest was one held in Newcastle East in January 1923, where the Labour nominee was Arthur Henderson, whose goodwill was vital to electoral co-operation between Liberals and Labour if it was to be carried beyond scattered local pacts. The Liberal, Harry Barnes, had voted for a capital levy in 1919, and he joined Labour in 1931, so he was no diehard anti-socialist. Barnes had been opposed by a Lloyd Georgian and Labour in 1922; the two Liberals had taken 56.8 per cent to Labour's 43.2 per cent. Since the total Liberal poll had exceeded Labour's, and since Barnes had been the M.P. up to 1922, it was too much to expect him to withdraw in favour of Henderson, especially

* Excluding the Portsmouth South by-election of December 1922, which had two candidates, both Conservatives.

when there was no rival Liberal candidate in the by-election. The Liberals frequently faced similar difficulties in the 1920s, as it was hard to stop ex-M.P.s who wished to contest their old seats even when this conflicted with their party's overall strategy.

These by-elections, and the varying attitude of Liberal spokesmen showed that Liberal-Labour relations were undecided even after the 1922 election. The two parties might have collaborated on a limited basis, but the effects of the 1922 election had hardly worn off when the 1923 election came almost without warning. In 1923 Liberals and Labour again conflicted in only half the seats. In the other half, their co-operation was a little more noticeable than in 1922, but it was still unofficial, because the two parties had not determined what their relations would be, as the Conservative victory of 1922 had seemed to shelve the need for considering coalitions for several years.

The most obvious result of the 1922 election for Labour was its great increase in seats. Some Conservatives welcomed the emergent Labour Party: as the Duke of Northumberland had put it earlier in 1922, 'the advent of the Labour Party to power would indeed be a boon; it would rally all the opposing elements'. The duke's views may have been unusual, but fear of Labour was undoubtedly a major factor in Conservative success between the wars. The reverse effect of this was that many voters who became dissatisfied with the performance of Conservative governments turned to Labour, frequently because Labour was the chief opposition group rather than because of conversion to socialism. This negative aspect in the rise of Labour has been emphasised less than the more positive contributions of Labour policy, organisation and leadership, but it is likely that antagonism to the Conservatives helped Labour at least as much as political and economic theories. This was especially noticeable after the 1922 election, for the Bonar Law-Baldwin Government proved less adequate than most, and it probably would have fallen at any of half a dozen different points in 1923 if it had depended on the Lloyd George Liberals or Chamberlainite Conservatives. However the 1922 election produced a definite Conservative majority, and this led to a political polarisation which might have taken some years to develop if the non-socialists had formed a series of shifting coalitions.[5]

The strength of the new Conservative Government lay in the

size of its parliamentary majority, not in the prestige of its ministers; but that parliamentary majority rested on an insecure foundation. With a 38.5 per cent of the vote, the Conservatives won more than half the seats. Not only was this a lower percentage than that obtained by any other majority government during this century; it was also 5.2 per cent less than the Conservatives had taken in the Liberal landslide of 1906. This comparison shows that there was no great surge to the Conservatives in 1922, but that they depended on the continuance of the division between Liberals and Labour. It was only in later elections that the Conservatives advanced much in terms of votes: in the other two elections of the 1920s in which all three parties contested two-thirds or more of the seats, the results were :*

Election	Con. % of vote	Con. seats	Con. % of seats
1922	38.5%	343	55.8%
1923	38.1	258	41.9
1929	38.2	260	42.3

The Conservatives nominated fewer candidates in 1922 than in 1923 or 1929, but they contested nearly all the seats where they had much chance, so that the three elections were roughly comparable. The table shows that there was a 'basic' Conservative vote of just over 38 per cent in the 1920s. This was a strong starting-point for a political party in a three-party system, but it was unlikely to yield a majority except in the unusual circumstance where the Opposition was both evenly divided and unable to make electoral agreements. In each of these elections the Conservatives won more seats than their percentage of votes entitled them to: in 1923 they won 23, and in 1929 25 more seats; but in 1922 they won 110 more. The Conservatives took 95 seats in 1922 on minority votes, and a further 19 in straight fights where their candidates had majorities of under 1000 votes, for a total of 114 seats which were insecure by usual reckoning. Nevertheless, however insecure individual seats were, the overall majority frustrated the possibilities of coalition which had been so widely discussed during the election, and this seemed to confirm the views of those Conservatives who had said they could

* The 1924 results were not comparable, as the Liberals contested fewer seats than in the three elections considered.

keep office by standing on their own. In fact the Conservatives did rule, apart from two interludes totalling three years, until 1945; but regardless of how it is considered, 38 per cent is not a majority, and the Chamberlainites were accurate when they said that the Conservatives needed Liberal assistance. It was a paradox that the Conservatives retained power in this election by relying on Liberals in many close fights, but that the politicians who wished to make definite arrangements to keep that backing lost face in their own party as a result of the Conservative victory.

Just after the election, the Conservative Party shifted to the right, and two Diehards, Colonel Gretton and A. B. Boyd-Carpenter, displaced two supporters of the old coalition on the executive of the National Unionist Association. In March 1923 Bonar Law appointed two other strong opponents of the Coalition, Sir Reginald Hall and F. S. Jackson, two important posts in the Conservative organisation, and he dismissed two others of more dubious loyalty, Sir Malcolm Fraser and Lord Farquhar. The attitudes of Sir George Younger and T. W. H. Inskip were also revealing. At a dinner in late 1922 Younger 'nearly jumped out of his chair and said Austen would *never* get into [Bonar Law's] government and that the country would not stand him at any price'. Younger had opposed continuance of the Lloyd George regime, but T. W. H. Inskip had supported it and had pledged to co-operate with the Lloyd George Liberals after the election, even though he was Bonar Law's solicitor-general. By mid-1923 Inskip had apparently sensed the change in Conservative circles, for he announced that Lloyd George was always 'crying stinking fish'.[6]

Yet it soon became obvious that the Government required a large majority to carry on : about two dozen Conservative M.P.s continued to support Chamberlain, and the comparatively inexperienced ministers in the new Government involved it in several setbacks in 1923 which would have toppled most governments with narrow majorities. During the 1922 election, Winston Churchill had labelled Bonar Law's cabinet as 'the second eleven', and Birkenhead had described the new ministers as second-class intellects. Birkenhead's brains had gone to his head, as Lady Asquith commented, but there was much to his and Churchill's descriptions. Most of the new ministers were inexperienced in high office, and several of them had rather limited ability. Bonar Law himself had told Sir Archibald Salvidge that he expected to have to replace some of them quickly; this was even before he had appointed them. His forecast proved accurate.[7]

A month and a half after the election, Stanley Baldwin left for the United States to discuss war debts with the American Government. Bonar Law thought that settlement of American claims should wait until the Americans agreed to all-round cancellation of war debts due to and from Britain, or until the interest rate on the American loan was reduced substantially. Baldwin was not authorised to conclude an agreement, but he did so anyway, and accepted an interest rate which was 1 per cent higher than Bonar Law thought it possible to pay. While this might seem a small difference, it amounted to well over £800 million during the sixty-two years the agreement was supposed to last. Moreover Baldwin had failed to get an assurance from the Americans that British payments to the United States would depend on French payments to Britain, even though the American debt had been contracted by Britain on behalf of France. Finally, on his way back from the United States, Baldwin told reporters that his difficulties had come from senators from the middle and western states, who did not understand the problem. This remark did not make revision of the terms easier. In his examination of this affair, Robert Blake labelled the debt negotiations as 'Baldwin's blunder', and he revealed that Bonar Law seriously considered resigning rather than agreeing to Baldwin's terms. This would have precipitated an unpredictable crisis in the Conservative Party, for Law was the only really strong man in the Government at that point. However he agreed under pressure to stay on, and contented himself with an anonymous denunciation of Baldwin's policy in *The Times*, under the pseudonym of 'a Colonial correspondent'.[8]

While the Government was trying to settle the war debt, the French invaded the Rhineland, ostensibly because Germany had failed to deliver 100,000 telephone poles as part of her reparations payments. The issue was only a pretext : the Germans could have delivered the poles, but wished to force re-examination of the entire question of reparations; and the French would have found another excuse to occupy the Rhineland, since their real reason for the invasion was not to acquire telephone poles, but to prevent Germany from rising again. The Government drifted throughout this episode, and despite almost constant prodding from all three opposition groups, it appeared to be following Bonar Law's dictum of October 1922, when he had said, 'We must leave things alone more or less where we can'.[9]

Although the cabinet had vacillated on the German problem, it took more positive action in February 1923 on the rent increases which had been collected in defiance of the 1920 rent controls. The courts had decided in favour of the tenants, and the issue had been a major election topic in central Scotland; but the Government introduced legislation which let the landlords keep the illegal increases anyway. The Asquithian and Lloyd George Liberals joined Labour in denouncing the retroactive principle involved, as well as the anti-tenant aim of the legislation. On the question of removing rent controls, the government indecision led directly to the loss of three by-elections. Sir Arthur Griffith-Boscawen, who as minister of health was responsible for rents and housing, had failed to win a seat in the general election, as had two junior ministers. In the three by-elections held in the first week of March, all three failed to keep hitherto safe Conservative seats.[10]

Only a week later the Government blundered once more on an issue which united the Opposition. The home secretary had authorised the arrest and deportation of over a hundred Irishmen, without specific charges being laid. As the civil war was still in progress in Ireland, the home secretary's action laid the deportees open to considerable risk. The courts declared the deportations illegal, which left the home secretary, W. C. Bridgeman, open to personal lawsuits by the deportees. Bridgeman told the commons that he saw nothing wrong with the mass arrests; the Government thereupon introduced a bill which retroactively protected Bridgeman, or any other minister, from lawsuits arising from this, or any similar illegal action committed while working on behalf of the Government. After vehement denunciations by the leaders of all three opposition groups, the Government limited the bill to this one case.[11]

In April 1923 the Government was defeated in the commons on a question relating to the employment of ex-servicemen. This was not a vote of confidence, but taken in conjunction with the

Government's fumbling over war debts, the occupation of the Rhineland, rents, housing the Irish deportations and similar matters during the first three months of the year, it showed that the Government was losing its grip. The Government retained little support from the independent sectors of the Press which had backed it in the 1922 election, and even the clerk of the privy council, Sir Almeric Fitzroy, reflected the general disenchantment. In his diary Fitzroy called Bonar Law 'a weary valetudinarian' and his cabinet 'well-intentioned and amiable gentlemen whose virtues are more impressive than their intellects'. He added that the Government could not cope with the 'problems of such menacing urgency' which it faced.[12]

Bonar Law realised the need to recruit new talent, and in mid-April he asked Austen Chamberlain, via Lord Beaverbrook, to join his cabinet with a promise of the succession as premier. Chamberlain refused, but only a few weeks later Bonar Law had to resign because of ill-health. Chamberlain would have been the obvious successor, but as he and his followers had not rejoined the Government, they needed in effect to be politically rebaptised as Conservatives when Law resigned. Baldwin's luck returned to him at this point. He had been promoted rapidly in October 1922, and although his handling of the American debt had been the most notable fiasco of early 1923, he had then presented a popular budget in April. In it Baldwin was merely reaping the fruit of Sir Robert Horne's savage fiscal cuts of 1922, and it took little to produce decreased taxes in 1923. But in such a government, even modest success shone in comparison with the general mediocrity. Thus Baldwin became, with Curzon, one of the two available choices as premier, not so much because of a good record as because of a stroke of luck.

Another minister benefiting from the change in government was Neville Chamberlain. At the beginning of the year he had been postmaster-general, not an office which usually provides much scope for initiative. With the defeat of Sir Arthur Griffith-Boscawen in March, Bonar Law needed a new minister of health at once. Chamberlain was moved in to fill the gap, and during his short tenure at the post, he showed that he had more drive than his predecessor. When Baldwin became prime minister in May, his first choice as chancellor of the exchequer was Sir Robert Horne, but Horne refused the offer. His second choice, Reginald

McKenna, also an ex-chancellor, accepted on condition that Baldwin found him a safe seat in the commons. Because of the by-election reverses, Baldwin could consider only invulnerable seats; from his viewpoint, Sir Frederick Banbury was dispensable, and his City of London seat was safe enough even in a period of deep Conservative unpopularity. But Banbury refused to withdraw for any Liberal. Baldwin, who had been acting as chancellor himself for three months, then gave the post to Neville Chamberlain. Thus both Baldwin and Neville Chamberlain owed their quick rise to the fact, fortunate for them, that Bonar Law's majority in 1922 had been so large that he had not needed to count on the former Coalition ministers. Both men had been rather small beer before 1922, but both survived the débâcle of 1923 to keep control of the Conservative machine throughout the interwar years, and this was one of the more important results of the 1922 election.[13]

From its election in November 1922 until Bonar Law's retirement in May 1923, the Government drifted without apparent aim from one crisis to another. When Baldwin took over this was less obvious, mostly because the new cabinet did not face so many urgent problems; but there was little evidence that Baldwin's Government had more positive goals than Law's had had. The by-election defeats in March were the only sign of the decreasing popularity of the Government. A more significant indicator was the attitude of the Lloyd George Liberals, who began voting more often with the Opposition. The Press also turned from the Government, and during the 1923 election, the Beaverbrook and Rothermere newspapers, which had stood by Bonar Law in 1922, backed Lloyd George. Taken together, these were all signs that November 1922 was an artificially propitious moment for the Conservatives, and that their victory depended on a favourable combination of chances.

The 1922 election had demonstrated one major difference between the Liberal and Conservative leaders. While the leaders of the ex-Coalitionist groups in each party were on bad terms with the leading opponents of the Coalition, only the Liberals let this conflict come into the open. The Chamberlainites formed a separate group in the commons, as did the Lloyd George Liberals, and they mostly stayed out of Bonar Law's Government. When Baldwin became premier, Birkenhead's view was

that the Government would 'fall through weakness and in-
capacity', and that it was best to remain out until this happened.
But few even among strong supporters of Chamberlain agreed,
and most concurred with Sir Laming Worthington-Evans, that
if Baldwin's Government failed, 'then the Tory party fails'. Most
backbenchers in both the Conservative and Liberal Parties shared
Worthington-Evans's viewpoint; in the Conservative Party this
desire to keep the party united triumphed, but in the Liberal
Party it did not. Part of the Conservative advantage derived
from the patronage at the disposal of the party leaders: for
instance Worthington-Evans joined Baldwin's administration as
did several other Chamberlainites. But part was due to the
positive wish of the dissident Conservatives to keep their party
united. In May 1923 Austen Chamberlain offered to release his
supporters from pledges to keep out of the Government, although
Baldwin neglected to get this release, apparently from inexperience rather than malice. During the 1923 election even Birkenhead campaigned vigorously for the Conservatives, despite his
ill-treatment by his party during the previous year. This was a
sharp contrast to the Liberal Party, where most of the M.P.s
wanted reunion, but where the leaders of one of the factions
continued to block it even after the 1922 election.[14]

The election resulted in no clear-cut decision on the Liberal
factional question, for as Roy Jenkins put it in his biography
of Asquith, 'the anti-Pope was almost as strong as the Pope'.
The problem of leadership became even more acute during 1923
than it had been during 1922, because the end of the Coalition
removed what ostensibly had been the major obstacle to reunion.
Open supporters of Lloyd George numbered 47, while 15 prefixless Liberals, Constitutionalists and independents were also inclined towards him. Open Asquithians numbered 41, and 15
prefixless Liberals and independents tendeds towards Asquith.
Two more M.P.s were not clearly associated with either leader.
A few supporters of Lloyd George shifted to Asquith fairly
quickly, and a few others joined the Conservatives, but this still
left each leader with about the same number of M.P.s. The even
split in the party accentuated the difficulty Liberals had in forming alliances with Labour or the Conservatives, and it also made
reunion harder to achieve than if either leader had won an
obvious majority.[15]

Because of the decisiveness of the Conservative majority, there seemed to be no urgency for resolving the leadership question. The *Liberal Magazine* anticipated that each Liberal group would be 'outwardly unchanged for some years, each retaining its own organisation and its own officers', but gradually merging in the constituencies. Baldwin's decision to call an election in December 1923 reduced the breathing space of 'some years' to twenty-four days (13 November–6 December 1923), and the reunion achieved in this short period did not go very deep as far as the leading Asquithians were concerned.[16]

Few Liberals wanted two separate parties, and continuance of the cleavage depended on the attitude of the leaders. There had been a few prefixless Liberals even before the Carlton Club Meeting, but the fall of Lloyd George encouraged more to take this position, and 95 candidates ran without prefix. Most of them said they would follow whichever Liberal leader won majority support at a post-election party meeting of all Liberal M.P.s. These suggestions for a post-election meeting came from all parts of the country, and their similarity suggests that they emanated from the same source, probably one of the leaders. However the candidates proposing such a meeting, many of whom evidently believed it had already been arranged, came from all factions, and the prefixless movement was probably spontaneous.

Asquith and Lloyd George each made lukewarm references to reunion during the election, but Lloyd George was more concerned with his prospects of resuming an alliance with the Conservatives, and Asquith with increasing the strength of his own small group. Thus in some ways it was surprising that the projected post-election meeting actually took place. Shortly after the results were declared, George Lambert, M.P. for South Molton, called a meeting of M.P.s to examine the situation. Lambert had chaired a similar meeting in February 1919 which had failed to achieve much. Lloyd George told Lambert on 24 November that he was 'very willing at any time' to discuss reunion, 'either with the leaders or at a general meeting of Liberals'. But though he would interpose no obstacle himself, he thought it best to secure wide support for reunion before proceeding. Asquith notified Lambert four days later that 'the most promising road [to reunion] would appear to me to be by cooperation in debate and in the division lobby'. Asquith used this argument throughout 1923 to dismiss attempts at reunion.[17]

The meeting, held on 27 November 1923, was convened by Maxwell Thornton, M.P. for Tavistock (contiguous to Lambert's constituency), a right-wing Liberal who seceded in 1925 because he regarded Liberal reunion as still incomplete even then. The meeting elected Lambert chairman, and, according to the official account, about sixteen of the 'nearly one hundred' Liberal M.P.s present spoke in favour of reunion, while none spoke against. The meeting did not select a party leader, which according to the prefixless Liberals had been its chief aim. Two days later C. A. McCurdy, Lloyd George's chief whip, stated that he favoured reunion, and that Lloyd George would be 'perfectly prepared to serve under Mr. Asquith's leadership'.[18]

Admittedly it was in Lloyd George's interest that reunion should come quickly, so long as the conditions of reunion left him some power. In March 1923 he offered again to serve under Asquith, if no questions were asked. He probably expected to get the Liberal leadership when Asquith, then over seventy, retired; and formal Liberal reunion would make it almost impossible for the Asquithians to make an alliance with the Conservatives which would leave him out. His newspaper, the *Chronicle*, had suggested during the election that such a move might take place; it had cited as evidence some lunches Asquith had with Sir George Younger in the middle of the campaign. The suggestion of a Conservative-Asquithian *rapprochement* was not entirely ridiculous, since the leading Asquithians had been in the 1915–16 Coalition; they supported the Conservatives during the 1926 general strike, while Lloyd George did not; and nearly all of them became Liberal Nationals after the election of 1931. Lloyd George wished to forestall any such coalition. During the 1922 election he had sought continued alliance with the Conservatives, but he became convinced afterwards that this was improbable for at least a few years, and he shifted his ground to get the maximum political leverage. Because there was no immediate opening with the Conservatives, he took the only opening he saw, towards the Asquithian Liberals. By achieving reunion quickly he could take his group into the Independent Liberal camp as a bloc, but delay would probably cause his group to disintegrate slowly, as individual members of it joined either the Conservatives or Asquithians. According to C. P. Scott, in late April 1923 Lloyd George was 'keen on reunion', and he was not going to speak as the leader of a group, but as an ordinary Liberal. But he added, 'I will not crawl. I will not crawl on my belly.'[19]

Lloyd George's political views seemed to change quickly in the few months after the election of 1922. During his alliance with the Conservatives, and especially from mid-1921 until his fall in October 1922, he had followed a policy of anti-socialism, and he had introduced few domestic reforms in that period. This may have been because he was preoccupied with foreign and Irish affairs, but it was contrary to his previous career and to his subsequent one. The development of his domestic policy after his fall was shown forcefully in his comments on a speech by F. E. Guest, who had been his chief whip during most of the Parliament elected in 1918. In June 1923 Guest threatened to secede if the Liberals supported nationalisation. He felt that they should become the left wing of 'a great national party to keep the Socialists out'. This was virtually what Lloyd George's own policy had been in the months preceding the Carlton Club Meeting, but in 1923 he called it 'a poor, sorry, sterile, and selfish policy unless you have something to put up instead'. During the 1920s he gradually shifted to the left, and developed, along with J. M. Keynes and others, the radical Liberal social and economic platform of 1929. By 1926 Lloyd George was even regretting, in a conversation with J. M. Kenworthy, that he was not joining Labour; of course Labour would not have had him, but he expressed the same regret to H. L. Nathan in 1934. In 1923 his ideas were not fully formulated, but he recognised that his previous policy was insufficient for a reformist party. On the other hand he regarded the Asquithian programme as 'a dish of stale flapdoodle'.[20]

By itself this remark was unlikely to counteract the movement towards reunion if Asquith and his colleagues supported it sincerely. However, despite the definite overtures from both Lloyd George and the backbench Liberal M.P.s, Asquith made no open move towards reunion. In fact one result of the back-bench meeting was that he dismissed the joint Liberal whip, J. M. Hogge, because he backed reunion. Asquith replaced him with his secretary, Vivian Phillipps, who had no parliamentary experience, but who opposed reunion. Asquith's friends then ridiculed Hogge: C. F. G. Masterman, one of the strongest Liberal opponents of Lloyd George, called Hogge 'the worst type of Lowland Scot, and corrupt'. Viscount Gladstone added that Hogge was a drunken womaniser who had become involved with a House of Commons waitress known as 'the fairy'. It was significant that Asquith and his associates had expelled George Lambert from their group in 1919 because he had favoured reunion, in much the same way as they deposed Hogge in 1923.[21]

Asquith rejected reunion unless it was couched in terms of surrender and repentance on the part of the former Coalition Liberals. This general drift of Liberalism was towards his position, mainly because the Lloyd Georgians were political mermaids, neither Coalitionists nor wholly Liberal. Thus Asquith could expect to isolate Lloyd George after a few years of gradual attrition, and overly rapid reunion could frighten away prospective Labour supporters of electoral pacts: MacDonald and Henderson disagreed on many things, but both detested Lloyd George. But the most important factor influencing Asquith against quick reunion was his personal dislike of Lloyd George and his desire for vengeance. He revealed his feelings at the time in letters which he wrote to Mrs Hilda Harrison of Oxford, and which were published after his death under the title of *H.H.A.: The Letters of the Earl of Oxford and Asquith to a Friend*. Just after the 1922 election he wrote, 'The thing that gives me most pleasure is to gloat over the corpses which have been left on the battlefield, Winston [Churchill], Hamar Greenwood, Freddie Guest, [Edwin] Montagu, [F. D.] Kellaway—all of them renegades.'[22]

Another strong opponent of reunion was Sir John Simon. According to C. P. Scott, who as editor of the *Manchester Guardian* had an entrée into most Liberal circles, Simon was 'not much interested in what relations could be established' with Lloyd George's followers. In May 1923 Simon said there were three major obstacles to reunion. The Lloyd Georgians had set up new organisations which it would be difficult to merge with the regular party groups. In addition the Coalition Liberals had given electoral pledges to the Conservatives which could hinder parliamentary co-operation between the Liberals. However his real objection arose from[23] a certain instability or uncertainty in the political character of the genius who was the previous Prime Minister. That is to say, it is always easier to be confident that that most distinguished man will find a way out of his difficulties than to prophesy in advance which way he will take.

Asquith still maintained in public that the thing preventing reunion was 'not a question of persons', but continued lack of co-operation between the two Liberal groups in Parliament. The Liberals should vote together, he said, 'but are they in fact doing so?' He mentioned two divisions, in one of which the handful of Lloyd Georgians present had been divided evenly. He did not mention that in the second division which he used as an example of non-co-operation, the Asquithians had been divided. Asquith's own supporters refuted his argument: the *Liberal Magazine* provided statistics showing that the Lloyd Georgians voted with the Asquithians three-quarters of the time. It listed 65 divisions, 25 of which were on unimportant topics, or else on ones where personal views were decisive, for instance one on matrimonial clauses. In the remaining 40 divisions, which dealt with tariffs, land values, old age pensions, trade union 'emancipation' and similar subjects, the Lloyd Georgians voted with the Asquithians on 30, against them on 8 and were split on 2. Moreover on all but one of the divisions where they opposed the Lloyd Georgians, the Asquithians were divided. The contention that there was conflict in Parliament between the two factions was fallacious, and as Sir John Simon said, 'We are in fact cooperating'.[24]

Even if there had been much to Asquith's demand for greater co-operation in Parliament, before he could consider reunion, he showed in an exchange of letters with Colonel H. K. Stephenson, M.P. for Sheffield (Park) that he was unlikely to forgive Lloyd George. Stephenson told Asquith that he wished to work with him, and requested the Independent Liberal whip to be sent to him. He also said that as a backbencher, he needed no special treatment, but that it would help greatly if Asquith made a small positive gesture towards Lloyd George. Asquith offered to send Stephenson the whip, but said nothing about Lloyd George or reunion. During the rest of 1923 reunion proceeded slowly, but when Baldwin called an election for December 1923, Asquith agreed to immediate reunion. On 13 November he and Simon conferred with Lloyd George and Sir Alfred Mond, and agreed to present a united front against the Conservatives. Despite the prediction of the *Liberal Magazine* that there would never be a moment when the Liberal leaders would meet on a stage to exchange tokens of forgiveness, such a tableau took place in Asquith's constituency when Lloyd George spoke on his behalf. However the tableau did not represent Asquith's true feelings, and reunion at the top never really came, although there were hardly any conflicts in the constituencies. Asquith told Mrs Harrison, 'I have rarely felt less exhilaration than when we got to the platform amid wild plaudits and a flashlight film was taken, "featuring" me and Ll G. separated only by the chairman'.[25]

In addition to being incomplete, Liberal reunion came too late to be fully effective. The chief issue of the 1923 election, tariffs, was as favourable ground as the Liberals could hope for, but they had spent 1923 in fighting each other rather than in convincing uncommitted voters to support them instead of Labour or the Conservatives. Though the Liberal seats rose from 117 to 159 (or from 121 to 161 counting the independents),* their overall vote rose only 0.5 per cent from 29.1 per cent to 29.6 per cent. The elections of 1922 and 1923 could not be compared precisely, because of the party split in 1922, when many Lloyd Georgians had Conservative backing. However the figures from constituencies which had Liberal-Conservative straight fights in 1918, 1922 and 1923 were comparable. There were twenty-five such contests, and the Liberal percentages were :

	1918	1922	1923
17 agricultural seats	42.0%	50.0%	51.7%
8 urban seats	29.1	43.9	52.7
Mean, 25 seats	37.9	48.4	52.0
Overall change, 25 seats		+10.5	+3.8

These figures show the Liberal gains in 1923 in a slightly more favourable light, but they also show that the great advance in

* These figures include the Liberal by-election gain of Tiverton.

Liberal support came in 1922, not in 1923. One reason why the Liberals gained comparatively little in 1923 was the long delay in achieving reunion. Another result of this delay in re-union was that the Liberals did not lay the ground for the period after the election, nor did they even solve their relations with the other parties in the election. In 1923, as in 1922, there was no general understanding between the Liberals and Labour. They did not conflict in half the seats, but they might have co-operated more openly if the two parties had had time to ponder their position, or if the Liberals had been uninhibited and undistracted by factional disputes from pushing towards an alliance.

Compounding this problem was the fact that Asquith did not seem to have a policy of his own on economic matters. Lloyd George's epithet of 'stale flapdoodle' was unfair in the sense that Asquith based his programme on a *mélange* of ideas produced by the numerous Liberal workshops on economics. However the uninspiring way in which Asquith presented this mixture shows that he was more interested in the mainly political issues, such as Home Rule and the supremacy of the commons, which had been the chief concerns of his previous career. Some historians, concentrating on the Asquithian leaders, such as Asquith himself, Viscount Gladstone, Simon, Runciman, McKenna and Grey, have concluded that the Liberals were out of date in the post-war period. In some respects these men were out of date, as in 1926 when they behaved like frightened middle-class lawyers with little comprehension of the needs of the working classes; but there were many more advanced Liberals. Indeed, if economic and social ideas or policies had been truly decisive in the 1920s, the Liberals would have fared better than they did, for much of the debate on such questions came within the Liberal Party, where men of differing temperaments came together to frame party policies on an empirical basis. In the other two parties, such debates were often restricted by the need to follow an official party dogma, free enterprise or nationalisation. The proof that Liberal ideas were not outdated came after 1945, when both Labour and the Conservatives accepted the notion of a mixed economy, with limited nationalisation and a welfare state side by side with private industry. The Liberals had propounded this during the interwar years, while Labour and the Conservatives (apart from a few young politicians such as Robert Boothby and

Harold Macmillan) had rejected it. Ramsay MacDonald, who was scarcely a socialist extremist, termed the mixed economy an unworkable 'medley' in an article in 1920, and his attitude typified that of most Labour and Conservative politicians.[26]

The election of 1922 was not the final round for the Liberals : they won forty more seats in 1923 than in 1922, and they took some in 1929 which they had not won in any previous interwar election. Nevertheless 1922 was a turning-point in Liberal fortunes, for the near-equality in numbers of the two factions discouraged rapid reunion. The Carlton Club Meeting had freed Lloyd George from the ties binding him to the Conservatives. He was the most likely leader of a revived Liberal Party, as Asquith and his associates did not have the emotional zest or the political flexibility required in a changing situation. If Lloyd George had won clearly, he could probably have taken the Liberals his way; on the other hand, if Asquith had won clearly, he could have afforded to give Lloyd George a subordinate post, and utilise his talents, because he would not be so much of a threat. The even distribution of the Liberal M.P.s between the factions meant that each leader had some power, but not enough to force his rival to give way. Thus the factional disputes continued during a year in which the political situation changed gradually from the flux which had characterised late 1922, to the relatively stable alignment of late 1923.

This chapter, like this book, has been based on contemporary views rather than on later ones. It has shown that many trends later taken for granted were in fact the results of chance, and that Britain could easily have taken a different path in 1922. This was the view, not only of the leading politicians, but of hundreds of candidates in the Liberal and Conservative Parties, and of many newspapers with different political commitments. The contemporary records exhibited much more uncertainty than later memoirs, which tended to play down the three weeks of confusion in their examination of two decades of overwhelming Conservative predominance. The Carlton Club Meeting overshadowed the election in most later accounts, and on the surface the election seemed unexciting, as there were few outstanding issues and no real debate. But behind this façade the election of 1922 was one of the most interesting, and certainly the most influential, of this century.

Many passing chances helped the Conservatives win their majority in this election. The role of Bonar Law was important, for if his health had broken down in October 1922 instead of in April 1923, the Conservative opponents of Lloyd George would have been virtually leaderless, though they would probably still have had their way at the Carlton Club. A delay in calling the election would also have hurt the Conservative cause, for it would have given the new ministers time to demonstrate their inexperience, as they did in the first few months of 1923. Even a negative policy, as Bonar Law called it during the election, is not possible all the time, and sooner or later the new Government would have taken a stand on an important issue such as rent controls, on which there was no national consensus. Almost any positive action would have alienated some floating voters, but as chapter 7 demonstrated, the Conservatives needed all the floating voters they could get, for their majority rested on only 3738 voters in close fights. Moreover, even when Bonar Law did call an early election, he could not have expected the events of the campaign to favour his party as uniformly as they did. As it was, the campaign helped the Conservatives with the uncommitted, but they still took less than two-fifths of the total vote, and many of their victories were narrow.

Both the Labour and Conservative Parties were likely to be strong, but their exact strength was not easily predicted in advance of the election. Yet it mattered greatly to the future alignment of parties whether the Conservative got just over, or just under, a bare majority, and whether Labour got a few more, or a few less, seats than the combined Liberal factions. Even granting the debatable point that Labour was destined to be the second party, the isolation and rapid disappearance of the Liberals as an effective political force was not certain.

The Liberal decline was more noticeable in seats than in votes : even in their setback of 1924, the Liberals won almost 3,000,000 votes, and in 1929 they won over 5,000,000 : that is more than the Conservatives got in 1922, though meanwhile there was a slight expansion of the franchise. However they lost three-quarters of their seats in 1924, and regained only a few in 1929. Another important factor in the Liberal decline was that it did not happen at once, but took place over the ten years after the 1922 election. Despite the declining Liberal prospects, there was never a great rush out of the party, and the men who did secede did so only a few at a time, rather than in droves. A solid Liberal defeat in 1922 would have encouraged the Liberal seceders to join the other parties; but the prospect of a Liberal revival held them where their talents were wasted.

No country can isolate a quarter of its politicians without some harmful effects, especially a country faced with problems which require reconsideration of the basis of its economy and of its foreign policy. The difficulties confronting Britain in the interwar years were at least as great as those it had faced in the nineteenth century, and in many ways they were more complex. Yet after 1922 the Liberal politicians, economists, social theorists and voters were virtually cut off from both the Government and the official Opposition. It would be an exaggeration to say that the Liberals had all the able men : there were many young and far-sighted Conservatives, such as the Boothby-Macmillan group; and there were many in the Labour Party too. The most senior Conservative and Labour leaders also had much to offer. However the Liberals had more than their share of experienced and able men in the middle ranks, partly because they had been in office for sixteen years and had attracted the ambitious, and partly because the middle position of the Liberal Party gave it an appeal which the more doctrinaire stances of Labour and the Conservatives lacked. As late as 1928 the socialist publicist H. N Brailsford commented that the Liberals had 'by far the ablest general staff, and much the most gifted group of thinkers, economists and journalists'. During and after the Second World War there was no such large-scale isolation of able men in a political necropolis as there had been between the wars, and there is little question but that both Conservative and Labour governments since 1945 have been more effective than their interwar counterparts.[27]

One of the main contentions of this book is that a great many informed politicians expected that the Conservatives would just fail to win a majority in 1922, and that this would lead to some form of Conservative-Liberal collaboration, whether or not such a coalition had Lloyd George in it. Obviously this mattered greatly to the politicians concerned, but did it matter to the country? Considerations of possible coalition would be relatively unimportant if the policies of the Government were the same regardless of the parties composing it. However there are several indications that the revival of coalition after the 1922 election would indeed have led to different solutions to the political and social problems of the day. For one thing there would have been a broader consensus, and as just pointed out, a coalition government would have had a wider range of experience to draw on than a one-party Conservative regime. A second consideration is that if the Conservatives had depended on the Liberals they would have kept more alert. The large majority they won in 1922 allowed them to grow indolent with much endangering their position. Also the polarisation of politics, especially after 1924, tempted the Conservatives to rest on their oars, for they could always rely on ideological repulsion from Labour to make up deficiencies in their own record.

Yet another factor which must be considered when dealing with the possibility of revived coalitions is that neither Stanley Baldwin nor Neville Chamberlain was likely to gain quick advancement except in a purely Conservative government. In 1922 Baldwin, though one of Lloyd George's ministers, was practically unknown, and Neville Chamberlain was known only for his failure as minister of national service during the war. In November 1922 both men were dispensable, and probably would have been dropped if the Conservative Government had depended on the support of the Lloyd George Liberals. The election of 1922 confirmed both of them in office, and led to the premiership of Baldwin, which lasted with two breaks for fourteen years (counting the four years during which Baldwin was mayor of the palace under the *roi fainéant* MacDonald). During this period Baldwin hesitated on many important occasions, after the manner of the French Radicals of the period, whose view seemed to be that the art of politics lay in postponing decisions until the problems were no longer relevant. This may be satisfactory enough in a time of peace and repose, but unfortunately for both Britain and France between the wars, pressing problems remained. Lloyd George and the cabinet he had built up had had the potential and the understanding to deal with many of these problems, but the crisis of 1922 and the Conservative majority in the election thrust him and his party into the wilderness for good.

APPENDIX I

The Carlton Club Meeting,
19 October 1922

This appendix lists the vote at the Carlton Club Meeting of all
Conservative M.P.s It is based on a list in the Austen Chamberlain Papers (AC/33/2/92), and has been checked against public
statements by the M.P.s of their votes at the meeting. In two
cases the public statements disagreed with Chamberlain's list.
They were Sir R. Greene (Hackney North) and C. Erskine-Bolst
(Hackney South). Chamberlaine's list said that Greene supported
the Coalition, while Erskine-Bolst opposed it. The two men
indicated that they had the opposite opinion, and their votes may
have been transposed in Chamberlain's list.

The appendix gives information on the attitude of Conservative M.P.s towards the Coalition before the Carlton Club Meeting, and it also lists some M.P.s who were present but who
according to Chamberlain did not vote.

R. R. James, using a different source, published a list of the
M.P.s voting at the Carlton Club (*Memoirs Of A Conservative*,
130–3). He gave the total vote as 185 opponents of the Coalition,
and 88 supporters, and he lists 184 opponents of the Coalition.
M.P.s who were listed differently from Chamberlain's accounting
were :

H. C. Brown (Chamberlain, anti; James, absent)
C. Carew (Chamberlain, absent; James, pro)
G. L. Palmer (Chamberlain, absent; James, anti)
H. Ratcliffe (Chamberlain, absent; James, pro)

N. Raw (Chamberlain, absent; James, anti)
R. G. Sharman-Crawford (Chamberlain, anti; James, absent)
R. Terrell (Chamberlain, anti; James, absent)
T. G. Tickler (Chamberlain, anti; James, absent)
C. Yate (Chamberlain, anti; James, absent)

The following abbreviations have been used :
Pro   : voted for continuance of the Coalition.
Anti   : voted against continuance of the Coalition.
Diehard : longtime opponent of the Coalition who signed one or both of the Diehard manifestos. Unless otherwise stated, the reference is to *Gleanings and Memoranda* (July 1922) 98.
At Chamberlain's dinner : listed in *The Times* (24 October 1922) as having attended the dinner for Chamberlain after the Carlton Club Meeting.

[1] Adair, T. B. S. (Glasgow-Shettleston). Anti. Diehard.

[2] Agg-Gardener, J. T. (Cheltenham). Pro.

[3] Ainsworth, C. (Bury). Absent on government business. *Bury Guardian* (28 October 1922).

[4] Allen, W. J. (Armagh North). Anti.

[5] Amery, L. C. M. S. (Birmingham-Sparbrook). Anti. Anti before meeting. Amery, *My Political Life*, II 237.

[6] Archer-Shee, M. (Finsbury). Anti. Diehard.

[7] Armstrong, H. B. (Mid-Armagh). Absent.

[8] Ashley, W. (Lancs-Fylde). Anti. Diehard.

[9] Astbury, F. W. (Salford West). Absent.

[10] Astor, Lady (Plymouth-Sutton). Supported Coalition, but did not attend meeting. *Western Evening Herald* (19 October 1922).

[11] Atkey, A. R. (Nottingham Central). Pro.

[12] Austin, H. (Birmingham-King's Norton). Absent.

[13] Bagley, E. A. (Lancs.-Farnworth). Pro.

[14] Baird, J. L. (Warwick-Rugby). Anti.

[15] Baldwin, S. (Worcs.-Bewdley). Anti. Anti before meeting. Harris, *Forty Years in and out of Parliament*, 93; Amery, *My Political Life*, II 236.

[16] Balfour, G. (Hampstead). Anti. Diehard. Cf. *Morning Post* (13 October 1922).

[17] Banbury, F. (City of London). Anti. Diehard.

[18] Banner, J. S. Harmood- (Liverpool-Everton). Pro. At Chamberlain's dinner.

[19] Barlow, C. A. M. (Salford South). Absent on government business. *South Wales Argus* (20 October 1922).

[20] Barnett, R. W. (St Pancras South-west). Anti. Said before the meeting that he would stand as a non-coalition Conservative. *West London News* (18 October 1922); *St Pancras Guardian* (27 October 1922).

[21] Barnston, H. (Cheshire-Eddisbury). Pro, but did not sign the ministerial letters of support for Chamberlain. *Liverpool Post* (30 October 1922).

[22] Beckett, G. (Yorks-Scarborough and Whitby). Anti before meeting and present at it, but according to Chamberlain's list did not vote. *Yorkshire Post* (2 September and 27 October 1922).

[23] Bell, W. C. H. (Wilts.-Devizes). Anti. Anti since late 1921. *Swindon Evening Advertiser* (26 October 1922).

[24] Bellairs, C. W. (Kent-Maidstone). Pro. At Chamberlain's dinner. Implied to his constituents that he had been against the Coalition. *Southeastern Gazette* (27 October 1922).

[25] Benn, A. S. (Plymouth-Drake). Anti.

[26] Benn, I. H. (Greenwich). Absent.

[27] Bennett, T. J. (Kent-Sevenoaks). Anti. Anti before meeting. *Southeastern Gazette* (11 April 1922); *Morning Post* (13 and 14 October 1922).

[28] Bentinck, Lord H. Cavendish- (Nottingham South). Absent.

[29] Betterton, H. B. (Notts.-Rushcliffe). Anti. Later implied that he had supported the Coalition, and defended it strongly. *Bulwell Local News* (11 November 1922).

[30] Bigland, A. (Birkenhead East). Anti.

[31] Birchall, J. D. (Leeds North-east). Anti. Anti before meeting. *Yorkshire Post* (11 October 1922).

[32] Bird, R. (Wolverhampton West). Pro.

[33] Bird, W. (Sussex-Chichester). Anti.

[34] Blades, G. R. (Surrey-Epsom). Anti.

[35] Blair, R. (Poplar-Bow and Bromley). Anti.

[36] Blane, T. A. (Leicester South). Anti.

[37] Borwick, G. O. (Croydon North). Pro. At Chamberlain's dinner.

[38] Boscawen, A. S. T. Griffith- (Somerset-Taunton). Anti. Anti shortly before meeting. Griffith-Boscawen, *Memories*, 252.

[39] Bowles, H. F. (Middlesex-Enfield). Anti. In 1918 had been connected with the National Party. *Wargrave Papers*, undated letter on the 1918 election by Sir Henry Page Croft.

[40] Bowyer, G. E. W. (Bucks.-Buckingham). Anti. Anti before meeting.

[41] Boyd-Carpenter, A. B. (Bradford North). Anti. Longtime opponent of the Coalition. *The Times* (27 March, 1 June and 3 November 1922).

[42] Brassey, H. L. C. (Northants-Peterborough). Pro. At Chamberlain's dinner.

[43] Bridgeman, W. C. (Salop-Oswestry). Anti. Anti before meeting. *Wellington Journal and Shrewsbury News* (4 November 1922).

[44] Briggs, W. J. H. (Manchester-Blackley). Pro.

[45] Brittain, H. (Middlesex-Acton). Present at Meeting, but not listed by Chamberlain as having voted. *Pall Mall Gazette* (19 October 1922).

[46] Brotherton, E. A. (Wakefield). Pro. At Chamberlain's dinner.

[47] Brown, D. C. (Northumberland-Hexham). Anti. Anti for a year before meeting. *Hexham Herald* (28 October 1922).

[48] Brown, H. C. (Berks.-Newbury). Anti. Anti before meeting. *Berkshire Chronicle* (27 October 1922).

[49] Bruton, J. (Gloucester). Anti. According to Liberal accusations, Bruton did not make up his mind until the meeting. Bruton neither confirmed nor denied this. *Gloucester Journal* (28 October 1922).

[50] Buchanan, A. L. H. (Lanark-Coatbridge). Pro.

[51] Buckley, A. (Lancs.-Waterloo). Anti. Anti before meeting. *Bootle Herald* (28 October 1922); *Liverpool Post* (26 October 1922).

[52] Bull, W. (Hammersmith South). Pro. At Chamberlain's dinner.

[53] Burdon, R. (Durham-Sedgefield). Anti.

[54] Burgoyne, A. (Kensington South). Absent. Had been a member of the National Party in 1918, according to a pamphlet in the *Wargrave Papers*.

[55] Burn, C. R. (Devon-Torquay). Anti. Diehard.

[56] Burn, T. H. (Belfast-St Anne's). Absent. *Morning Post* (23 October 1922).

[57] Butcher, J. G. (York). Anti. Diehard. *Gleanings and Memoranda* (April 1922) 402.

[58] Campbell, J. G. D. (Kingston-on-Thames). Pro.

[59] Campion, W. R. (Sussex-Lewes). Anti.

[60] Carew, C. (Devon-Tiverton). Absent.

[61] Carter, R. A. (Manchester-Withington). Pro.

[62] Cautley, H. S. (Sussex-East Grinstead). Anti.

[63] Cayzer, H. R. (Portsmouth South). Absent because of illness. *Morning Post* (4 November 1922).

[64] Cecil, E. (Birmingham-Aston). Anti. Cecil told Bonar Law on 18 October, 'I contemplate standing myself as a Conservative in the broadest sense at the election'. *Bonar Law Papers*, 107/2/69.

[65] Cecil, Lord H. (Oxford University). Anti. Diehard. *Gleanings and Memoranda* (April 1922) 402.

[66] Cecil, Lord R. (Herts-Hitchin). Anti before meeting, but not invited to it, as he had ceased to be a Coalitionist. *Asquith Papers*, Box 34, f. 7 [Cecil to Asquith, 1 July 1921].

[67] Chadwick, R. B. (Barrow). Anti for over a year before meeting, but attended Chamberlain's dinner. *Liverpool Post* (25 October 1922).

[68] Chamberlain, A. Neville (Birmingham-Ladywood). In Canada for meeting. Feiling, *Neville Chamberlain*, 100.

[69] Chamberlain, J. Austen (Birmingham West). Pro.

[70] Cheyne, W. (Scottish Universities). Absent.

[71] Chilcott, H. W. S. (Liverpool-Walton). Pro. At Chamberlain's dinner.

[72] Child, H. (Staffs.-Stone). Anti.

[73] Churchman, A. (Suffolk-Woodbridge). Anti.

[74] Clarry, R. (Newport). Elected as a Diehard on 18 October, and unable to be present at meeting.

[75] Clay, H. H. Spender- (Kent-Tonbridge). Anti. Had supported a coalition election early in 1922, but later turned against the Lloyd George regime. *Austen Chamberlain Papers*, AC/33/2 [Clay to Chamberlain, 11 January 1922]; *Sevenoaks Chronicle* (3 November 1922).

[76] Clough, R. (Yorks.-Keighley). Pro before meeting, but abstained at it. *Yorkshire Post* (16 October 1922); *Memoirs of a Conservative*, ed. R. R. James, 133.

[77] Coats, S. (Surrey East). Pro. At Chamberlain's dinner.

[78] Cobb, C. (Fulham West). Anti.

[79] Cockerill, G. K. (Surrey-Reigate). Anti. Plans to oppose Cockerill because of his support for the Coalition fell through. In July 1922, Cockerill assured his constituents that the Coalition would end. He broke with Chamberlain because he felt that Chamberlain had misled him. *Wandsworth Borough News* (14 July 1922); *Austen Chamberlain Papers*, AC/33/2/76 [Cockerill to Chamberlain, 17 October 1922]; *Morning Post* (30 October 1922).

[80] Cohen, J. B. B. (Liverpool-Fairfield). Anti before meeting, but was in the U.S.A. for it. *Liverpool Post* (31 October and 9 November 1922).

[81] Colfox, W. P. (Dorset North). Anti. Anti for a year before meeting. *Dorset County Chronicle* (8 June 1922).

[82] Colvin, R. (Essex-Epping). Anti.

[83] Conway, W. M. (Combined English Provincial Universities). Pro. At Chamberlain's meeting.

[84] Cooper, R. (Walsall). Anti. Diehard.

[85] Coote, W. (Tyrone South). Absent campaigning in Canada and the U.S.A. against Sinn Fein propaganda. *West Middlesex Times* (14 October 1922).

[86] Cope, J. (Glamorgan-Llandaff and Barry). Anti. Anti before meeting. *South Wales Evening Express* (20 October 1922).

[87] Cory, J. H. (Cardiff South). Absent.

[88] Courthorpe, G. L. (Sussex-Rye). Anti.

[89] Craig, G. C. (Antrim South). Anti.

[90] Craik, H. (Scottish Universities). Anti. Diehard.

[91] Croft, H. Page- (Bournemouth). Anti. Diehard.

[92] Curzon, Viscount (Battersea South). Anti. Diehard.

[93] Dalziel, D. (Lambeth-Brixton). Absent, but supported the Coalition. *Austen Chamberlain Papers*, AC/33/2/81 [Dalziel to Chamberlain, 18 October 1922].

[94] Davidson, J. C. C. (Herts.-Hemel Hempstead). Anti. In August Davidson told Bonar Lar, 'I hope that the election will be postponed, but if it comes, the Tories *must* go separately to the country'. *Bonar Law Papers*, 107/2/2a [Davidson to Law, 13 August 1922].

[95] Davidson, J. H. (Hants-Fareham). Anti.

[96] Davies, A. T. (Lincoln). Anti. Before the meeting, and also after it, said 'I am the advocate and friend of no man who would rush our country into war, whether it was Lloyd George or anyone else, however able'. *Lincoln Gazette* (14 October and 4 November 1922).

[97] Davies, T. (Gloucs.-Cirencester and Tewkesbury). Anti. Anti before meeting. *Tewkesbury Register* (25 March 1922).

[98] Davison, W. H. (Kensington South). Anti. Diehard. Wrote an anti-Coalition letter to *The Times* (23 February 1922); also cf. *Gleanings and Memoranda* (April 1922) 402.

[99] Dawson, P. (Lewisham West). Anti. An anti-waste opponent withdrew before the election. *Morning Post* (28 October and 7 November 1922).

[100] Dean, P. T. (Blackburn). Anti.

[101] Denison-Pender, H. C. (Wandsworth-Balham and Tooting). Absent.

[102] Dennis, J. W. (Birmingham-Deritend). Absent.

[103] Denniss, E. R. B. (Oldham). Pro.

[104] Dewhurst, H. (Cheshire-Northwich). Anti.

[105] Dixon, H. (Belfast-Pottinger). Absent.

[106] Dockrell, M. (Dublin). Absent.

[107] Donald, T. (Belfast-Victoria). Absent.

[108] Doyle, N. Grattan (Newcastle North). Did not vote at meeting, but may have been a teller for the minority, as he said later that he had supported Chamberlain. *North Star* (27 October 1922).

[109] Du Pre, W. B. (Bucks.-Wycombe). Anti.

[110] Edgar, C. B. (Richmond-Surrey). Anti.

[111] Ednam, Viscount (Hornsey). Anti. Renounced the Coalition in 1921. *Hornsey Journal* (28 October 1921).

[112] Elliot, W. E. (Lanark-Lanark). Pro. At Chamberlain's dinner.

[113] Elliott, G. S. (Islington North). Anti.

[114] Elveden, Viscount (Southend). Anti.

[115] Erskine, J. M. M. (Westminster-St George's). Diehard. Excluded from meeting. *Scotsman* (18 October 1922); *The Times* (20 October 1922).

[116] Erskine-Bolst, C. (Hackney South). Anti. Not strictly a Conservative M.P., but a Coalitionist. In 1922 he ran as a

Constitutionalist supporting renewed coalition. *Hackney Gazette* (1 November 1922).

[117] Eyres-Monsell, B. M. (Worcs.-Evesham). Anti. Anti before meeting. *Evesham Journal* (28 October 1922).

[118] Falcon, M. (Norfolk East). Anti. Anti before meeting. Walding, *Who's Who in the New Parliament, 1922*, 70

[119] Falle, B. (Portsmouth North). Anti.

[120] Fell, A. (Great Yarmouth). Anti.

[121] Fitzroy, E. A. (Northants-Daventry). Anti. Supported the Coalition in July 1922, in a speech to the Coalition Liberals in his constituency. Later there were rumours of a Diehard candidature against him. After the Carlton Club Meeting, Fitzroy reverted to his previous pro-coalition attitude. *Northampton Daily Chronicle* (21 July, 20 and 28 October and 4 November 1922); *Daventry Express* (4 November 1922).

[122] Flannery, J. F. (Essex-Maldon). Pro.

[123] Ford, P. J. (Edinburgh North). Pro. At Chamberlain's dinner.

[124] Foreman, H. (Hammersmith North). Anti, but attended Chamberlain's dinner.

[125] Forestier-Walker, C. (Monmouth-Monmouth). Anti. His speech of 31 October implied that he had opposed the Coalition for some time. *Monmouthshire Beacon* (3 November 1922).

[126] Foxcroft, C. T. (Bath). Anti. Diehard.

[127] Fraser, K. (Leics.-Harborough). Anti.

[128] Frece, W. de (Ashton-under-Lyne). Pro. At Chamberlain's dinner.

[129] Fremantle, F. E. (Herts.-St Albans). Anti.

[130] Ganzoni, J. F. C. (Ipswich). Anti. In April 1922 told his constituents that he would support the Coalition until it fell. After the Carlton Club Meeting said he had made up his mind that it would fall anyway. *Suffolk Chronicle and Mercury* (28 April and 1 November 1922).

[131] Gardner, E. (Berks.-Windsor). Pro. Supported Bonar Law as soon as the result of the meeting was known. *Maidenhead Advertiser* (1 November 1922).

[132] Gee, R. (Woolwich East). Anti. Elected as a Coalitionist in 1921, but told an audience in Bodmin in January 1922 that he was 'not a Coalition Member of Parliament'. On 16 October told his constituents that he was 'no blind follower' of Lloyd

George, that he would stand as a straightforward Conservative in the ensuing election, and that he felt that Lloyd George would serve under either Bonar Law or Austen Chamberlain. *Newquay Express* (24 February 1922); *Kentish Independent* (20 October 1922).

[133] Gibbs, G. A. (Bristol West). Pro.

[134] Gilmour, J. (Glasgow-Pollock). Pro. At Chamberlain's dinner.

[135] Glyn, R. (East Stirlingshire). Pro.

[136] Goff, R. P. (Yorks.-Cleveland). Voted against the Government forty-seven times, but was absent in Constantinople on 19 October on government business. *Yorkshire Post* (26 October 1922).

[137] Gould, J. C. (Cardiff Central). Anti. Probably anti before meeting. *Monmouthshire Beacon* (27 October 1922).

[138] Goulding, E. (Worcester). Pro. At Chamberlain's dinner.

[139] Grant, J. A. (Cumberland-Whitehaven). Anti. May have made up mind at the meeting. *West Cumberland News* (28 October 1922).

[140] Gray, E. (Accrington). Supported the Coalition, but did not vote at the meeting. He had disliked the Coalition's attitude to teachers' pensions, but had agreed with it otherwise. *Accrington Gazette* (28 October 1922).

[141] Grayson, H. M. (Birkenhead West). Absent.

[142] Green, A. (Derby). Absent on world tour. *Derby Daily Telegraph* (10 November 1922).

[143] Greene, W. R. (Hackney North). Pro.

[144] Greenwood, W. (Stockport). Anti. Refused to say anything about his vote to his constituents. *Cheshire Daily Echo* (4 November 1922).

[145] Greer, H. (Somerset-Wells). Pro.

[146] Grenfell, E. C. (City of London). Anti.

[147] Gretton, J. (Staffs.-Burton). Anti. Diehard.

[148] Gritten, W. G. H. (Hartlepools). Anti. Diehard.

[149] Guinness, W. E. (Suffolk-Bury St Edmunds). Opposed the Coalition for some months before the meeting, but was not recorded in Chamberlain's list as having voted at it. *Cambridge Independent Press, Ely Edition* (3 November 1922).

[150] Gwynne, R. S. (Sussex-Eastbourne). Anti. Diehard.

[151] Hacking, D. H. (Lancs.-Chorley). Anti. Later defended the Coalition. *Chorley Guardian* (4 November 1922).

[152] Hailwood, A. (Manchester-Ardwick). Anti.

[153] Hall, D. B. (Isle of Wight). Anti before meeting, but did not vote at it. *Isle of Wight Observer* (9 September 1922).

[154] Hall, F. (Camberwell-Dulwich). Absent.

[155] Hall, R. (Liverpool-West Derby). Anti. Diehard.

[156] Hambro, A. V. (Dorset South). Supported the Coalition, but absent from Carlton Club Meeting because of illness. *Austen Chamberlain Papers*, AC/33/2/128 [Hambro to Chamberlain, 22 October 1922].

[157] Hamilton, G. (Cheshire-Altrincham). In Brazil as a member of a parliamentary delegation. *The Times* (13 November 1922).

[158] Hanna, G. B. (Antrim East). Absent.

[159] Hannon, P. J. H. (Birmingham-Moseley). Anti. Stated after the Carlton Club Meeting that he had opposed the Coalition before it. *Birmingham Post* (31 October 1922).

[160] Harmsworth, E. C. (Kent-Thanet). Anti. Diehard. *Gleanings and Memoranda* (April 1922) 402.

[161] Harris, H. P. (Paddington South). Anti.

[162] Hayes, H. (Down West). Absent.

[163] Henderson, V. L. (Glasgow-Tradeston). Pro.

[164] Hennessey, J. R. G. (Hants-Winchester). Anti.

[165] Herbert, A. N. H. M. (Somerset-Yeovil). Diehard. Not at meeting.

[166] Herbert, D. (Herts.-Watford). At meeting, but left before vote was taken, because of a business commitment. Hemingford, *Backbencher And Chairman*, 42.

[167] Hickman, T. E. (Wolverhampton-Bilston). Anti.

[168] Higham, C. F. (Islington South). Present at meeting, but did not vote. Earlier in 1922, he stated that he liked Lloyd George personally, and that 'if there was an election he would stand by him'. *Holloway Press* (4 February 1922); *Pall Mall Gazette* (19 October 1922).

[169] Hilder, F. (Essex South-east). Absent.

[170] Hills, J. W. (Durham-Durham). Anti. Anti before meeting. *Sunderland Daily Echo* (17 October 1922).

[171] Hoare, S. (Chelsea). Anti. Anti before meeting. *Buckingham Advertiser* (21 October 1922).

[172] Hohler, F. (Rochester-Gillingham). Pro. Also marked as anti on Chamberlain's list, but 'pro' was evidently intended.

[173] Holbrook, A. (Hants-Basingstoke). Anti. Anti before meeting. He announced his intention to run independently of the Coalition in early 1921, when elected in a by-election. *The Times* (27 March 1922); *Hants and Berks Gazette* (21 October and 4 November 1922).

[174] Hood, J. (Wimbledon). Anti.

[175] Hope, H. (Stirlingshire West). Pro.

[176] Hope, J. A. (Midlothian North). At meeting, but did not vote, since he felt that he should not take part in factional disputes because of his position as president of the Scottish Unionist Association. *Scotsman* (20 October 1922).

[177] Hope, J. F. (Sheffield Central). Present but did not vote. *Swindon Evening Advertiser* (19 October 1922).

[178] Hopkins, J. W. (St Pancras South-east). Anti.

[179] Horne, R. S. (Glasgow-Hillhead). Pro. At Chamberlain's dinner.

[180] Horne, W. E. (Surrey-Guildford). Not at meeting, but later at Chamberlain's dinner. Horne retired from politics before the Carlton Club Meeting. *Surrey Weekly Press* (20 October 1922).

[181] Hotchkin, S. V. (Lincs.-Horncastle). Anti.

[182] Houfton, J. P. (Nottingham East). Absent, but told Chamberlain that he supported the Coalition in spirit. *Austen Chamberlain Papers*, AC/33/2/86 [Houfton to Chamberlain, 19 October 1922].

[183] Houston, R. P. (Liverpool-West Toxteth). At meeting but did not vote. *Swindon Evening Advertiser* (19 October 1922).

[184] Hudson, R. M. (Sunderland). Pro.

[185] Hume-Williams, E. (Notts.-Bassetlaw). Pro. At Chamberlain's dinner.

[186] Hunter, A. (Lancs.-Lancaster). Anti.

[187] Hunter-Weston, A. (Bute and North Ayrshire). Pro.

[188] Hurd, P. (Somerset-Frome). Anti. Probably made up his mind at the meeting. *Somerset and Wiltshire Journal* (3 November 1922).

[189] Hurst, G. B. (Manchester-Moss Side). Absent.

[190] Inskip, T. W. H. (Bristol Central). Pro.

[191] Jackson, F. S. (Yorks.-Howdenshire). Anti. Voted against the Government in several Diehard motions in 1922; also opposed

the Coalition generally before 19 October. *Howdenshire Gazette* (3 November 1922).

[192] James, C. (Bromley). Anti. Diehard.

[193] Jameson, J. G. (Edinburgh West). Pro.

[194] Jellett, W. (Dublin University). Absent. Diehard. *Gleanings and Memoranda* (April 1922) 402.

[195] Jephcott, A. R. (Birmingham-Yardley). Pro. At Chamberlain's dinner.

[196] Jodrell, N. P. (Norfolk-King's Lynn). Pro. At Chamberlain's dinner.

[197] Johnson, L. S. (Walthamstow East). Anti.

[198] Jones, G. W. H. (Stoke Newington). Absent.

[199] Joynson-Hicks, W. (Middlesex-Twickenham). Anti. Diehard.

[200] Kelley, F. (Rotherham). In South Africa for meeting. *Yorkshire Telegraph and Star* (27 October 1922).

[201] Kerr-Smiley, P. K. (Antrim North). Anti.

[202] Kidd, J. (Linlithgow). Anti. Said after the meeting that the general opinion of Conservative M.P.s had been against the Coalition for some weeks, but that Bonar Law's speech had influenced a few M.P.s. *Scotsman* (20 October 1922).

[203] King, H. D. (Norfolk North). Anti. Contested the 1918 election as an Independent; during the 1922 election ran against a Diehard in Paddington South. In 1922 King supported Bonar Law, Chamberlain and Lloyd George simultaneously. *The Times* (2, 6, 7 and 14 November 1922).

[204] Kinloch-Cooke, C. (Plymouth-Devonport). Anti.

[205] Knight, E. A. (Worcs.-Kidderminster). Anti.

[206] Lane-Fox, G. R. (Yorks.-Barkston Ash). Ani. Anti before meeting. He 'often told my constituents that at the next election I should ask them to let me stand as before, as a Conservative independent of any Coalition'. He seconded the motion to break with the Lloyd George Coalition at the Carlton Club Meeting. *Bonar Law Papers*, 107/2/68 [Lane-Fox to Bonar Law, 14 October 1922]; *Yorkshire Post* (13 September and 13 and 20 October 1922).

[207] Larmor, J. (Cambridge University). Anti.

[208] Law, A. Bonar (Glasgow Central). Anti.

[209] Law, A. J. (Rochdale). Pro.

[210] Leigh, J. (Wandsworth-Clapham). At meeting, but did not

vote. During a May 1922 by-election, Leigh promised to support Chamberlain, Balfour and Bonar Law. However he was 'no slavish supporter of anybody' and might back Lloyd George. *Wandsworth Borough News* (12 May 1922); *Southern Daily Echo* (19 October 1922).

211 Lindsay, W. A. (Belfast-Cromac). Anti.

212 Lloyd, G. B. (Salop-Shrewsbury). Absent.

213 Lloyd-Graeme, P. (Middlesex-Hendon). Anti. In early 1922 he was an 'unrepentant Coalitionist', but he turned against the Coalition before the Carlton Club Meeting, and requested Chamberlain to let him resign. Beaverbrook, *Decline of Lloyd George*, 102; *Holloway Press* (4 February 1922); *The Times* (2 November 1922).

214 Locker-Lampson, G. L. (Middlesex-Wood Green). Anti before the meeting, but not present at it. Walding, *Who's Who in the New Parliament, 1922*, 107.

215 Locker-Lampson, O. S. (Huntingdonshire). Pro. At Chamberlain's dinner.

216 Lorden, J. W. (St Pancras North). Anti.

217 Lort-Williams, J. (Bermondsey-Rotherhithe). Pro. At Chamberlain's dinner.

218 Lowe, F. W. (Birmingham-Edgbaston). Pro. At Chamberlain's dinner.

219 Lowther, General C. (Cumberland-Penrith and Cockermouth). Pro.

220 Lowther, Colonel C. (Lancs.-Lonsdale). Anti. Said in April 1920 that he was 'not wholly in agreement with the Coalition'. In July 1921, withdrew from the Coalition but was nonetheless present at the Carlton Club Meeting. *Newcastle Daily Chronicle* (19 April 1920); *Liberal Magazine* (August 1921) 418.

221 Lowther, Major C. (Cumberland North). Pro. In May 1920 wrote to the executive of the North Cumberland Liberal Association that he had become 'a Critic of the Government'. He later became Austen Chamberlain's private secretary and a supporter of the Coalition. *Minutes of the North Cumberland Liberal Association*, letter to the executive, 5 May 1920.

222 Lloyd, A. T. (Berks-Abingdon). Anti. Anti before meeting. One of the few sitting Conservatives opposed by a Lloyd George Liberal in the 1922 election. *North Berks Herald* (4 November 1922).

[223] Lyle, C. E. L. (West Ham-Stratford). Anti.

[224] Lynn, R. J. (Belfast Woodvale). In Ulster for the meeting. In 1923, Lynn claimed the credit for keeping Lord Birkenhead out of the Government. *Morning Post* (23 October 1922); *Manchester Guardian* (19 November 1923).

[225] McConnell, T. E. (Belfast-Duncairn). In Ulster for the meeting. *Morning Post* (23 October 1922).

[226] Macdonald, B. F. P. (Wallasey). Absent, but supported the Coalition. *Austen Chamberlain Papers*, AC/33/2/80 [Macdonald to Chamberlain, 18 October 1922].

[227] McGuffin, S. (Belfast-Shankill). Labour-Unionist M.P. Absent.

[228] Mackinder, H. J. (Glasgow-Camlachie). Pro.

[229] McLaren, R. (Lanark North). Absent.

[230] McLean, C. (Lincs.-Brigg). Absent.

[231] Macleod, J. M. (Glasgow-Kelvingrove). Pro.

[232] Macnaghten, M. (Londonderry County North). Anti.

[233] McNeill, R. (Kent-Canterbury). Anti. Diehard. Open antagonist of the Coalition in 1921. *The Times* (14 November 1921).

[234] Macquisten, F. A. (Glasgow-Springburn). Absent.

[235] Maddocks, H. H. (Warks.-Nuneaton). Anti. Left the Coalition 'some time' before 19 October. *Coventry Herald* (3–4 November 1922).

[236] Magnus, P. (London University). Pro. At Chamberlain's dinner.

[237] Maitland, A. Steel- (Birmingham-Erdington). Anti. Renounced the Coalition in August 1921. To Asquith, he expressed his 'disgust' with the Lloyd George Government. *Asquith Papers*, Box 34, f. 26 [Steel-Maitland to Asquith, 29 July 1921]; *Liberal Magazine* (September 1921) 526.

[238] Mallaby-Deely, H. (Willesden East). Anti.

[239] Malone, P. B. (Tottenham South). Pro.

[240] Manville, E. (Coventry). Anti. During the election, Manville stated that he had come out against the Coalition only because of the split in the Conservative leadership. If the leadership had not been split, he would have continued, he said, to support Chamberlain; but he was sure that Conservatives and Liberals would continue to work together. *Coventry Herald* (3–4 November 1922).

241 Marriott, J. A. R. (Oxford City). Anti. Diehard.

242 Meysey-Thompson, E. C. (Birmingham-Handsworth). Anti.

243 Mildmay, F. B. (Devon-Totnes). Pro. Received a peerage in Lloyd George's resignation honours list.

244 Mitchell, W. Lane- (Wandsworth-Streatham). Anti. According to the *Chronicle* (11 November 1922), Lane-Mitchell made up his mind to oppose the Coalition at the meeting. According to P. J. Ford, Lane-Mitchell felt the anti-Coalition amendment at the meeting was 'substantially in agreement' with Chamberlain's own views. *Austen Chamberlain Papers*, Box 32 [Ford to Chamberlain, 19 October 1922].

245 Moles, T. (Belfast-Ormeau). In Ulster for the meeting. *Morning Post* (23 October 1922).

246 Molson, J. E. (Lincs.-Gainsborough). Pro. At Chamberlain's dinner.

247 Moore, N. (Islington North). In Canada for the meeting, but told Chamberlain that he continued to support the Coalition. *Hornsey Journal* (3 November 1922); *Austen Chamberlain Papers*, AC/33/2/78 [Moore to Chamberlain, 17 October 1922].

248 Moore-Brabazon, J. (Rochester-Chatham). Pro. At Chamberlain's dinner.

249 Morden, W. G. (Middlesex-Brentford). Pro.

250 Morrison, H. (Wilts.-Salisbury). Anti. Anti before meeting. *Salisbury Times* (27 October 1922).

251 Morrison-Bell, A. C. (Devon-Honiton). Diehard. In Brazil for the meeting.

252 Murchison, C. K. (Hull East). Anti. Anti before the meeting, but a waverer. *Huntingdonshire Post* (19 and 26 October and 2 November 1922).

253 Murray, C. D. (Edinburgh South). Pro. At Chamberlain's dinner.

254 Murray, Gideon (Glasgow-St Rollox). Anti. Diehard.

255 Murray, W. (Dumfries). Pro.

256 Nall, J. (Manchester-Hulme). Anti.

257 Nelson, R. F. W. R. (Lanark-Motherwell). Absent.

258 Newman, J. R. P. (Middlesex-Finchley). Anti. Anti before the meeting. By early 1922 Newman was a member of the Diehard group led by Lord Salisbury. *Finchley Press* (27 July and 3 November 1922); *Southern Daily Echo* (17 October 1922).

259 Newman, R. H. S. D. L. (Exeter). Pro. At Chamberlain's

dinner. In 1918, Newman had been nominated by a local Liberal-Conservative coalition. In 1922 he ran successfully as an independent Conservative; in 1923 he won Exeter as a Conservative free trader. In 1929 he won as an Independent against official Conservative opposition. *Times House of Commons, 1919*; *Exeter Express and Echo* (21 October 1922); *Manchester Guardian* (19 November 1923).

[260] Newson, P. (Warks.-Tamworth). Pro. At Chamberlain's dinner.

[261] Newton, D. (Cambridge). Repudiated the Coalition during a March 1922 by-election. In Brazil for the Carlton Club Meeting. *Cambridge Independent Press* (3 March 1922).

[262] Newton, H. K. (Essex-Harwich). Pro.

[263] Nicholl, E. (Cornwall-Penryn and Falmouth). Pro.

[264] Nicholson, J. S. (Westminster-Abbey). Anti. Diehard.

[265] Nicholson, W. G. (Hants-Petersfield). Anti. Anti 'some time' before the Carlton Club Meeting. *Morning Post* (8 November 1922).

[266] Nield, H. (Ealing). Anti. Diehard. Opposed by another Diehard in the 1922 election.

[267] Norris, H. G. (Fulham East). Anti.

[268] Norton-Griffiths, J. (Wandsworth Central). In Brazil for the Carlton Club Meeting.

[269] Oman, C. (Oxford University). Anti. Diehard.

[270] O'Neill, R. (Mid-Antrim). In Ulster for the meeting. *Morning Post* (23 October 1922).

[271] Ormsby-Gore, G. W. A. (Staffs.-Stafford). Anti. Anti before the meeting. *Staffordshire Chronicle.* (21 October 1922).

[272] Pain, W. H. (Londonderry County South). Absent.

[273] Palmer, G. L. (Wilts.-Westbury). Absent.

[274] Parkinson, A. L. (Blackpool). Absent.

[275] Pease, H. P. (Darlington). Present at the meeting, but did not vote. Pease may have been a teller for the minority, since he refused Bonar Law's offer of the postmaster-generalship, the office he had previously held. Pease did not discuss the Carlton Club Meeting during the election in speeches reported in the *Evening Despatch*, the local newspaper. *Southern Daily Echo* (19 October 1922); *Yorkshire Post* (1 November 1922).

[276] Peel, S. (Middlesex-Uxbridge). Convalescing in Scotland

from an operation at the time of the Carlton Club Meeting. *Middlesex Advertiser* (27 October and 3 November 1922).

²⁷⁷ Pennefather, de F. (Liverpool-Kirkdale). Anti. Diehard.

²⁷⁸ Percy, C. (Tynemouth). Absent.

²⁷⁹ Percy, Lord E. (Hastings). Anti. Anti by May 1922. During the election, Percy announced that he would not take the whips of any party if elected. *National Review* (May 1922), 437; *The Times* (11 November 1922).

²⁸⁰ Perkins, W. F. (Hants-New Forest and Christchurch). Pro. At Chamberlain's dinner.

²⁸¹ Perring, W. G. (Paddington North). Anti.

²⁸² Philipps, O. (Cheshire-City of Chester). At the meeting, but did not vote. *Southern Daily Echo* (19 October 1922).

²⁸³ Pickering, E. W. (Dewsbury). Anti.

²⁸⁴ Pilditch, P. (Middlesex-Spelthorne). Announced in March 1922 that he would not support the Coalition unless it stated its policy. At the annual fête of the Spelthorne Unionist association, it was announced that he would stand as 'a Conservative pure and simple'. However he would not follow a revolt against the elected party leaders, and spoke vigorously in favour of the Coalition at the Middlesex divisional council of the National Unionist Association; he got the council to shelve an anti-Coalition proposal by 45 votes to 33. In September he told Chamberlain that he had weathered three Diehard crises in his constituency in 1921 and 1922. He was in Brazil during the Carlton Club Meeting. *The Times* (23 March 1922); *Middlesex Advertiser* (22 September 1922); *Austen Chamberlain Papers*, AC/33/2/16–17 [Pilditch to Chamberlain, 7 and 19 September 1922].

²⁸⁵ Pinkham, C. (Willesden West). Anti.

²⁸⁶ Polson, T. A. (Kent-Dover). Diehard and anti-waster. Excluded from the Carlton Club Meeting. *Morning Post* (19 October 1922).

²⁸⁷ Pollock, E. (Liverpool-Excange). Pro. At Chamberlain's dinner.

²⁸⁸ Pownall, A. (Lewisham East). In Italy at the time of the Carlton Club Meeting. *Lewisham Borough News* (25 October 1922).

²⁸⁹ Prescott, W. H. (Tottenham North). Pro. Despite his support for the Coalition, Tottenham Lloyd George Liberals opposed

Prescott during the election. *Tottenham and Edmonton Weekly Herald* (10 November 1922).

[290] Preston, W. (Stepney-Mile End). Pro. At Chamberlain's dinner.

[291] Pretyman, E. G. (Essex-Chelmsford). Anti; proposed the motion at the Carlton Club Meeting to end the Coalition. Anti before the meeting. *Buckingham Advertiser* (21 October 1922).

[292] Raeburn, W. H. (Dumbartonshire). Pro.

[293] Ramsden, G. T. (Yorks-Elland). Anti. Anti for months before the meeting. *Yorkshire Post* (25 October 1922).

[294] Randles, J. S. (Manchester-Exchange). Absent.

[295] Rankin, J. S. (Liverpool-East Toxteth). Absent.

[296] Raper, A. B. (Islington East). Detained in Norway at the time of the Carlton Club Meeting because of his wife's illness. *Islington Daily Gazette* (25 October 1922); *Hornsey Journal* (3 November 1922).

[297] Ratcliffe, H. B. (Bradford Central). Absent.

[298] Raw, N. (Liverpool-Wavertree). Absent.

[299] Rawlinson, J. F. P. (Cambridge University). Anti.

[300] Reid, D. D. (Down East). Anti.

[301] Remer, J. R. (Cheshire-Macclesfield). Pro.

[302] Remnant, J. F. (Holborn). Anti. Disgruntled with Austen Chamberlain's leadership from June 1921 onwards. *Bonar Law Papers*, 107/1/31 [Remnant to Law, 1 June 1921].

[303] Renwick, G. (Newcastle Central). Pro. At Chamberlain's dinner. Renwick refused to be bound by the decision of the Carlton Club Meeting, and ran in 1922 as an independent Conservative. *Yorkshire Post* (30 October 1922).

[304] Richardson, A. (Kent-Gravesend). Anti. Anti before the meeting, but, according to P. J. Ford, he thought that the motion to end the Coalition was 'substantially in agreement' with Chamberlain's views. *Chatham, Rochester and Gillingham News* (27 October 1922); *Austen Chamberlain Papers*, AC/33/2/102 [Ford to Chamberlain, 19 October 1922].

[305] Richardson, P. (Surrey-Chertsey). In Brazil for the meeting. Richardson had been elected as a non-Coalition Conservative in a March 1922 by-election. *The Times* (13 March 1922).

[306] Roberts, S. (Sheffield-Ecclesall). Pro. Made a privy councillor in Lloyd George's resignation honours list.

[307] Roberts, S. (Herefordshire-Hereford). Anti. Anti before

the meeting. When elected in a June 1921 by-election, Roberts said that he did not intend to give the Coalition any more than 'general support'. He went to the Carlton Club Meeting 'with his mind fully made up'. *Hereford Journal* (7 November 1922); *Ross Gazette* (2 November 1922).

[308] Rothschild, L. N. de (Bucks.-Aylesbury). Pro. At Chamberlain's dinner.

[309] Roundell, R. F. (Yorks.-Skipton). Pro.

[310] Royden, T. (Bootle). Absent.

[311] Royds, E. (Lincs.-Grantham). Pro. At Chamberlain's dinner.

[312] Rutherford, J. (Lancs.-Darwen). Pro. At Chamberlain's dinner.

[313] Rutherford, W. (Liverpool-Edge Hill). Anti, but attended Chamberlain's dinner.

[314] Samuel, A. (Surrey-Farnham). Anti.

[315] Samuel, H. (Lambeth-Norwood). Pro. At Chamberlain's dinner.

[316] Samuel, S. (Wandsworth-Putney). Anti. Prior to the meeting, he told his constituents that he was 'not willing to support the Coalition government', but that he felt some arrangements would have to be made with the Liberals. He was opposed in the 1922 election by a Diehard. *Wandsworth Borough News* (13 October 1922).

[317] Sanders, R. A. (Somerset-Bridgwater). Anti. Anti before the meeting, and submitted his resignation to Chamberlain, but put it off until the decision of the Carlton Club Meeting was known. *Scotsman* (18 October 1922).

[318] Sassoon, P. A. G. D. (Hythe). Pro. Told Lloyd George of the result of the Carlton Club Meeting. At Chamberlain's dinner. *Leicester Daily Mercury* (19 October 1922).

[319] Scott, L. (Liverpool-Exchange). Pro. At Chamberlain's dinner.

[320] Scott, S. (St Marylebone). Anti.

[321] Sharman-Crawford, R. G. (Mid-Down). Anti.

[322] Shaw, W. T. (Forfar). Pro.

[323] Simms, Major-General Rt Revd. J. M. (Down North). Absent.

[324] Smith, A. M. (Croydon South). Absent.

[325] Smith, H. (Warrington). Pro. At Chamberlain's dinner.

[326] Smithers, A. W. (Kent-Chislehurst). Anti.

[327] Sprot, A. (Fife East). Anti. Diehard.

[328] Stanley, G. F. (Preston). Anti.

[329] Starkey, G. R. (Notts.-Newark). Anti.

[330] Steel, S. Strang- (Kent-Ashford). Anti. Anti before the meeting. *Southeastern Gazette* (24 January and 21 March 1922).

[331] Stevens, M. (Eccles). Absent, but supported the Coalition. *Austen Chamberlain Papers*, AC/33/2/82 [Stevens to Chamberlain, 18 October 1922].

[332] Stewart, G. (Wirral). Anti. Diehard, but wished to cooperate with Lloyd George if Lloyd George became a Conservative. *Birkenhead and Cheshire Advertiser* (4 November 1922).

[333] Sueter, M. F. (Herts.-Hertford). Diehard and anti-waster. Excluded from the Carlton Club Meeting. *Scotsman* (18 October 1922).

[334] Sugden, W. H. (Lancs.-Royton). Pro.

[335] Surtees, H. C .(Gateshead). Pro.

[336] Sykes, A. J. (Cheshire-Knutsford). Anti.

[337] Terrell, G. (Wilts.-Chippenham). Anti. Said before the Carlton Club Meeting that he intended to stand independently of the Coalition, but that he would back it until the general election. *North Wilts. Herald* (13 October 1922).

[338] Terrell, R. (Oxon.-Henley). Anti. Anti before the meeting. *Berkshire Chronicle* (2 June 1922).

[339] Thomas-Stanford, C. (Brighton). Anti. Anti before the meeting. *Brighton Evening Argus* (25 October 1922).

[340] Thompson, W. Mitchell- (Glasgow-Maryhill). Pro. At Chamberlain's dinner.

[341] Thomson, F. C. (Aberdeen South). Pro.

[342] Thorpe, J. H. (Manchester-Rusholme). Anti.

[343] Tickler, T. G. (Grimsby). Anti.

[344] Townley, M. (Mid-Beds.). Anti.

[345] Townshend, C. (Salop-Wrekin). Anti. Townshend ran as an independent in the 1920 by-election, and defeated the Coalitionist. He joined the Conservative Party in 1922. Anti before the meeting. *Wolverhampton Chronicle* (15 February 1922); *Southern Daily Echo* (19 October 1922).

[346] Tryon, G. C. (Brighton). Anti. Anti before the meeting. *The Times* (31 October 1922).

[347] Turton, E. R. (Yorks.-Thirsk and Malton). Absent, but opposed continued coalition. *Yorkshire Post* (25 October 1922).

[348] Vickers, D. (Sheffield-Hallam). Absent.

[349] Waddington, R. (Rossendale). Supported continued coalition before the meeting and also afterwards, but could not attend it. Although he had announced his intention to withdraw from politics in April 1922, he rejected Bonar Law's leadership and supported Lloyd George and Austen Chamberlain during the election. *Accrington Gazette* (4 November 1922); *Bacup Times* (18 March and 21 October 1922).

[350] Ward, L. (Hull North-west). In Italy during the Carlton Club Meeting. *Yorkshire Post* (1 November 1922).

[351] Ward-Jackson, C. L. A. (Herefordshire-Leominster). Anti. Ward-Jackson left Leominster in 1921 because his association wished him to run as an independent Conservative. Although he voted against the Coalition on 19 October, he later supported it in his new constituency, Harrow. *Harrow Observer* (3 November 1922); *Middlesex Advertiser* (3 November 1922).

[352] Warren, A. (Edmonton). Pro. During the election campaign, Warren was on the platform of a Lloyd George meeting, but not of any ministerial one. *The Times* (6 November 1922).

[353] Weston, J. W. (Westmorland). Did not vote. Weston said in late September 1922 that the Conservatives should stay with the Coalition. *Yorkshire Post* (30 September 1922).

[354] Wheler, G. C. H. (Kent-Faversham). Anti.

[355] White, G. D. (Southport). Anti. Anti before the meeting. *Southport Guardian* (25 October 1922).

[356] Whitla, W. (Belfast University). Absent.

[357] Wild, E. (West Ham-Upton). Absent.

[358] Willey, F. V. (Bradford South). During mid-October was in the U.S.A. on semi-official business. Anti before the meeting and a member of the National Party in 1918. *Exeter Express and Echo* (30 October 1922); *Yorkshire Post* (11 October 1922); pamphlet in the *Wargrave Papers*.

[359] Williams, C. (Devon-Tavistock). Absent.

[360] Williams, R. (Dorset West). Absent.

[361] Willoughby, C. (Lincs.-Rutland and Stamford). Did not vote, although he was present at the meeting. Signed the Diehard manifesto of March, but not that of June 1922. *Southern Daily*

Echo (19 October 1922); *Gleanings and Memoranda* (April 1922) 402 and (July 1922) 98.

[362] Wills, G. (Somerset - Weston-super-Mare). Anti.

[363] Wilson, A. S. (Yorks.-Holderness). Anti. He 'was a Diehard and proud of it'. *The Times* (27 March 1922); *Yorkshire Post* (23 October 1922); *Beverley Guardian* (4 November 1922).

[364] Wilson, L. O. (Reading). Anti. Anti before the meeting. *Austen Chamberlain Papers*, Box 32 [Wilson to Chamberlain, 21 September and 11 October 1922].

[365] Wilson, M. J. J. (Yorks.-Richmond). Anti.

[366] Wilson, M. R. H. (Bethnal Green South-west). Absent.

[367] Windsor, Viscount (Salop-Ludlow). Anti. Made up his mind to oppose the Coalition before the meeting, but had not decided to break with Chamberlain, as he had not known Chamberlain's views about a second coupon election. *Ludlow Advertiser* (4 November 1922).

[368] Winterton, Earl (Sussex-Horsham and Worthing). In India on government business at the time of the meeting. Dubious in early 1922 about maintaining the Coalition. *Morning Post* (31 October 1922); Beaverbrook, *Decline of Lloyd George*, 134.

[369] Wise, F. (Ilford). Anti. Had an independent Conservative opponent in 1922.

[370] Wolmer, Viscount (Hants-Aldershot). Anti. Diehard.

[371] Wood, E. F. L. (Yorks-Ripon). Anti. Anti before the meeting. *Austen Chamberlain Papers*, AC/33/2/83 [Aide-memoire by Chamberlain, 17 October 1922].

[372] Wood, J. (Cheshire-Stalybridge and Hyde). Anti.

[373] Wood, H. Kingsley (Woolwich West). Pro.

[374] Woods, S. Hill- (Derbyshire-High Peak). Absent.

[375] Woods,(R. (Dublin University). Absent.

[376] Worsfold, T. C. (Surrey-Mitcham). Anti.

[377] Worthington-Evans, L. (Essex-Colchester). Pro. At Chamberlain's dinner.

[378] Yate, C. E. (Leics.-Melton). Anti. Diehard.

[379] Young, F. (Wilts.-Swindon). Anti.

[380] Younger, G. (Ayr District). Anti. Anti before the meeting. *Austen Chamberlain Papers*, AC/33/2/20 [Younger to Chamberlain, 16 September 1922].

APPENDIX II

Liberal–Conservative
Co-operation in the 1922
Election

In the 1922 election, over two hundred Liberal and Conservative candidates ran under the aegis of two or more parties. This appendix lists such candidates under four categories :

a Prefixless Liberals : that is, Liberals who did not stand as straightforward Asquithians or Lloyd Georgians. In most cases they pledged to back whichever Liberal leader had the support of the majority of Liberal M.P.s after the election.

b Constitutionalists : that is, candidates officially nominated by the Conservative or Liberal organisations, but who contested the election under labels of their own choosing.

c Conservatives with Liberal support.

d Liberals with Conservative support.

a Prefixless Liberals

* indicates that the candidate had Conservative support.

Bedfordshire :
 Luton—*Chronicle* (1 November 1922).
 Mid—*Chronicle* (17 November 1922).
Berkshire :
 Abingdon—*North Berks Herald* (4 and 11 November 1922).
Buckinghamshire :
 Wycombe—*Chronicle* (1 November 1922).

Cambridgeshire—*Scotsman* (30 October 1922); *Cambridge Independent Press* (17 March and 3 November 1922).

Cumberland :
 Carlisle—*The Times* (27 October 1922); *Yorkshire Post* (4 November 1922).
 Penrith—*Yorkshire Post* (4 November 1922).

Derbyshire :
 *Belper—*Nottingham Guardian* (30 October 1922).
 *Chesterfield—*Chronicle* (31 October and 6 November 1922); Williams, *Derbyshire Miners*, 816.
 Ilkeston—*Nottingham Guardian* (4 November 1922).
 South—*Derby Daily Telegraph* (30 October 1922).

Devon :
 South Molton—*Chronicle* (7 November 1922).
 Tiverton—*Chronicle* (7 November 1922).
 Torquay—*Torbay Express* (11 November 1922).

Dorset :
 North—*Three Shires Advertiser* (10 November 1922).

Durham :
 *Bishop Auckland—*Northeastern Daily Gazette* (30 October and 1 November 1922).

Essex :
 East Ham North—There were five candidates in 1922, a Conservative, a Lloyd Georgian, an Asquithian, a prefixless Liberal and Labour.

Gloucestershire :
 Gloucester—*Gloucester Journal* (11 November 1922).
 Thornbury—A Rendall, elected as a Coalitionist in 1918, withdrew from the Coalition in 1920, but during the 1922 election supported Lloyd George and ran without prefix. *South Gloucestershire Chronicle* (22 and 29 November 1918); *Bristol Evening News* (27 October and 10 and 11 November 1922).

Hampshire :
 Isle of Wight—*Isle of Wight Observer* (11 November 1922).
 Southampton (2 seats)—*Chronicle* (11 November 1922).

Hertfordshire :
 Hertford—*Chronicle* (7 November 1922); *Herts Record* (10 November 1922).

Lancashire :
*Heywood and Radcliffe—*Radcliffe Times* (4 November 1922).
Manchester (7 seats)—*The Times* (26 October 1922).
Nelson and Colne—*Nelson Leader* (3 November 1922).
Rochdale—*Carnarvon and Denbigh Herald* (3 November 1922).
Salford North and West—*Manchester Evening News* (3 and 6 November 1922).
London and Middlesex :
Holborn—*Chronicle* (7 November 1922).
Kensington South—[Ind. Lloyd Georgian] *Chronicle* (11 November 1922).
Tottenham North—*Tottenham and Edmonton Weekly Herald* (10 November 1922).
Uxbridge—*Middlesex Advertiser* (10 November 1922).
Willesden East—*Willesden Citizen* (17 November 1922).
Norfolk :
Eastern—*Eastern Daily Press* (31 October 1922).
Northants :
*Wellingborough—Joint nominee of the local Liberal and Conservative associations. *Northampton Daily Chronicle* (25 and 28 October 1922).
Nottinghamshire :
*Mansfield—*Nottingham Guardian* (27 October 1922); *Chronicle* (4 November 1922).
Nottingham East—*Nottingham Guardian* (3 November 1922).
Shropshire :
Ludlow—*Ludlow Advertiser* (11 November 1922).
Shrewsbury—*Worcester Herald* (4 November 1922).
Somerset :
Bath—*Chronicle* (2 November 1922).
Taunton—*Chronicle* (17 November 1922).
Suffolk :
*Eye—Two prefixless Liberals. *Suffolk and Essex Free Press* (2 November 1922); *Suffolk Chronicle and Mercury* (6 October 1922).
Great Yarmouth—*Morning Post* (7 November 1922).
Surrey :
Kingston-on-Thames—[Independent on Liberal platform] *The Times* (10 November 1922).

Richmond—*Chronicle* (3 November 1922).

Sussex :

Brighton (1 seat)—*Morning Post* (7 November 1922).

Salisbury—*Salisbury Times* (27 October and 3 November 1922).

Yorkshire :

Batley and Morley—*Chronicle* (31 October and 7 November 1922).

Colne Valley—*The Times* (6 November 1922); *Manchester Guardian* (10 November 1922).

Doncaster—*Doncaster Gazette* (3 November 1922).

*Don Valley—*Yorkshire Post* (3 November 1922).

Elland—*The Times* (1 November 1922).

*Halifax—[The speaker, unopposed].

Holderness—*Chronicle* (17 November 1922).

**Leeds South and West (2 seats)—*The Times* (1 November 1922); *Yorkshire Post* (7 November 1922).

Leeds Central, North, North-east and South-east (4 seats)—*The Times* (1 November 1922).

Pontefract—*Goole Journal* (8 November 1922).

Pudsey and Otley—*Pudsey and Stanningley News* (3 November 1922).

Wales :

Anglesey—*Chronicle* (3 November 1922).

Cardiff (3 seats)—All three Liberals stood without prefix. In Cardiff South, Lieutenant-Colonel Freyberg, though nominated by the Liberal association, ran as an independent. Singleton-Gates, *General Lord Freyberg*, 90–2; *Chronicle* (4 November 1922).

Carmarthen—J. Hinds. An Asquithian also ran. *Chronicle* (8 November 1922).

*Carnarvon—*Carnarvon and Denbigh Herald* (3 November 1922).

*Merioneth—*Chronicle* (8 November 1922); *The Times* (13 November 1922).

*Montgomery—*Montgomery County Times* (4 November 1922); *Liverpool Post* (1 November 1922).

Pontypool—*South Wales Argus* (9 November 1922).

*Swansea East—*Chronicle* (7 November 1922).

Swansea West—*Chronicle* (28 November 1922).

Scotland :
  Aberdeenshire West—*Aberdeen Daily Journal* (26 October
    and 2 November 1922).
  *Ayrshire South—*Largs and Millport Weekly News* (4 Novem-
    ber 1922).
  *Banff—*Chronicle* (6 November 1922).
  Berwick and Haddington—The local Conservative and Lloyd
    George Liberal associations repudiated J. D. Hope, the
    sitting M.P., as he had not made a single speech during his
    twenty-four years in Parliament. Lord Balfour wrote Hope
    a letter of support under the impression that he was still
    Lloyd George's nominee; he later retracted the letter. Hope
    supported Bonar Law as an Independent Lloyd Georgian.
    There was also an official Lloyd Georgian. *The Times* (1
    November 1922); *Scotsman* (1 and 2 November 1922).
  Caithness and Sutherland—2 prefixless Liberals. *Scotsman* (28
    October 1922); *Northern Times* (2 and 9 November 1922);
    Chronicle (7 November 1922).
  Edinburgh North—*Scotsman* (3 October 1922).
  Galloway—*Lloyd George Liberal Magazine* (June 1922) 847,
    and (December 1922) 236.
  *Inverness—There was also an Asquithian Liberal. *Football
    News* [Inverness] (4 November 1922); *Aberdeen Daily
    Journal* (27 October 1922).
  Kilmarnock—*Glasgow Herald* (10 November 1922).
  *Kinross and West Perth—*Scotsman* (30 October 1922).
  *Moray and Nairn—T. Guthrie, the Lloyd Georgian, said it
    was 'unfair' to tie a candidate to a leader in the 1922
    election. He has an Asquithian opponent. *Dundee Adver-
    tiser* (26 October and 1 November 1922).
  Refrew East—*Scotsman* (28 October 1922).
  Western Isles—Dr D. Murray, the Asquithian, ran without
    prefix; he had a Lloyd Georgian opponent. *Stornoway
    Gazette* (9 November 1922).

b. **Constitutionalists**

* Indicates that the candidate was elected. Independent Conservatives are not listed here, unless they ran as Constitutionalists or under some similar label.

*Barnard Castle—J. E. Rogerson, 'Liberal-Labour-Unionist'. *Newcastle Daily Chronicle* (10 November 1922).

Bishop Auckland—E. A. Jones, 'I am as much a Labour man, as much a Liberal, as much a Unionist in the true and honest sense, as any man could be'. He had Liberal and Conservative support. *Northeastern Daily Gazette* (30 October and 1 November 1922).

Bootle—Sir A. Bicket, Constitutionalist. *Liverpool Post* (27 and 28 October 1922).

Cannock—J. Parker said, 'I cannot call myself a Conservative and I cannot call myself a Liberal'. He had Conservative and Liberal support. *Chronicle* (3 and 9 November 1922).

*Dartford—G. Jarrett, Constitutionalist. He also ran as a Constitutionalist in Dartford in 1923. *Dulwich Gazette* (31 October 1922); *West Kent Advertiser* (27 October); *Dartford Chronicle* (23 November 1923).

Doncaster—R. Nicholson, 'Constitutional Democrat'. *Chronicle* (7 November 1922); *Doncaster Gazette* (3 November 1922).

Don Valley—J. Walton, 'Constitutional Labour'. He also said he was running 'as plain Jim Walton'. *Yorkshire Post* (3 November 1922); *Doncaster Gazette* (3 and 10 November 1922).

*Gravesend—Sir A. Richardson, Constitutionalist. *Gravesend and Dartford Reporter* (4 November 1922).

*Hackney South—C. Erskine-Bolst, Constitutionalist. *Hackney Gazette* (24 July and 1 November 1922).

*Lambeth-Kennington—F. Harrison, Conservative Anti-waster. *Northeastern Daily Gazette* (27 October 1922); *Morning Post* (8 November 1922).

Merthyr—Sir R. Mathias, Independent Anti-Socialist with official Liberal and Conservative support. *Manchester Guardian* (3 November 1922).

Saffron Walden—Sir A. Beck, Constitutionalist. *Cambridge Independent Press* (10 November 1922).

*Tottenham South—P. B. Malone, Constitutionalist. *Hornsey Journal* (3 November 1922).

c. Conservatives with Liberal support

* Indicates that the Asquithian Liberals supported the Conservatives. In all other instances in this list, the Lloyd George Liberals provided the Liberal support.

Cheshire :

City of Chester—*Scotsman* (30 October 1922).

Eddisbury—*Scotsman* (30 October 1922).

Northwich—*Scotsman* (30 October 1922).

Stockport (1 seat)—*Cheshire Daily Echo* (28 October 1922).

Wallasey—*Liverpool Post* (7 November 1922).

Devon :

Exeter—Sir R. Newman ran as the 'official independent Unionist' with Lloyd Georgian support. *The Times* (30 October 1922).

*Plymouth-Sutton—*Western Independent* (22 October 1922).

Durham :

Chester-le-street, Gateshead—*Sunderland Daily Echo* (31 October 1922).

Gloucestershire :

Bristol Central and West—*Bristol Evening News* (3 and 11 November 1922).

Lancashire :

Blackburn (1 seat)—*Yorkshire Post* (6 November 1922).

Bolton (1 seat)—*Bolton Evening News* (7 and 8 November 1922).

Liverpool (4 seats)—Seats involved were East Toxteth, Edge Hill, Exchange and Wavertree. *Liverpool Post* (7 November 1922).

Oldham (1 seat)—F. Blundell stood as a 'Unionist and agriculturist' with Lloyd George Liberal support. *Stratford-upon-Avon Herald* (27 October 1922); *Liverpool Post* (7 November 1922).

St Helen's—*Liverpool Post* (7 November 1922).
Southport—*Liverpool Post* (7 November 1922).
Widnes—*Liverpool Post* (7 November 1922).
Leicestershire :
Leicester South—*Chronicle* (2 November 1922).
London and Middlesex :
Balham and Tooting—*Balham, Tooting and Mitcham News* (27 October 1922).
Stoke Newington—*The Times* (9 November 1922.)
Northamptonshire :
Kettering—*Northampton Daily Chronicle* (8 November 1922).
Peterborough—*Peterborough Citizen* (19 September and 24 October 1922).
Northumberland :
Newcastle Central—Sir G. Renwick nominated himself as an independent Conservative supporter of Lloyd George, and left it to the local Conservative association to nominate him, which it did. *Chronicle* (1 November 1922).
Newcastle North—*Chronicle* (31 October 1922).
Yorkshire :
Sheffield (3 seats)—Seats involved were : Central, Ecclesall, and Hallam. *The Times* (31 October 1922).
*Thirsk and Malton—*The Times* (31 October 1922).
Wales :
Rhondda West—*Radnor Express* (2 November 1922).
Scotland :
Aberdeen South—*Aberdeen Daily Journal* (20 October 1922).
Aberdeenshire Central—*Aberdeen Daily Journal* (31 October 1922).
Ayr District, Dumbartonshire—*Scotsman* (31 October 1922); *Dumbarton Herald* (1 November 1922).
Edinburgh (3 seats)—Seats involved were North, South and West. *Scotsman* (26 and 31 October and 1 November 1922).
Glasgow (9 seats)—*Scotsman* (21 October 1922); *Glasgow Herald* (28 October 1922).
Greenock—*Scotsman* (31 October 1922).
Hamilton—*Scotsman* (8 November 1922).

d. Liberals with Conservative support

* Indicates that the Conservatives supported a prefixless Liberal. In all other instances in this list, they supported a Lloyd Georgian.

Cheshire :
 Crewe—*Scotsman* (30 October 1922).
 Stockport (1 seat)—*Cheshire Daily Echo* (28 October 1922).
Cornwall :
 Camborne—*Cornish Post* (11 November 1922).
 Northern—*Morning Post* (31 October 1922).
Derbyshire :
 *Belper—*Nottingham Guardian* (30 October 1922).
 *Chesterfield—*Chronicle* (31 October 1922).
Dorset :
 East—The executive of the East Dorset Conservative Association officially supported F. E. Guest, the sitting Lloyd George Liberal. However the Poole Conservative Club nominated G. R. Hall Caine to oppose him. H. Page Croft later maintained that he had engineered Hall Caine's nomination. Lord Beaverbrook appeared on Caine's platform, but denied that he or his newspaper had anything to do with nominating 'Mister Haa-al Cai-ne'. *Dorset County Chronicle* (26 October and 9 November 1922); *East Dorset Herald* (23 November 1922); Croft, *My Life Of Strife*, 165; Beaverbrook, *Decline of Lloyd George*, 214.
Durham :
 *Bishop Auckland—[Liberal-Labour-Unionist] *Northeastern Daily Gazette* (30 October and 1 November 1922).
 South Shields—*Newcastle Daily Chronicle* (2 November 1922).
 Stockton—*Newcastle Daily Chronicle* (30 October 1922).
Essex :
 Romford—*Chronicle* (4 November 1922).
 Walthamstow West—*Chronicle* (31 October 1922).
Gloucestershire :
 Bristol East, North, and South—*Bristol Evening News* (3 November 1922).

Kent :

Dartford—*Woolwich Gazette* (31 October 1922); *West Kent Advertiser* (27 October 1922); *Chronicle* (2 November 1922).

Lancashire :

Blackburn (1 seat)—*Yorkshire Post* (6 November 1922).

Bolton (1 seat)—*Bolton Evening News* (21 and 23 October 1922).

*Heywood and Radcliffe—*Chronicle* (31 October 1922); *Radcliffe Times* (4 November 1922).

Middleton and Prestwich—*Northampton Daily Chronicle* (6 November 1922).

Oldham (1 seat)—*The Times* (14 November 1922).

Stretford—*Manchester Guardian* (3 November 1922).

Westhoughton—*Chronicle* (4 November 1922).

Leicestershire :

Leicester East—*Leicester Daily Mercury* (1 November 1922).

Loughborough—*Leicester Daily Mercury* (4 November 1922).

London and Middlesex :

Battersea North—*Morning Post* (6 November 1922); *Chronicle* (8 November 1922).

Bermondsey West—The local Conservative association and also the Conservative central office both supported a Lloyd George Liberal against an unofficial Conservative. *Chronicle* (9 November 1922).

Camberwell North-west—*Scotsman* (30 October 1922); *Chronicle* (10 November 1922).

Hackney Central—*Hackney Gazette* (9 June 1922); *The Times* (9 November 1922).

Shoreditch—*Chronicle* (1 November 1922).

Southwark (3 seats).—*The Times* (1 November 1922); *Chronicle* (9 November 1922).

Stepney-Limehouse—*Pall Mall Gazette* (1 November 1922).

Norfolk :

Norwich (2 seats)—*Norwich Mercury* (4 November 1922).

Southwestern—*Chronicle* (4 November 1922).

Northamptonshire :

Northampton—*Northampton Daily Chronicle* (1 November 1922).

*Wellingborough—*Northampton Daily Chronicle* (25 and 28 October 1922).

Northumberland :

Berwick-upon-Tweed—*Newcastle Daily Chronicle* (3 November 1922).

Newcastle East—*Chronicle* (31 October 1922).

Newcastle West—*Newcastle Daily Chronicle* (1 November 1922).

Nottinghamshire :

*Mansfield—*Chronicle* (4 November 1922).

Staffordshire :

Cannock—*Chronicle* (3 and 9 November 1922).

Kinswinford—*Chronicle* (3 November 1922).

Lichfield—*Chronicle* (3 November 1922).

Newcastle-under-Lyme—Bealey, et al., *Constituency Politics*, 108.

Stoke (3 seats)—*Chronicle* (3 November 1922).

Suffolk :

*Eye—Of the two prefixless Liberals, the Conservatives supported G. Howard. *Suffolk and Essex Free Press* (2 November 1922).

Yorkshire :

Barnsley—Despite 'great pressures' from outside to support the sitting Lloyd George Liberal, the Barnsley Conservatives sought a candidate of their own. However they did not find one before nominations closed, and they therefore gave the Lloyd Georgian reluctant backing. *Barnsley Independent* (8 July and 11 November 1922).

*Don Valley—*Doncaster Gazette* (3 and 10 November 1922).

*Halifax—[The speaker, unopposed.]

Hemsworth—*Doncaster Gazette* (3 November 1922).

Huddersfield—*Chronicle* (28 October 1922).

**Leeds South and West—*The Times* (1 November 1922); *Yorkshire Post* (7 November 1922).

Sheffield (4 seats)—The four seats were : Attercliffe, Central, Hillsborough and Park. *The Times* (31 October 1922).

Shipley—*The Times* (3 November 1922).

Wales :

Aberdare—*Radnor Express* (2 November 1922).

Brecon and Radnor—*Radnor Express* (9 November 1922).

Cardigan—*Cambrian News* (3 November 1922).

*Carnarvon—*Montgomery County Times* (4 November 1922).

Carnarvon District—*Montgomery County Times* (4 November 1922).

Gower—*Manchester Guardian* (3 November 1922).

Llanelly—*Llanelly Argus* (11 November 1922).

*Merioneth—H. H. Jones did not have official Conservative support, but most of the local Conservative executive appeared on his platform. He was unopposed. *Liverpool Post* (1 November 1922); *Montgomery County Times* (4 November 1922); *Chronicle* (8 November 1922); *The Times* (13 November 1922).

*Montgomery—*Liverpool Post* (November 1, 1922); *Montgomery County Times* (4 November 1922).

Neath—*Chronicle* (31 October 1922).

Rhondda East—*Chronicle* (3 November 1922).

*Swansea East—*Chronicle* (7 November 1922).

Pembroke—*Carnarvon and Denbigh Herald* (3 November 1922).

Scotland :

Aberdeen North—*Aberdeen Daily Journal* (20 October 1922).

Aberdeenshire East—*Scotsman* (11 November 1922).

Aberdeenshire West—*Scotsman* (11 November 1922).

Argyll—*Scotsman* (1 November 1922).

*Ayrshire South—*Largs. and Millport Weekly News* (4 November 1922).

*Banff—The prefixless Liberal was unopposed.

Berwick and Haddington—Conservatives supported the official Lloyd Georgian. *Berwick Mercury* (4 November 1922).

*Caithness and Sutherland—The Caithness Conservatives supported Sir Archibald Sinclair on condition that he gave general support to Bonar Law. *Scotsman* (28 October 1922); *Chronicle* (7 November 1922).

Dumbarton District—*Dumbarton Herald* (8 November 1922).

Dundee (2 seats)—*Aberdeen Daily Journal* (27 October 1922); *Dundee Advertiser* (15 November 1922).

Edinburgh Central, East—*Scotsman* (26 and 31 October and 1 November 1922).

Glasgow (4 seats)—The four seats concerned were : Bridgeton,

Gorbals, Govan and Partick. *Scotsman* (21 October 1922); *Glasgow Herald* (28 October 1922).

*Inverness—*Football News* [Inverness] (4 November 1922); *Aberdeen Daily Journal* (27 October 1922).

*Kinross and West Perth, Kirkcaldy District—*Scotsman* (27 October 1922).

 Montrose District—*Dundee Advertiser* (31 October and 1, 2 and 3 November 1922).

*Moray and Nairn—*Dundee Advertiser* (26 October and 1 November 1922).

Motherwell—*Lloyd George Liberal Magazine* (June 1922) 848.

Orkney and Shetland—*Chronicle* (10 November 1922).

Renfrew West—*Johnstone Advertiser* (3 November 1922).

Ross and Cromarty—*Chronicle* (2 November 1922).

Roxburgh and Selkirk—*Hawick News* (3 November 1922).

Rutherglen—*Scotsman* (1 November 1922).

References

Chapter 1 Lloyd George and political change, 1919–22

[1] *Frondirion MSS.*, Nat. Library of Wales, 10865 E; Hammond, *C. P. Scott of the Manchester Guardian*, 205; 'Centurion', 'Truth and falsehood in high places', *National Review* (June 1922) 554.

[2] Shakespeare, *Let Candles Be Brought In*, 48; *Nation* (24 January 1920) 556.

[3] Chamberlain, *Down the Years*, 244–5.

[4] Beveridge, *Power and Influence*, 163; *Lord Riddell's War Diary*, 153.

[5] Liddell Hart, *Memoirs*, I 373; d'Abernon, *Ambassador Of Peace*, I 140; *H. A. L. Fisher Papers*, Diary (3 June 1921).

[6] *Lloyd George Papers*, F/24/4/14 [synopsis of meeting between Coalition and Independent Liberal M.P.s, 2 June 1921]; Chamberlain, *Down the Years*, 137.

[7] Petrie, *Chapters of Life*, 90; A. P. Nicholson, *The Real Men in Public Life*, 63; *Manchester Guardian* (22 March 1921).

[8] *D. R. Daniel Papers*, MS. biography of Lloyd George in Welsh, 8–10.

[9] Jones, *Lloyd George*, 279–80; Liddell Hart, op. cit., I 361; Brockway, *Socialism Over Sixty Years*, 88; Shakespeare, op. cit., 44.

[10] *Beatrice Webb's Diaries, 1912–1924*, ed. M. Cole, 94n; *Lloyd George Papers*, F/27/3/15 [Henderson to Lloyd George, 11 August 1917].

[11] *Bonar Law Papers*, 84/3/1. The draft and its consequences are discussed in Blake, *Unknown Prime Minister*, 382; Countess Lloyd-George, *The Years That Are Past*, 137.

[12] *Bonar Law Papers*, 107/1/29 and 107/1/40 [Goulding to Law, 30 May and 11 June 1921].

[13] *Daily News* (28 March 1922).

[14] *Lloyd George Papers*, F/34/3/12 [Lloyd George to C. A. McCurdy, 14 June 1921].

[15] *5 H.C. Debates*, 130, col. 78 [7 June 1920]; *10 & 11 Geo. V*, Ch. 76, clause 1 (1); *Lloyd George Papers*, F/5/4/7 [Griffith Boscawen to Lloyd George, 16 December 1921]; Griffith-Boscawen, 'The decontrol of agriculture', *Lloyd George Liberal Magazine* (July 1921) 488–9.

[16] *Lloyd George Papers*, F/5/4/9–10; *Austen Chamberlain Papers*, AC/35/2/46–49 [Griffith-Boscawen to Lloyd George, 2 and 9 October 1922; to Chamberlain, 9, 10 and 12 October 1922; Chamberlain to Griffith-Boscawen, 11 October 1922].

[17] *H. A. L. Fisher Papers*, Diary, 21 February, 29 April and 19 June 1918; *Cabinet Minutes*, CAB 23/6 [5 April 1918].

[18] Callwell, *Field-Marshal Sir Henry Wilson*, II 263.

[19] Jones, op. cit., 181; d'Abernon, *Portraits and Appreciations*, 35.

[20] *5 H.C. Debates*, 114, cols. 2942 and 3022 [16 April 1919]; *Cabinet Minutes*, CAB 23/11 [12 August 1919].

[21] *H. A. L. Fisher Papers*, Diary, 9 July, 23 September and 3 November 1919; *Liberal Magazine* (December 1919) 672; *Cabinet Minutes*, CAB 23/29 [27 March 1922] & CAB 23/32 [1 November 1922]; *5 H.C. Debates*, 130 col. 177 [7 June 1920].

[22] *Nation* (October 1922) 6–7.

[23] *Daily Mail*, 19 July 1922; *Coalville Times*, 10 November 1922.

[24] *Daily News*, 28 April 1922; Keynes, *A Rivision of the Treaty*, 2.

[25] *5 H.C. Debates*, 105, col. 2358 [9 May 1918]; Harmsworth and Pound, *Northcliffe*, 377; Clarke, *My Northcliffe Diary*, 377.

[26] *5 H.C. Debates*, 114, col. 2953 [16 April 1919].

[27] Beaverbrook, *Politicians and the Press*, 22, 49.

[28] *H. A. L. Fisher Papers*, Diary, 2 August 1921.

[29] *Manchester Guardian* (3 January 1919;) Croft, *My Life of Strife*, 151.

[30] *Liverpool Post* (16 November 1922); *Chatham, Rochester and Gillingham News* (10 November 1922); *Goole Journal* (28 October 1922); *The Times* (15 November 1922); *Manchester Guardian* (8 November 1922).

[31] Birkenhead reprinted his 1920 articles in *Points of View*, II 192–219.

Chapter 2 Liberals and Conservatives in the early twenties

[1] *The Call to Liberalism*, 76.

[2] Four anti-war Liberal M.P.s who were refused renomination were E. T. John (Denbigh), H. B. Lees-Smith (Northampton), R. L. Outhwaite (Hanley) and C. P. Trevelyan (Elland).

[3] *Reports of the Annual Conferences of the Labour Party* [hereafter R.A.C.L.P.] (1919) 128–32; (1920) 147–53; (1921) 179–81; *Passfield Papers*, Beatrice Webb's Diary [unpublished extract, 4 January 1922]; *E. T. John Papers* [John to Beriah Evans, 2 January 1920].

[4] Gray, *Confessions of a Candidate*, 38; Fenby, *The Other Oxford*, 136–8.

[5] Wilson, *The Downfall of the Liberal Party*, 384–7.

[6] A. J. P. Taylor, *Lloyd George, Rise and Fall*, 27.

[7] A. J. P. Taylor, *English History, 1914–1945*, 69.

[8] Davies, *The Prime Minister's Secretariat, 1916–1920*, 36.

[9] H. A. Taylor, *Sir Robert Donald*, 123.

[10] *Elibank Papers*, MS. 8804, ff. 193–4 [aide-memoire by Alexander Murray, Lord Murray of Elibank, 2 October 1918]; Lloyd George, *The Truth about the Peace Treaties*, 175–6.

[11] Margot Asquith, *Autobiography*, II 302–3.

[12] Wilson, op. cit., 143; *The Times* (4 and 12 December 1918); *Midland Counties Express* (23 November 1918).

[13] Some supporters of Lloyd George successfully contesting former Conservative seats were J. Gardiner (Kinross and West Perth), Sir Thomas Bramsdon (Portsmouth Central) and S. G. Howard (Sudbury). Cf. *Kinross-shire Advertiser* (23 and 30 November 1918; *Evening News* [Portsmouth] (27 November 1918); and *Suffolk and Essex Free Press* (9, 20 and 27 November 1918).

[14] Jenkins, *Asquith*, 481.

[15] *Asquith Papers*, Box 18, ff. 39, 41 [8 and 11 January 1919]; *Edinburgh Evening News* (14 February 1923).

[16] *H. A. L. Fisher Papers*, Diary, 9 January 1919.

[17] Ibid., Diary, 9 January and 21 February 1919; 31 January and 4 February 1920.

[18] MacCarthy, *Letters of the Earl of Oxford and Asquith to a Friend*, I 114.

[19] *Minutes of the North Cumberland Liberal Association*, 24 March 1918; *Manchester Guardian* (8 January and 26 February 1921); *Viscount Gladstone Papers*, Add. MSS., 46085, ff. 103–4 [F. Barter to Gladstone, 20 April 1923]; *Lloyd George Liberal Magazine* (October 1920) 24; *Newcastle Daily Chronicle* (31 May 1920); *Lloyd George Papers*, F/22/2/20 [report on party organisation, 16 November 1920].

[20] *Minutes of the Scottish Liberal Federation*, Eastern minute books (1909–20) 467, 527 [2 October 1918 and 3 March 1920]; (1920–30) 14 [15 March 1921]; Western minute books (1908–25) 432–40 [22 November 1920]; *Newcastle Daily Chronicle* (1 May 1920); *Lloyd George Liberal Magazine* (November 1920) 95.

[21] Kinnear, *The British Voter*, 88–90, lists Liberal associations supporting the Coalition. Some gave it only partial support.

[22] *Lloyd George Papers*, F/35/1/9 [McCurdy to Lloyd George, 4 March, 1922].

[23] Butler, *The Electoral System in Britain, 1918–1950*, 148; Kinnear, *The British Voter*, 119–24, gives the percentage of middle-class and agricultural voters in each constituency in the 1921 census. For the purpose of this analysis, 'middle-class' and 'agricultural' constituencies are defined as those having more than 20 per cent engaged in the relevant occupations.

[24] Ibid., 70–2.

[25] Gough, *Soldiering On*, 182–204; *The Times* (27 October 1922).

[26] *Lloyd George Papers*, F/35/1/39 [Sutherland to Lloyd George, 8 March 1922].

[27] *Austen Chamberlain Papers*, AC/33/1/51 & AC/32/4/1a [Derby to Chamberlain, 22 March 1922, and Fraser to Chamberlain, 31 December 1921]; AC/5/1/249 [Chamberlain to Ida Chamberlain, 24 September 1922]; *Reading Papers*, EUR E/238/5 [Peel to Reading, 11 October 1922]; Griffith-Boscawen, *Memories*, 60.

[28] Mackenzie, *British Political Parties*, 22.

[29] *Austen Chamberlain Papers*, AC/33/2/114 [Chamberlain to H. Pike Pease, 20 October 1922].

[30] Birkenhead, *Contemporary Personalities*, 73.

[31] Ibid., 67; *Gleanings and Memoranda* (June 1921) 623.

[32] G. Murray, *A Man's Life*, 259; *Lloyd George Liberal Magazine* (April 1922) 697.

[33] Young, *Arthur James Balfour*, 428; *The Times* (24 October 1922); *Austen Chamberlain Papers*, AC/33/2/116 [Chamberlain to Newman, 20 October 1922].

[34] Kenworthy, *Sailors, Statesmen—and Others*, 200; Snell, *Men, Movements, and Myself*, 246; Tillett, *Memories and Reflections*, 273; Kirkwood, *My Life of Revolt*, 202; Clynes, *Memoirs*, I 339; Griffith-Boscawen, *Memories*, 222.

[35] McDowell, *British Conservatism, 1832–1914*, 9; *Daily News* (6 January 1922).

[36] Beaverbrook, *Decline of Lloyd George*, 182.

[37] *Austen Chamberlain Papers*, AC/32/2/11 and AC/32/2/23 [Younger to Chamberlain, 4 December 1921 and 9 January 1922].

[38] Ostrogorski, *Democracy and the Organisation of Political Parties*, 227–30.

Chapter 3 Conservative constituency parties and the coalition

[1] *The Times* (13 November 1922).

[2] Beaverbrook, *Decline Of Lloyd George*, 241.

[3] Rentoul, *This is my Case*, 87; Petrie, *Austen Chamberlain*, II 199–200; *South Wales Argus* (12, 13 and 17 October 1922).

[4] Cooper, *Old Men Forget*, 128; Wignall, *The Life of Commander Sir Edward Nicholl*, 219–24; *Tewkesbury Register* (25 March and 11 November 1922); *P. J. Hannon Papers*, Box 62 ['Secret Fund']. A. E. Beck, J. Havelock Wilson and Christabel Pankhurst each received £1000 in campaign expenses in 1918. The others mostly got £500. The British Commonwealth Union also subsidised the National Democratic Party (previously known as the British Workers' League) at the rate of £300 monthly during 1919 and 1920.

[5] [Islington] *Daily Gazette* (24 October 1922); *Fulham Chronicle* (3 and 10 November 1922). In 1923 Norris supported the Liberal candidate in East Fulham. *Manchester Guardian* (29 November 1923).

[6] *Hereford Journal* (28 October 1922); *Middlesex Advertiser* (6 and 22 October 1922); *Manchester Guardian* (15, 20, 23 and 29 November 1923).

[7] *Worcester Herald* (24 June and 22 July 1922).

[8] *The Times* (30 October 1922).

[9] *Bristol Evening News* (3 November 1922); *Leicester Daily Mercury* (1 November 1922); *Scotsman* (20 and 21 October and 1 and 3 November 1922); *Glasgow Herald* (26 October 1922); *The Times* (1 November 1922).

[10] *Steel-Maitland Papers*, Box 95, file 3 [Steel-Maitland to his local party officers, 23 April 1923]; *Morning Post* (4 November 1922).

[11] *Nottingham Guardian* (4 November 1922); *Eastwood Observer* (10 November 1922).

[12] *Austen Chamberlain Papers*, AC/32/4/16 [Fraser to Chamberlain, 30 December 1921].

[13] *Daventry Express* (27 May 1922); *Northampton Daily Chronicle* (21 July, 28 October and 4 November 1922).

[14] *Who's Who in Worcestershire*, 18, 93, 110; *Who's Who in Gloucestershire*, 186; *Altrincham Advertiser* (25 August 1922).

[15] Bealey, Blondel and McCann, *Constituency Politics*, 111, 263, 402; Jones, *Borough Politics*, 55; Birch, *Small Town Politics*, 46, 50, 81; Ranney, *Pathways to Parliament*, 69; Patterson, *The Selectorate*, 15, 66.

[16] Ranney, op. cit., 64–5, 68, 75–86; Courtney, *Sailor in a Russian Frame*, 189–213.

[17] *Peterborough Citizen* (19 September 1922); *Western Independent* (6 August 1922); *Hexham Herald* (16 September 1922); *North Wilts Herald* (6 November 1922).

[18] Bridges, *Reminiscences of a Country Politician*, 170.

[19] *Finchley Press* (3 November 1922).

[20] *Templewood Papers*, EUR E/240/111 [Hoare to Lord Willingdon, 3 March 1933].

Chapter 4 The Conservative MPs and the Coalition

[1] 5 *H.C. Debates*, 144, col. 2127 [19 July 1921] and 154, col. 326 [16 May 1922].

[2] *Wandsworth Borough News* (20 October 1922).

[3] *Lloyd George Papers*, F/35/1/36 and 39 [Sutherland to Lloyd George, 16 and 18 March 1922].

[4] Ross, *Parliamentary Representation*, 2nd ed., 36.

[5] Birkenhead, *Contemporary Personalities*, 5; 5 *H.C. Debates*, 140, cols 1988, 1998, 2009 [20 April 1921]; *Liverpool Post* (6 October 1922); S. Salvidge, *Salvidge Of Liverpool*, 207; *Three Shires Advertiser* (19 May 1922); *National Review* (November 1921) 344–5.

[6] *Gleanings and Memoranda* (July 1922) 97; *National Review* (June 1922) 554.

[7] *Western Independent* (30 July and 6 August 1922).

[8] Birkenhead, *Contemporary Personalities*, 180–2; 5 *H.C. Debates*, 150, cols 1595–8 [23 June 1922]; Croft, *My Life Of Strife*, 70; Murray, *A Man's Life*, 263.

[9] 5 *H.L. Debates*, 26 cols 172–212 [7 August 1917]; *Wargrave Papers*, 1918 National Party election leaflets.

[10] In Dover, the Anti-Waste candidate was director of a bankrupt firm; in the Isle of Wight, part of the Conservative organisation supported one candidate, and another part supported the other candidate; in Richmond, there was considerable agitation about the parliamentary attendance of the M.P. *Gleanings and Memoranda* (June 1922) 612; *Isle of Wight Observer* (6 May and 9 September 1922); *The Times* (10 November 1922 and 27 September 1924); *Morning Post* (28 October 1922).

[11] *Austen Chamberlain Papers*, AC/32/4/16 [Fraser to Chamberlain, 30 December 1921].

[12] Table 4 is based on statements by Conservative M.P.s who are listed in Appendix I under the following numbers: 19, 23, 27, 38, 40, 43, 47, 51, 67, 75, 79, 111, 117, 121, 125, 127, 132, 137, 139, 151, 173, 191, 206, 222, 235, 237, 250, 252, 304, 307, 316, 329, 336, 337, 338, 355, 364, 367. Appendix I also gives the references, except for 27 (*Sevenoaks Chronicle*, 20 October 1922), 43 (*Liverpool Post*, 1 November 1922), 67 (*Liverpool Post*, 17 October 1922), 206 (*Howdenshire Gazette*, 9 November 1922), 127 (*Leicester Daiyl Mercury*, 30 October 1922), 336 (*Cheshire Daily Echo*, 23 October 1922), and 337, 338 (both *Swindon Evening Advertiser*, 18 October 1922).

[13] *Austen Chamberlain Papers*, AC/33/1/29 [Salvidge to Chamberlain, 17 March 1922].

[14] In *My Early Life* (Fontana ed.), 168–9, and 305–9, Churchill describes backbiting comments on himself before 1900.
[15] *Yorkshire Evening Press* (22 July 1922).
[16] H. A. L. *Fisher Papers*, Diary, 16 and 17 May 1922.

Chapter 5 The ebb of coalition

[1] *Beatrice Webb's Diaries, 1912–1924*, ed. M. Cole, 85; Amery, *My Political Life*, II 225.
[2] *Gleanings and Memoranda* (February 1921) 109–110; (March 1921) 202, 286; (September 1921) 264; R. Churchill, *Lord Derby*, 387; *Liberal Magazine* (February 1921) 41.
[3] H. A. L. *Fisher Papers*, Diary, 24 March 1921; *Morning Post*, 18 April 1921; *Liberal Magazine* (June 1921) 311.
[4] *Lloyd George Papers*, F/34/3/14 [Wallace to McCurdy, 22 June 1921].
[5] Beaverbrook, *Decline of Lloyd George*, 32, 38; H. A. L. *Fisher Papers*, Diary, 5 August 1921.
[6] *Bonar Law Papers*, 107/1/46 [Jones to Law, 22 July 1921].
[7] *Gleanings and Memoranda* (September 1921) 244; *5 H.C. Debates*, 147, col. 1402 [31 October 1921].
[8] *Manchester Guardian* (4 November 1921); *5 H.C. Debates*, 147, col. 2046 [3 November 1921].
[9] R. Churchill, *Lord Derby*, 422; Blake, *Unknown Prime Minister*, 433; *Manchester Guardian* (18 November 1921).
[10] Johnston, *A Hundred Commoners*, 287; *Manchester Guardian* (18 November 1921).
[11] R. Churchill, *Lord Derby*, 424; *Bonar Law Papers*, 107/1/71–728 [Salisbury and Younger to Law, 19 November 1921]; *Manchester Guardian* (18 November 1921).
[12] *Manchester Guardian* (18 November 1921).
[13] *Gleanings and Memoranda* (December 1921) 499–501, 536.
[14] *Manchester Guardian* (9 December 1921).
[15] H. A. L. *Fisher Papers*, Diary, 6 December 1921; *Liverpool Post* (12 December 1921); D. R. *Daniel Papers*, Diary, 6 December 1921. The two Coalition Liberals voting against the Irish Treaty were Sir Clifford Cory and Austin Hopkinson.
[16] S. Salvidge, op. cit., 225; *Austen Chamberlain Papers*, AC/32/2/3 [Austen to Neville Chamberlain, 21 December 1921]; Beaverbrook, *Decline of Lloyd George*, 125.

[17] *Austen Chamberlain's Papers*, AC/32/2/1, 2 and 12 [Chamberlain to Younger, 22 December 1921; Chamberlain to Younger, 28 December 1921 and 4 January 1922].

[18] Ibid., AC/32/4/1a [Fraser to Chamberlain, 31 December 1921]. Fraser predicted that 317 Conservatives and 96 Coalition Liberals would be elected. He suggested deducting 10 per cent which would have left 372 Coalitionists.

[19] *Lloyd George Papers*, F/34/4/27 and F/35/1/1–2 [McCurdy to Lloyd George, 26 December 1921 and 4 January 1922; Sutherland to Lloyd George, 2 January 1922].

[20] *Austen Chamberlain Papers*, AC/32/2/23 [Younger to Chamberlain, 3 January 1922]; *Manchester Guardian* (2 and 3 January 1922).

[21] Ibid. (6 January 1922).

[22] Ibid. (11 January 1922).

[23] *Lloyd George Papers*, F/35/1/3 [McCurdy to Lloyd George, 5 January 1922]; *Manchester Guardian* (11 January 1922).

[24] *Austen Chamberlain Papers*, AC/32/2/30 [Chamberlain to Younger, 11 January 1922]; *Lloyd George Papers*, F/35/1/3 [McCurdy to Lloyd George, 11 January 1922].

[25] *The Times* (23 January 1922).

[26] *H. A. L. Fisher Papers*, Diary, 17 and 18 January 1922; *Manchester Guardian* (17 and 21 January 1922).

[27] *Gleanings and Memoranda* (March 1922) 281; *Liberal Magazine* (February 1922) 98; Petrie, *Austen Chamberlain*, II 173; G. Murray, *A Man's Life*, 260–1.

[28] *Gleanings and Memoranda* (March 1922) 280.

[29] Ibid. (April 1922) 399–400; *Liberal Magazine* (March 1922) 100.

[30] *Gleanings and Memoranda*, March 22, 398; *Reading Papers*, EUR/E/238/4 [Montagu to Reading, 12 February 1922].

[31] *H. A. L. Fisher Papers*, Diary, 23 and 28 February 1922; Beaverbrook, *Decline of Lloyd George*, 136; Countess Lloyd-George, *The Years that are Past*, 197.

[32] *Daily News* (2 March 1922).

[33] Ibid. (4 March 1922).

[34] *Liberal Magazine* (April 1922) 190–2; *Lloyd George Papers*, F/45/1/4 [Sassoon to Lloyd George, 24 March 1922].

[35] *Daily News* (7 March 1922); *Austen Chamberlain Papers*, AC/33/1/2 and 24 [Leith to Chamberlain, 4 March, and Chamberlain to Leith, 7 March 1922].

[36] *H. A. L. Fisher Papers*, Diary, 5 October 1920 and 9 March 1922.

[37] *Lloyd George Papers*, F/35/1/30 and 34 [McCurdy to Lloyd George and Sutherland to Lloyd George, both 15 March 1922].

[38] *Austen Chamberlain Papers*, AC/33/1/46 [Chilcott to Chamberlain, 15 March 1922]; S. Salvidge, op. cit., 233.

[39] *Lloyd George Papers*, F/3/1/39 [Sutherland to Lloyd George, 18 March 1922].

[40] Ibid., F/36/1/19 and F/35/1/31 [Greenwood to Lloyd George, 21 March, and McCurdy to Lloyd George, 16 March 1922].

[41] *Manchester Guardian* (9 January 1922); *Economist* (29 April 1922) 799.

[42] *Liberal Magazine* (July 1922) 417.

[43] *5 H.C. Debates*, 155, cols 1717–23, 1730–7, 1742–9 and 1756–61 [26 June 1922].

[44] Amery, *My Political Life*, II 233.

[45] *H.C. Debates*, 157, cols 207 [4 August 1922].

[46] *Cabinet Minutes*, CAB 23/31 and 23/32 [7 September and 1 November 1922].

[47] Ibid., CAB 23/29 [20 March 1922].

[48] Ibid., CAB 23/31 [3 August 1922].

[49] Countess Lloyd-George, *The Years that are Past*, 206.

[50] Nicolson, *Curzon: The Last Phase*, 30.

[51] *Nelson Leader* (13 October 1922); *Yorkshire Post* (22 September 1922).

[52] *Yorkshire Post* (25 September 1922); *Austen Chamberlain Papers*, Box 32, Younger to Chamberlain (16 September 1922).

[53] *Doncaster Gazette* (13 October 1922); *Aberdeen Daily Journal* (2 October 1922).

[54] *Austen Chamberlain Papers*, AC/33/2/12–14 and 20 [Derby to Chamberlain, 1, 9 and 11 September 1922; Chamberlain to Derby, 7 September 1922; Younger to Chamberlain, 16 September 1922].

[55] Petrie, *Austen Chamberlain*, II 197–8.

[56] Ibid., II 200.

Chapter 6 The Carlton Club Meeting

[1] *Pall Mall Gazette* (13 October 1922).

[2] Ibid. (14 October 1922).

[3] *Bonar Law Papers*, 107/2/62 [G. Armstrong to Viscount Long of Wraxall, 30 September 1922, copy]; Beaverbrook, *Decline of Lloyd George*, 187; *Cabinet Minutes*, CAB 23/32 [7 November 1922].

[4] D'Abernon, *Portraits and Appreciations*, 34–5; *Lloyd George Papers*, F/35/1/31 [McCurdy to Lloyd George, 16 March 1922].

[5] *Bonar Law Papers*, 107/2/68 [Lane-Fox to Law, 14 October 1922]; *South Wales Argus* (17 and 18 October 1922).

[6] *Morning Post* (14 October 1922); *Austen Chamberlain Papers*, AC/33/1/41–43 and 70 [Wilson to Chamberlain, 11 October, Amery to Chamberlain, 18 October 1922, and Chamberlain to Wilson, 13 October 1922]; Griffith-Boscawen, *Memories*, 251–2.

[7] Amery, *My Political Life*, II 237.

[8] James, *Memoirs Of A Conservative*, 122–3; *Buckingham Advertiser* (21 October 1922); *West London Press* (27 October 1922; *Bonar Law Papers*, 107/2/69 [Sir Evelyn Cecil to Law, 18 October 1922].

[9] *Gleanings and Memoranda* (November 1922) 486.

[10] *Balfour Papers*, Add. MSS. 49693 [Minute of conversation between Balfour and Bonar Law, 22 December 1922]; A. C. Murray, *Master and Brother*, 185.

[11] *H. A. L. Fisher Papers*, Diary, 8 October 1922; Harris, *Forty Years in and out of Parliament*, 93; *Finchley Press* (3 November 1922); *Buckingham Advertiser* (4 November 1922); H. A. Taylor, *Jix*, 161; *Morning Post* (19 October 1922).

[12] *Cambridge Independent Press* (3 March 1922); *The Times* (13 and 23 March 1922); *Austen Chamberlain Papers* [Pilditch to Chamberlain, 7 and 19 September 1922]; *Middlesex Advertiser* (22 September 1922); *Torbay Express* (13 October 1922); *Western Independent* (22 October 1922).

[13] *Morning Post* (31 October 1922; Beaverbrook, *Decline of Lloyd George*, 134; *Yorkshire Post* (11 and 26 October 1922); *Exeter Express and Echo* (30 October 1922); *South Wales Argus* (20 October 1922).

[14] *Morning Post* (19 October 1922).

[15] G. Murray, *A Man's Life*, 263–4; *Morning Post* (31 October 1922).

[16] There are two slightly different accounts of this incident in G. Murray, op. cit., 264, and Beaverbrook, *Decline of Lloyd George*, 200.

[17] Blake, *Unknown Prime Minister*, 73; *Austen Chamberlain Papers*, AC/32/2/114 and AC/33/2/95 [Chamberlain to Pike Pease, 20 October 1922, and to Wilson, 22 November 1922].

[18] Unless otherwise stated, all references to the speeches at the Carlton Club Meeting come from *Gleanings and Memoranda*, November 1922, 487–95.

[19] Amery, *My Political Life*, II 238; *Ludlow Advertiser* (4 November 1922); Hemingford, *Backbencher and Chairman*.

[20] G. Murray, op. cit., 265; H. A. Taylor, *Jix*, 161; *H. A. L. Fisher Papers*, Diary, 19 October 1922; *Bonar Law Papers*, 107/2/72 [Fraser to Law, 20 October 1922].

[21] *Austen Chamberlain Papers*, AC/33/2/95 [Chamberlain to Wilson, 22 November 1922].

[22] Ibid., AC/33/2/102 [Ford to Chamberlain, 19 October 1922].

[23] The seven were M.P.s (numbered as in Appendix I): 29, 49, 75, 116, 139, 151 and 188. The five faced with independent Conservative opposition were: 99, 110, 121, 203 and 351.

[24] Beaverbrook, *Decline of Lloyd George*, 191.

[25] *Austen Chamberlain Papers*, AC/33/2/76 [Cockerill to Chamberlain, 17 October 1922].

Chapter 7 The uncertain trumpet: political confusion in early November 1922

[1] *Manchester Guardian* (13 November 1922); *J. L. Garvin Papers*, 1922 domestic politics notebook; *Nation* (11 November 1922).

[2] *The Times* (9 November 1922); *Daily Mail* (1 November 1922); *Doncaster Gazette* (10 November 1922).

[3] *South Wales Argus* (11 October 1922).

[4] *Gloucester Journal* (21 October 1922).

[5] See, for instance, the Diehard remarks on beer in *Yorkshire Post* (9 September and 8 November 1922); *Yorkshire Evening*

Press (1 July 1922); *Oxford Times* (3 November 1922); *Maidenhead Advertiser* (1 November 1922); *Gloucester Journal* (4 November 1922); *Huntingdonshire Post* (2 November 1922); and *Doncaster Gazette* (10 November 1922). The last also reported that some Doncaster Diehards extended their interest to ginger beer.

[6] Amery, *My Political Life*, II 241; *The Times* (24, 26 October and 1 November 1922).

[7] *Gleanings and Memoranda* (December 1922) 554; Gaunt, *Yield of the Years*, 278.

[8] *South Wales Argus* (12 and 17 October 1922); *Morning Post* (18 October 1922); *The Times* (11 and 14 November 1922); *Liverpool Post* (10 November 1922).

[9] *Scotsman* (30 October 1922); *The Times* (1 November 1922); *Pontefract Advertiser* (30 September, 1 and 4 November 1922).

[10] *Bristol Adventurer* (3 November 1922).

[11] *The Times* (1 November 1922); *Yorkshire Post* (7 November 1922); *Doncaster Gazette* (3 and 10 November 1922).

[12] Amery, *Thoughts on the Constitution*, 16.

[13] Salvidge, *Salvidge of Liverpool*, 238; *Reading Papers*, EUR/E/238/5 [Peel to Reading, 25 October 1922].

[14] *Bristol Evening News* (11 November 1922); *East London Observer* (11 November 1922); *The Times* (9 November 1922); *Stirling Observer* (26 October 1922); *Dumbarton Herald* (1 November 1922); *Accrington Gazette* (28 October 1922); *Maidenhead Advertiser* (1 November 1922).

[15] *Liverpool Post* (26 October 1922); *North Berks Herald* (1 November 1922); *Southeastern Gazette* (3 and 14 November 1922); *Berkshire Chronicle* (2 June 1922); *Oxford Mail* (10 November 1922).

[16] *Bulwell Local News* (11 November 1922); *Hackney Gazette* (1 November 1922).

[17] *Chorley Guardian* (4 November 1922); *Northampton Daily Chronicle* (21 July, 28 October, 3 and 6 November 1922).

[18] *Hexham Herald* (28 October 1922); *Monmouthshire Beacon* (27 October 1922); *Finchley Press* (7 July, 20, 30 October and 3 November 1922); *West Kent Argus* (3 November 1922); *Leicester Daily Mercury* (30 October 1922); *Salisbury Times* (27 October 1922).

[19] *Morning Post* (16 October 1922); *Southern Daily Echo* (19 October 1922).

[20] *Beckenham Journal* (11 November 1922).

[21] *Liverpool Post* (10 November 1922).

[22] The figures for turn-out in 1918 and 1922 which have been published previously have been based on the assumption that voters in the two-member constituencies each cast two votes. In fact there were numerous 'plumpers', and taking this into account affects the turn-out figures considerably. The figures given here count all 'plumpers'.

Chapter 8 The general election of 1922

[1] H. A. L. *Fisher Papers*, Diary, 19 October 1922.

[2] *The Times* (21 October 1922).

[3] *The Times* (23 October 1922); *Dundee Advertiser* (23 October 1922); H. A. L. *Fisher Papers*, Diary (22 October 1922); *Lloyd George Papers*, F/37/2/6 [Mond to Lloyd George, undated, but written during the 1922 election].

[4] Amery, *My Political Life*, II 241–2, 245.

[5] *The Times* (21 and 23 October 1922).

[6] *The Times* (24 October 1922).

[7] Ibid.

[8] *The Times* (28 October 1922); Croft, *My Life of Strife*, 165; *Morning Post* (6 November 1922).

[9] Unadjusted relief figures were published in *The Ministry of Labour Gazette*, December 1922; the figures cited here are based on November 1918 as 'full employment'. The local election results for London in 1922 were published in *The Times* (3 November 1922). Beatrice Webb's comments on Poplarism may be found in unpublished portions of her diary for 17 September 1920.

[10] *Worcester Herald* (2 November 1922).

[11] Young, *Balfour*, 428. Sassoon was noted as a political host for the Coalitionists.

[12] *Chronicle* (1 November 1922); *The Times* (2 November 1922).

[13] *The Times* (10 November 1922).

[14] *The Times* (10 and 11 November 1922).

[15] *The Times* (13 November 1922); *Westminster Record* (7 January and 4 February 1922).

[16] *The Times* (13 November 1922); R. Churchill, *Derby*, 467.

[17] *Manchester Guardian* (6 November 1922); R. Churchill, *Derby*, 465–70.

[18] *The Times* (4 and 6 November 1922).

[19] *Cabinet Minutes*, CAB 23/32 [1 November 1922].

[20] *Chronicle* (10 November 1922).

[21] *Chronicle* (8 November 1922); *The Times* (8 November 1922); *Manchester Guardian* (7 November 1922); *Cabinet Minutes*, CAB 23/32 [7 and 8 November 1922].

[22] *J. L. Garvin Papers*, 1922 domestic politics notebook; *Cabinet Minutes*, CAB 23/32 [1 November 1922].

[23] *Cabinet Minutes*, CAB 23/32 [7 November 1922].

[24] *The Times* (15 November 1922).

[25] *Sunderland Daily Echo* (9 November 1922); *The Times* (9 November 1922); *Beckenham Journal* (11 November 1922).

[26] Hicks, Hicks and Postan, *The Taxation of War Wealth*, 212; Macartney, *Hungary and her Successors*, 73–250, examines the Czech economy and national questions affecting the levy there.

[27] *Liberal Magazine* (February 1920) 21; Dalton, *The Capital Levy Explained*, 89; *The Times* (14 November 1917); 5 H.C. Debates, 101, col. 1502 [27 January 1918].

[28] 5 H.C. Debates, 116, cols 341–2 [20 May 1919]; 130, cols 323–6 [8 June 1920]; *Liberal Magazine* (June 1919) 262 and (April 1920) 133; *H.C. Paper* 102 of 1920.

[29] Pethick-Lawrence, *The Capital Levy*, 6; Hicks, Hicks and Postan, op. cit., 218.

[30] *The Times* (4 November 1922).

[31] *The Times* (7 November 1922); *The Campaign Guide, 1922*, 528. A second edition of this volume will shortly be published by the Harvester Press.

[32] Dalton, *The Capital Levy Explained*, 89.

[33] Cf. for instance, Nicholas, *The British General Election of 1950*, 284–5; Butler, *The British General Election of 1951*, 239; Butler and Rose, *The British General Election of 1959*, 105; and Butler and King, *The British General Election of 1964*, 208.

Chapter 9 Lloyd George and Welsh politics

[1] Morgan, *David Lloyd George*, 9.

[2] *E. T. John Papers*, Evans to John, 30 August 1920.

[3] Morgan, *Wales in British Politics, 1868–1922*, 109, 115.

[4] *Agricultural Statistics for England and Wales* (1921) iii 42–4.

[5] *J. Bryn Roberts Papers*, undated memorandum of *c*. 1923–4.

[6] Riddell, *More Pages from my Diary*, 64; *E. T. John Papers*, Evans to John (6 November 1920).

[7] *Liverpool Post* (5 April 1920 and 28 February 1921).

[8] *E. T. John Papers*, Evans to John, 19 March 1915 and 11 October 1920.

[9] Ibid., Evans to John, 19 March 1915.

[10] Ibid., Evans to John, 30 August 1920.

[11] *D. R. Daniel Papers*, MS. biography of Lloyd George, 12, 14 and 19.

[12] 2nd Earl Lloyd-George, *Lloyd George*, 56–7; *D. R. Daniel Papers*, MS. biography of Lloyd George, 65.

[13] *D. R. Daniel Papers*, MS. biography of Lloyd George, 9 and 18.

[14] Ibid., 38–41, 45, 47; Daniel's diary, 19 and 20 November 1917; 5 May and 11 November 1918; 14 July 1920; 2 March and 19 October 1922; undated memorandum at end of diary for 1922.

[15] *D. M. Richards Papers*, Reports of Aberdare Liberal Club, 1906–1912; *Liberal Magazine* (February 1921) 21.

[16] *Liberal Magazine* (February 1921) 21 and (March 1921) 135; *E. T. John Papers*, Evans to John, 30 August, 11 and 16 October and 15 November 1920.

[17] *Liverpool Post* (30 May 1921 and 16 and 30 January 1922); *E. M. Humphreys Papers*, D. M. Rees to Humphreys (7 August 1923).

[18] *E. T. John Papers*, Evans to John, 14 May 1920; *Liverpool Post* (31 May and 7 June 1920); *Manchester Guardian* (1 January 1921); *E. M. Humphreys Papers*, H. Rees to R. H. Davies, 16 June 1920 (copy).

[19] *Manchester Guardian* (12, 15 and 21 January 1921).

[20] Ibid. (26 January 1921).

[21] *Liverpool Post* (24 January, 1921).

272

[22] *Manchester Guardian* (27 and 28 January and 11, 15, 18 and 19 February 1921).

[23] Ibid. (8, 9, 11, 12 and 14 February 1921); *E. T. John Papers*, John to G. Davies, 14 April 1923.

[24] *Carnarvon and Denbigh Herald* (22 and 29 November and 13 December 1918).

[25] Ibid. (22 and 29 November and 6 December 1918).

[26] Ibid. (3 November 1922); *Liverpool Post* (24 October and 7 and 19 December 1921); *E. M. Humphreys Papers*, Davies to Humphreys 13 December 1921.

[27] *Carnarvon and Denbigh Herald* (1 and 29 November and 6 December 1918); 10 and 17 November 1922; *South Wales Evening Express* (10 November 1922).

Chapter 10 The victory of the second eleven

[1] Conservatives won because of Liberal splits in: East Ham North, Portsmouth Central, Sunderland (1) and Sudbury. Labour won because of Liberal splits in: Bermondsey West, Bradford East, Cannock, Clay Cross, Don Valley, Hanley, Leicester West, Newcastle East and West and Walthamstow North.

[2] *Nation* (25 November 1922) 308; *Pall Mall Gazette* (14 April 1923).

[3] *Torbay Express* (27 October 1922); *Birkenhead Advertiser* (28 October and 2 November 1922); *Manchester Guardian* (19 March 1921 and 18 January and 8 and 10 November 1922).

[4] *Liberal Magazine* (June 1922) 355, 358; (January 1923) 17; (August 1923) 453.

[5] *National Review* (February 1922) 784.

[6] Marchioness Curzon, *Reminiscences*, 170; *Gleanings and Memoranda* (October 1923) 351–2.

[7] Quoted by A. G. Gardiner in *Certain People of Importance*, 138; Salvidge, *Salvidge of Liverpool*, 239.

[8] Blake, *Unknown Prime Minister*, 494; Wrench, *Geoffrey Dawson and our Times*, 215.

[9] Eyck, *Weimar Republic*, I 231; *The Times* (27 October 1922).

[10] The House of Lords decided in favour of the tenants in the decision of *Kerr v. Bryde*; cf. *Journals of the House of Lords* (3 November 1922) 388.

[11] *5 H.C. Debates*, 164, cols 860 and 864 [28 May 1923].

[12] Fitzroy, *Diary*, II 795–6.

[13] *Annual Register, 1923*, 94.

[14] *Austen Chamberlain Papers*, AC/35/2/2 and 11a [Worthington-Evans to Chamberlain, 22 May 1923; memorandum by Chamberlain, 23 May 1923].

[15] Jenkins, *Asquith*, 496.

[16] *Liberal Magazine* (March 1923) 132.

[17] Ibid. (January 1923) 11.

[18] *The Times* (2 December 1925); *Liberal Magazine* (January 1923) 12.

[19] *Liberal Magazine* (January 1923) 12; (April 1923) 210; *Chronicle* (7 and 8 November 1922); *C. P. Scott's Diary*, ed. Wilson, 437, 8 March 1923.

[20] *Liberal Magazine* (July 1923) 383, 422–3; Kenworthy, *Sailors, Statesmen and Others*, 222; Hyde, *Strong for Service*, 113.

[21] *Edinburgh Evening News* (14 February 1923); *C. P. Scott's Diary*, ed. Wilson, 439–41 (9 March 1923); *Liberal Magazine* (May 1919) 213.

[22] *Letters from the Earl of Oxford and Asquith to a Friend*, II 37.

[23] *C. P. Scott's Diary*, ed. Wilson, 437 (29 January 1923); *Liberal Magazine* (June 1923) 357.

[24] *Liberal Magazine* (June 1923) 354–7.

[25] Ibid. (March 1923) 123; (July 1923) 421–2; *Letters from the Earl of Oxford and Asquith to a Friend*, II 84–5.

[26] *Nation* (29 May 1920) 273.

[27] *Foreign Affairs* (October 1928) 59.

Bibliography

I Manuscript Sources

H. H. Asquith Papers, Bodleian Library, Oxford.
A. J. Balfour Papers, British Museum.
General MSS. 1125, University of Bangor.
A. Bonar Law Papers, Beaverbrook Library, London.
C. E. Breese Papers, National Library of Wales, Aberystwyth.
James Bryce Papers, Bodleian Library, Oxford.
Cabinet Office Records, Public Record Office.
Carnarvon Boroughs Voters Lists, Bangor.
Carnarvonshire Local Information Committee Records, Bangor.
Cecil of Chelwood Papers, British Museum.
Austen Chamberlain Papers, Birmingham University Library.
Viscount d'Abernon Papers, British Museum.
Hugh Dalton Papers, London School of Economics.
D. R. Daniel Papers, National Library of Wales.
G. M. Lloyd-Davies Papers, National Library of Wales.
Denbigh and Flint Boroughs Amalgamation letters, 1917, National Library of Wales.
Sir Richard Denman Papers, Newcastle University Library.
Viscount Elibank Papers [A. C. Murray], National Library of Scotland, Edinburgh.
J. L. Garvin Papers, University of Texas Library, Austin, Texas.
Ellis Griffith Papers, National Library of Wales.
A. D. Evans Papers, National Library of Wales.
T. J. Evans Papers, National Library of Wales.
Vincent Evans Papers, National Library of Wales.
H. A. L. Fisher Papers, Bodleian Library.
Frondirion Miscellany, National Library of Wales.
Viscount Gladstone Papers, British Museum.

E. Morgan Humphreys Papers, Bangor.

R. B. Haldane Papers, National Library of Scotland.

P. J. Hannon Papers, Beaverbrook Library.

E. T. John Papers, National Library of Wales.

H. Haydn Jones Papers, National Library of Wales.

William Jones Papers, Bangor.

Labour Club Records, Fitzwilliam Library, Cambridge.

Lancashire, Cheshire, and Northwestern Liberal Federation Records, Offices of the Federation, Manchester.

George Lansbury Papers, London School of Economics.

Leeds Liberal Federation Records, Leeds Central Library.

Leicester Liberal Federation Records, Leicester Museum.

Llandwynda Liberal Association Records, National Library of Wales.

Sir John Lloyd Papers, Bangor.

David Lloyd George Papers, Beaverbrook Library.

Marquess of Lothian Papers, Scottish Record Office, Edinburgh.

T. J. Macnamara Speeches (1921), National Library of Wales.

Viscount Milner Papers, Bodleian Library.

Miscellany 10362 E, National Library of Wales.

Edwin Montagu Papers, India Office Library, London.

E. D. Morel Papers, London School of Economics.

Sir John Morris-Jones Papers, Bangor.

Murray of Elibank Papers [Alex Murray], National Library of Scotland.

North Cumberland Liberal Association Minutes, Offices of the association, Carlisle.

Viscount Pontypridd Papers, Cardiff Central Library.

Marquess of Reading Papers, India Office Library.

J. Bryn Roberts Papers, National Library of Wales.

Scottish Liberal Federation Records, Edinburgh University Library.

J. A. Spender Papers, British Museum.

Sir Arthur Steel-Maitland Papers, Scottish Record Office.

Sheffield Trades and Labour Council Records, Offices of the council, Sheffield.

Society of Certified and Associated Liberal Agents Records, Leeds Central Library.

Viscount Templewood Papers, India Office Library.

E. L. H. Turner Miscellany, National Library of Wales.

C. P. Trevelyan Papers, Newcastle University Library.
Lord Wargrave Papers, Beaverbrook Library.
Beatrice Webb Papers, London School of Economics
Yorkshire Liberal Federation Records, Leeds Central Library.

II Newspapers (short titles)

National metropolitan newspapers : *Daily Chronicle, Daily Express, Daily Herald, Daily Mail, Morning Post, Daily News, Pall Mall Gazette, Sunday Chronicle, Sunday Graphic, Sunday Pictorial, Daily Telegraph, The Times, Westminster Gazette.*

Bedfordshire : *Bedford County Record* (Bedford), *Bedfordshire Standard* (Bedford), *Luton News.*

Berkshire : *Berkshire Chronicle* (Reading), *Maidenhead Advertiser, Newbury Weekly News, North Berks Herald* (Abingdon), *Reading Standard.*

Buckinghamshire : *Buckingham Advertiser.*

Cambridgeshire : *Cambridge Independent Press.*

Cheshire : *Altrincham Advertiser, Birkenhead Advertiser, Cheshire Daily Echo* (Stockport), *Crewe Chronicle.*

Cornwall : *Cornish Echo* (Falmouth), *Cornish Post* (Camborne), *Newquay Express.*

Cumberland : *West Cumberland News* (Whitehaven).

Derbyshire : *Derby Daily Telegraph, Derbyshire Courier* (Chesterfield), *North Cheshire and North Derbyshire Advertiser* (Glossop).

Devon : *Express and Echo* (Exeter), *Tavistock Gazette, Tiverton Gazette, Torbay Express* (Torquay), *Western Evening Herald* (Plymouth), *Western Independent* (Plymouth).

Dorset : *Blandford and East Dorset Herald, Dorset County Chronicle* (Dorchester).

Durham : *Northern Evening Despatch* (Darlington), *Hartlepools Labour News* (November & December 1922 only), *Morpeth Herald, Northern Daily Mail* (West Hartlepool), *North Star* (Darlington), *Seaham Weekly News, Sunderland Daily Echo, Washington Labour News.*

Essex : *Epping Advertiser, Essex Chronicle* (Chelmsford), *Essex Newsman* (Chelmsford), *Ilford Argus, Leytonstone Express and Independent, Walthamstow Monitor, West Essex Gazette* (Epping). Also see under London local newspapers.

Gloucestershire : *Bristol Adventurer, Bristol Evening News, Gloucester Journal, Gloucestershire Echo* (Cheltenham), *South Gloucestershire Chronicle* (Thornbury), *Stroud News, Tewkesbury Register, Western Daily Press* (Bristol).

Hampshire : *Aldershot Gazette, Hants and Berks Gazette* (Basingstoke), *Southern Daily Echo* (Southampton), *Evening News* (Portsmouth).

Herefordshire : *Hereford Journal, Ross Gazette.*

Hertfordshire : *Hertfordshire Record* (Hertford), *West Herts Post* (Watford).

Huntingdonshire : *Huntingdonshire Post.*

Isle of Ely : *Cambridge Independent Press, Ely Edition.*

Isle of Wight : *Isle of Wight Observer* (Ryde).

Kent : *Bromley Mercury, Chatham, Rochester and Gillingham News, Dartford Chronicle, Gravesend and Dartford Reporter, Kentish Express* (Ashford), *Rochester, Chatham and Gillingham Journal, Sevenoaks Chronicle, Sevenoaks Courier, Southeastern Gazette* (Maidstone), *West Kent Advertiser* (Dartford).

Lancashire : *Accrington Gazette, Accrington Observer, Ashton-under-Lyne Herald, Bacup Times, Barrow Guardian, Blackburn Catholic News, Blackburn Times, Blackburn Weekly Telegraph, Bolton and Bury Catholic Herald, Bolton Evening News, Bootle Herald, Burnley Express, Bury Guardian, Chorley Guardian, Clitheroe Advertiser, Lancashire Daily Post* (Preston), *Leigh Chronicle, Liverpool Daily Post, Manchester Evening News, Manchester Guardian, Nelson Leader, Newton Guardian, Oldham Chronicle, Radcliffe Times, Southport Guardian, Southport Journal, Western Telegraph* (Urmston).

Leicestershire : *Coalville Times, Hinckley Times, Leicester Chronicle, Leicester Daily Mercury, Leicester Mail, Melton Mowbray Times.*

Lincolnshire and Rutland : *Boston Guardian, Grimsby Daily Telegraph, Horncastle News, Lincoln Gazette, Stamford and Rutland News* (Stamford).

London local newspapers : *Balham Tooting and Mitcham News, Daily Gazette* (Islington), *Dulwich Reporter, East London Observer* (Stepney), *Fulham Chronicle, Hackney Gazette, Hampstead Advertiser, Holloway Press, Ilford Recorder, Kentish Independent* (Woolwich), *Lewisham Borough News, Marylebone Record, St. Pancras Chronicle, St. Pancras Guardian, South*

London Observer (Camberwell), *South London Press* (South-wark), *Southwark and Bermondsey Recorder, Southwark Labour News* (March 1921 only), *Southwestern Star* (Battersea), *Wandsworth Borough News, West Ham Express, West London Press* (Chelsea), *Westminster Record, Woolwich Gazette, Woolwich Herald.* Also see under Essex, Kent, Middlesex, and Surrey.

Middlesex : *Finchley Press, Harrow Observer, Hornsey Journal, Middlesex Advertiser* (Uxbridge), *Tottenham and Edmonton Herald, West Middlesex Times* (Staines), *Willesden Citizen.* Also see under London local newspapers.

Norfolk : *Eastern Daily Press* (Norwich), *Holt Post, Lynn News, Norfolk Chronicle* (Norwich), *Norwich Mercury.*

Northamptonshire : *Daventry Express, Daily Echo* (Northampton), *Northampton Daily Chronicle, Peterborough Citizen.*

Northumberland : *Blyth News, Hexham Courant, Hexham Herald, Newcastle Daily Chronicle.*

Nottinghamshire : *Mansfield Reporter, Nottingham Guardian, Nottingham and Bulwell Local News, Nottinghamshire Guardian* (Nottingham).

Oxfordshire : *Banbury Guardian, Henley Standard, Oxford Chronicle, Oxford Times.*

Shropshire : *Ludlow Advertiser, Shrewsbury Outlook, Wellington Journal.*

Somerset : *Bath Chronicle, Pulman's Weekly News* (Yeovil), *Somerset Journal* (Frome), *Three Shires Advertiser* (Yeovil), *Wells Journal, Weston-super-Mare Gazette.*

Staffordshire : *Hanley Evening Sentinel, Midland Counties Express* (Wolverhampton), *Staffordshire Chronicle* (Hanley), *Staffordshire Sentinel* (Stafford), *Wolverhampton Chronicle.*

Suffolk : *Bury and Norwich Post* (Bury St. Edmunds), *Framlingham Weekly News, Lowestoft Journal, Suffolk and Essex Free Press* (Sudbury), *Suffolk Chronicle and Mercury* (Ipswich).

Surrey : *Beckenham Journal, Croydon Advertiser, Surrey Weekly Press, Surrey Weekly Press, Guildford Edition.* Also see London local newspapers.

Sussex : *Chichester Observer, Evening Argus* (Brighton), *Horsham Guardian.*

Warwickshire : *Birmingham Gazette, Birmingham Post, Coventry Herald, Nuneaton Chronicle, People's Tribune* (Nuneaton), *Rugby Observer, Stratford-upon-Avon Herald, Warwick Advertiser.*

Westmorland : *Westmorland Gazette* (Kendal).

Wiltshire : *North Wilts Herald* (Swindon), *Salisbury Times, Swindon Evening Advertiser, Wiltshire Gazette* (Devizes), *Wiltshire Times* (Trowbridge).

Worcestershire : *County Express* (Stourbridge), *Evesham Journal, Worcester Herald.*

Yorkshire : *Barnsley Independent, Batley Reporter, Beverley Guardian, Bradford Daily Argus, Brighouse Free Press, Doncaster Gazette, Goole Journal, Howdenshire Chronicle* (Pocklington), *Howdenshire Gazette* (Goole), *Hull Daily Mail, Northeastern Daily Gazette* (Middlesbrough), *Pateley Bridge and Nidderdale Herald, Pontefract Advertiser, Pudsey and Stanningley News, Ripon Observer, Sheffield Independent, Shipley Times, Todmorden Advertiser, Todmorden and District News, Yorkshire Evening News* (Leeds), *Yorkshire Evening Press* (York), *Yorkshire News* (York), *Yorkshire Telegraph and Star* (Sheffield), *Yorkshire Weekly Post* (Leeds), *Wetherby News.*

Wales : *Cambrian News* (Aberystwyth), *Cardiff Times, Carnarvon and Denbigh Herald, Denbighshire Free Press, Llanelly Argus, Merioneth County Times, Monmouthshire Beacon, Montgomery County Times, North Wales Guardian* (Wrexham), *Radnor Express, Rhyl Guardian, South Wales Argus* (Newport), *South Wales Evening Express* (Cardiff), *Welsh Gazette* (Aberystwyth), *Western Mail* (Cardiff).

Scotland : *Aberdeen Daily Journal, Alloa Journal, Berwick Mercury, Dumbarton Herald, Dundee Advertiser, Dundee and District Jute and Flax Workers' Guide, Edinburgh Evening News, Falkirk Herald, Football Times* (Inverness; not a sports newspaper), *Glasgow Herald, Greenock Herald, Hawick News, Highland News* (Inverness), *Johnstone Advertiser, Kinross-shire Advertiser* (Kinross), *Largs. and Millport Weekly News, Northern Times* (Caithness), *Red Commune* (Glasgow; suppressed after one issue of February 1921), *Scotsman* (Edinburgh), *Socialist* (Glasgow), *Stirling Observer, Stornoway Gazette, The Worker* (Glasgow).

Other periodicals : *Army Quarterly, Cavalry Journal, C.O.'s Hansard* (wartime), *Economist, Fortnightly Review, Royal United Services Institution Journal, Labour Monthly, Nation,*

National Review, New Statesman, Nineteenth Century and After, Ploughshare (wartime), *Punch, Review of Reviews, Saturday Review, Socialist Standard, Spectator, Tribunal* (wartime), *Wipers Times* (retrospective series).

III Official and Party publications

1   OFFICIAL PUBLICATIONS

Agricultural Statistics.
Census of 1921
House of Commons Debates, 5th Series (referred to as *5 H.C. Deb.*).
House of Commons Journals.
House of Lords Debates, 5th Series (referred to as *5 H.L. Deb.*).
House of Lords Journals.
Ministry of Labour Gazette.

2   PARTY PUBLICATIONS

Campaign Guide, 1922. Conservative central office. New edition by M. Kinnear.
The Communist. Communist Party.
Essays on Liberalism. Liberal publication dept. [L.P.D.] (1922).
Gleanings and Memoranda. Conservative central office (monthly).
How to Conquer Unemployment. Labour Party (1929).
Labour and the New Social Order. Labour Party (1918).
Labour and the Russian–Polish War. Labour Party (1920).
Labour Speakers' Handbook. Labour Party (1922).
Liberal Magazine. L.P.D. (monthly).
Liberal Pamphlets and Leaflets. L.P.D. (annually).
Liberal Policy. L.P.D. (1918).
Liberal Year Book. L.P.D. (annually).
Lloyd George Liberal Magazine (published 1920–3).
1916–1920: The Lloyd George Coalition in war and peace. L. J. Gooding for the Lloyd George Liberals (1920).
Reports of the Annual Conferences of the Labour Party (referred to as R.A.C.L.P.).

IV Books on the Conservative Party

1 BOOKS ON AND BY CONSERVATIVES ACTIVE IN 1918–22

L. C. M. S. Amery (Birmingham-Sparkbrook, 1918 and 1922), *National Imperial Economics* (1923).

——, *A Plan of Action* (1932).

——, *The Forward View* (1935).

——, *The Framework of the Future* (1944).

——, *Thoughts on the Constitution* (1947).

——, *The Awakening* (1948).

——, *My Political Life*, 3 vols (1953 et seq.).

——, *A Balanced Economy* (1954).

Stanley Baldwin (Worcs.-Bewdley, 1918 and 1922), *Our Inheritance* (1928).

——, *Service of our Lives* (1937).
    My Father: The True Story, by A. W. Baldwin (1955).
    Stanley Baldwin, by J. Barnes and R. Middlemas (1969).
    Stanley Baldwin, A Tribute, by Sir Arthur Bryant (1937).
    Stanley Baldwin: Man or Miracle? by B. Roberts (1936).
    Stanley Baldwin, by A. G. Whyte (1926).
    Stanley Baldwin, by G. M. Young (1952).

A. J. Balfour (City of London, 1918, then peer), *Writings Speculative and Political* (New York, 1921).

——, *Chapters of Autobiography*, ed. B. Dugdale (1930).
    Arthur James Balfour, by B. Dugdale. 2 vols (1926).
    Balfour's Burden, by A. Gollin (1965).
    Lord Balfour: A Memory, by I. Malcolm (1930).
    Mr. Balfour, by E. T. Raymond (1920).
    Arthur James Balfour, by K. Young (1963).

Lord Beaverbrook, *Politicians and the Press* (n.d.).

——, *Politicians and the War*, 2 vols (1928 and 1932).

——, *Men and Power, 1917–1918* (1956).

——, *The Decline and Fall of Lloyd George and Great was the Fall Thereof* (referred to as *Decline of Lloyd George*) (1963).
    Beaverbrook, by T. Driberg (1956).

Lord Birkenhead, *Toryism* (New York, 1903).

——, *Speeches, 1906–1909* (Liverpool, 1910).

——, *Unionist Policy* (1913).

Lord Birkenhead, *The Destruction of Merchant Ships under International Law* (1917).
——, *Points of View*, 2 vols (1922 and 1923).
——, *Contemporary Personalities* (1924).
——, *Speeches* (1929).
——, *Last Essays* (1930).
    F.E., by 2nd Earl of Birkenhead, 2nd ed. (1959).
    The Glittering Prizes, by W. Camp (1960).
    Lord Birkenhead, by 'Ephesian' (B. Roberts) (1926).
R. Boothby, et al., *Industry and the State* (1927).
Sir H. Brittain (Middlesex-Acton, 1918 and 1922), *Happy Pilgrimage* (n.d.).
Sir W. Bull (Hammersmith South, 1918 and 1922), *Parliamentary Pocketbook* (1920).
Lord Carson (Belfast-Duncairn, 1918; life peer, 1921). *Life of Lord Carson*, by E. Marjoribanks and I. Colvin, 3 vols 1932–6).
Lord Cave. *Lord Cave: A Memoir*, by Sir Charles Mallet (1931).
Lord Hugh Cecil (Oxford University, 1918 and 1922), *Conservatism* (n.d.).
——, *Conservative Ideals* (1924).
Lord Robert Cecil (Herts.-Hitchen, 1918 and 1922), *The New Outlook* (1919).
——, *The Great Experiment: An Autobiography* (1941).
——, *All the Way* (1949).
J. Austen Chamberlain (Birmingham West, 1918 and 1922), and A. J. Balfour, *The Unionist Party and Future Policy* (1922).
——, *Peace in our Time* (Speeches to 1928) (1928).
——, *Politics from Inside* (1936).
——, *Down the Years* (1935).
    The Chamberlain Tradition, by Sir Charles Petrie (1938).
    The Life and Letters of the Right Hon. Sir Austen Chamberlain, by Sir Charles Petrie, 2 vols (1939).
A. Neville Chamberlain (Birmingham-Ladywood, 1918 and 1922).
    The Life of Neville Chamberlain, by K. Feiling (1946).
    Prime Minister Neville Chamberlain, by D. Keith-Shaw (1939).
    Neville Chamberlain, by I. Macleod (1961).

Neville Chamberlain, Man of Peace, by D. Walker-Smith (1939).

Lord Chaplin. *Henry Chaplin, A Memoir*, by Countess Londonderry (1926).

H. W. S. Chilcott (Liverpool-Walton, 1918 and 1922), *Political Salvation, 1930–1932* (1932).

Sir James Craig (Mid-Down, 1918; peer, 1921). *Craigavon: Ulsterman*, by St John Ervine (1949).

Henry Page Croft (Bournemouth, 1918 and 1922), *The War and After* (1919).

——, *My Life of Strife* (n.d.).

A. S. Cunningham-Reid (Warrington, 1922). *He Walks Alone: The Public and Private Life of Captain Cunningham-Reid, M.P., 1922–1945*, by R. J. Ellis (1945).

Marquess of Curzon. *Reminiscences*, by Marchioness Curzon (1955).

 Curzon: The Last Phase, by Harold Nicolson (1934).

 The Life of Lord Curzon, by Lord Ronaldshay, 3 vols (1928).

Earl of Derby. *Lord Derby, 'King' of Lancashire*, by R. Churchill (1959).

Walter Elliott (Lanark-Lanark, 1918 and 1922). *A Companion of Honour*, by Sir Colin Coote (1962).

Lord Ernle, *Whippingham to Westminster* (1938).

J. L. Garvin, *J. L. Garvin: A Memoir*, by K. Garvin (1948).

 The Observer and J. L. Garvin, by A. Gollin (1960).

Admiral Sir Guy Gaunt (Yorks.-Buckrose, 1922), *The Yield of the Years* (1940).

Sir Arthur S. T. Griffith-Boscawen (Dudley, 1918 and 1921; Taunton 1921 and 1922; Mitcham, 1923), *Fourteen Years in Parliament* (1907).

——, *Memories* (1925).

Admiral Sir Reginald Hall (Liverpool-West Derby, 1919 and 1922). *The Eyes of the Navy: A Biographical Study of Admiral Sir Reginald Hall*, by Admiral Sir William James (1955).

D. H. Herbert (Watford, 1918 and 1922), *Backbencher and Chairman* (1946).

W. A. S. Hewins (Swansea West, 1922), *Trade in the Balance* (1924).

W. A. S. Hewins, *Apologia of an Imperialist*, 2 vols (1929).
Sir Ellis Hume-Williams (Notts.-Bassetlaw, 1918 and 1922), *The World, the House, and the Bar* (1930).
Sir William Joynson-Hicks, *Jix*, by H. A. Taylor (1933).
P. K. Kerr-Smiley (Antrim North, 1918), *The Peril of Home Rule* (1922).
A. Bonar Law (Glasgow-Central, 1918 and 1922), *Ambition* (rectorial address, Glasgow University) (1921).
> *The Unknown Prime Minister: The Life and Times of Andrew Bonar Law, 1858–1923*, by Robert Blake (1955).
> *The Strange Case of Andrew Bonar Law*, by H. A. Tayor (n.d.) [?1932].

Viscount Lee of Fareham, *A Good Innings* (privately printed).
Walter Long (Westminster-St George's, 1918; peer, 1921), *Memories* (1923).
Sir J. A. R. Marriott (Oxford City, 1918 and 1922), *Economics and Ethics* (1923).
——, *Memories of Fourscore Years* (1946).
Lord Milner, *Questions of the Hour* (1923).
> *Proconsul in Politics*, by A. Gollin (1964).

Gidean Murray (Glasgow-St Rollox, 1918), *A Man's Life* (1934).
Sir Edward Nicholl (Cornwall-Penryn and Falmouth, 1918).
> *The Life of Commander Sir Edward Nicholl*, by T. C. Wignall (1921).

Sir Charles Oman (Oxford University, 1918 and 1922), *Things I Have Seen* (1933).
Lord Eustace Percy (Hull Central 1919; Hastings 1921 and 1922), *Democracy on Trial* (1931).
——, *Some Memories* (1958).
Sir Gervais Rentoul (Suffolk-Lowestoft, 1922), *This is my Case* (1945).
Sir Archibald Salvidge. *Salvidge of Liverpool*, by S. Salvidge (1934).
Lord Swinton (as Sir Philip Lloyd-Greame ran in Hendon 1918 and 1922; later known as Sir Philip Cunliffe-Lister), *I Remember* (n.d.).
Major-General Sir F. H. Sykes (Sheffield-Hallam, 1922), *From Many Angles* (1942).

Viscount Ullswater (Penrith, 1918; peer, 1921), *A Speaker's Commentaries*, 2 vols (1925).

Sir Herbert Williams (Combined English Universities, 1918; Wednesbury, 1922), *Politics Grave and Gay* (n.d.).

Field-Marshal Sir Henry Wilson (Down North, 1922 by-election).
Field-Marshal Sir Henry Wilson: His Life and Diaries, by Major-General Sir C. Callwell, 2 vols (1927).
Brasshat, by B. Collier (1961).

Earl Winterton (Sussex-Horsham, 1918 and 1922), *Prewar* (1932).

——, *Orders of the Day* (1953).

——, *Fifty Tumultuous Years* (1955).

——, *Near to Greatness* (1965).

E. F. L. Wood (Yorks.-Ripon, 1918 and 1922), *Halifax*, by 2nd Earl of Birkenhead (1965).

2 BOOKS ON THE CONSERVATIVE PARTY

G. D. M. Block, *A Source Book of Conservatism* (1964).

J. A. Bridges, *Reminiscences of a Country Politician* (1906).

Simon Haxey, *Tory M.P.* (1939).

J. D. Hoffman, *The Conservative Party in Opposition, 1945–1951* (1964).

R. B. McDowell, *British Conservatism, 1832–1914* (1959).

R. T. McKenzie and A. Silver, *Angels in Marble: Working class Conservatives in urban England* (Chicago, 1968).

E. A. Nordlinger, *The Working-Class Tories: Authority, Deference, and Stable Democracy* (1967).

Sir Charles Petrie, *Chapters of Life* (1950).

V Books on the Liberal Party

1 BOOKS ON AND BY LIBERALS ACTIVE IN 1918–22.

* Indicates that the politician concerned seceded from the Liberals.

*Christopher Addison (L.G.Lib., then prefixless Lib., Shoreditch, 1918 and 1922), *The Betrayal of the Slums* (1922).

——, *Politics from Within*, 2 vols (1924).

Christopher Addison, *A Policy for British Agriculture* (1939).
>   *Viscount Addison, Leader of the Lords*, by R. J. Minney (1958).

*Percy Alden (Lib., Tottenham North, 1918; Labour, Luton, 1922), *Housing* (1907).

——, 'Unemployment: its causes and remedies', in *Social Science and Social Service* (1909).

H. H. Asquith (East Fife, 1918; Paisley, 1920 and 1922), *Occasional Addresses, 1893–1916* (1918).

——, *The National Debt and the Nation's Duty* (1920).

——, *The Paisley Policy* (1920).

——, and R. McKenna, *Coalition Extravagance* (1920).

——, *The Genesis of the War* (1923).

——, *The Open Road* (1924).

——, *Studies and Sketches* (1924).

——, *Forward Liberalism* (1926).

——, *Scaliger* (1926).

——, *Fifty Years of Parliament*, 2 vols (1926).

——, *Speeches* (1927).

——, *Memories and Reflections*, 2 vols (1928).

——, *Letters from Lord Oxford to a Friend*, ed. D. McCarthy, 2 vols (n.d.).
>   *Mr. Asquith*, by J. P. Alderson (1905).
>   *Life of Herbert Henry Asquith, Lord Oxford and Asquith*, by C. Asquith and J. A. Spender, 2 vols (1932).
>   *Asquith*, by F. Elias (1909).
>   *Asquith*, by R. Jenkins (1964).
>   *Asquith*, by R. B. McCallum (1936).

Margot Asquith, *Autobiography*, 2 vols (1920–2).

——, *More Memories* (1933).

H. T. M. Bell (Asq. Lib., Westminster-St George's, 1918), *The Balance of Life*, by A. Smythe (1955).

Sir E. Benn, *Ernest Benn, Counsel for Liberty*, by D. Abel (1960).

Sir William Beveridge, *Unemployment: A Problem of Industry* (1930).

——, *Tariffs* (1932).

——, *Why I am a Liberal* (1945).

——, *Power and Influence* (1953).

*Winston L. S. Churchill (L.G.Lib., Dundee, 1918 and 1922), *The World Crisis*, 2 vols (1938).

——, *The Aftermath* (1929).

——, *Great Contemporaries* (1937; 1940 ed. used).

Winston Churchill as I Knew Him, by Lady Violet Bonham-Carter (1965).

Winston Churchill, by Randolph Churchill and Martin Gilbert (1966 et seq.) supersedes all previous biographies of Churchill.

A Bibliography of the Works of Sir Winston Churchill, by F. Woods (1963).

Sir Colin Coote (L.G.Lib., Isle of Ely, 1918 and 1922), *Editorial* (1965).

Viscount Cowdray. *Weetman Pearson*, by J. A. Spender (1930).

Marquess of Crewe. *Lord Crewe, 1858–1945: The Likeness of a Liberal*, by J. Pope-Hennessy (1955).

David Davies (prefixless Lib. Montgomery, 1918 and 1922), *Force* (1934).

——, *The Seven Pillars of Peace* (1945).

Sir Joseph Davies (L.G.Lib., Crewe, 1918 and 1922), *The Prime Minister's Secretariat, 1916–1920* (Newport, 1951).

Sir Robert Donald, *Sir Robert Donald*, by H. A. Taylor (n.d.).

H. A. L. Fisher (L.G. Lib., Combined English Universities, 1918 and 1922), *James Bryce*, 2 vols (1927).

——, *An Unfinished Autobiography* (1940).

Herbert Fisher, 1865–1940, by D. Ogg (1947).

B. Freyberg (prefixless Lib., Cardiff South, 1922). *General Lord Freyberg*, by P. Singleton-Gates (1963).

C. B. Fry (prefixless Lib., Brighton, 1922), *Life Worth Living* (1939).

David Lloyd George (L.G.Lib., Carnarvon District, 1918 and 1922), *The People's Budget* (1909).

——, *Through Terror to Triumph*, ed. F. Stevenson (1915).

——, *Is It Peace?* (1923).

——, *Liberalism and Liberty* (1924).

——, *Slings and Arrows, ed. P. Guedalla* (1929).

——, *The Truth about Reparations and War Debts* (New York, 1932).

——, *Organising Prosperity* (1935).

——, *The Truth about the Peace Treaties*, 2 vols (1938).

——, *War Memoirs*, 2 vols (1938).

The Wizard of Wales, by F. Burbridge (1943).

David Lloyd George, *The Man Who DIDN'T Win The War*, by 'Centurion' (1923).

My Lloyd George Diary, by T. Clarke (1939).

Lloyd George: The Man and his Story, by F. Dilnot (1921).

Marconi Scandal, by F. Donaldson (1962).

Life of David Lloyd George, by H. du Parq, 4 vols (1912).

David Lloyd George: The Man and the Statesman, by J. H. Edwards (n.d.).

David Lloyd George, by E. M. Humphreys (1943).

Lloyd George, by 2nd Earl Lloyd-George (1960).

My Brother and I, by William George (1958).

Lloyd George and the War, by 'Independent Liberal' (n.d.) [1917?]

Lloyd George, by T. Jones (1951).

Lloyd George and Co., by D. Low (cartoons) (n.d. [1921?]

The Mask of Merlin, by D. McCormack (1963).

Honours for Sale, by G. Macmillan (1954).

David Lloyd George: A Study, by Sir Charles Mallet (1930).

David Lloyd George, War Minister, by J. S. Mills (1924).

David Lloyd George: Welsh Radical as World Statesman, by K. O. Morgan, Cardiff (1963).

L.G., by B. Murray (1932).

Mr. Lloyd George's Future, by 'Northumbrian' (1920).

Tempestuous Journey, by F. Owen (1954).

The REAL Lloyd George, by G. E. Raine (1913).

Mr. Lloyd George, by E. T. Raymond [E. R. Thompson] (1922).

Mr. Lloyd George and Liberalism, by J. M. Robertson (1923).

Mr. Lloyd George and the War, by W. Roch (1920).

The Prime Minister, by H. Spender (1920).

The Real Lloyd George, by A. J. Sylvester (1947).

David Lloyd George, by M. Thomson (n.d.).

Lloyd George: Rise and Fall, by A. J. P. Taylor, Cambridge (1961).

The 'New' Lloyd George and the 'Old', by E. Walters (1916).

Mr. Lloyd George's Last Fight, by G. West (1930).

Mrs. D. Lloyd George. *Dame Margaret*, by 2nd Earl Lloyd-George (1947).

Countess Lloyd-George, *The Years that are Past* (1967).

Lord Gladstone. *Herbert Gladstone: A Memoir*, by Sir Charles Mallet (1932).

Sir Philip Guedalla (Asq. Lib., Hackney North, 1922), *The Industrial Future: A Liberal Policy* (1921).

Frank Gray (Asq. Lib., Oxford City, 1918 and 1922), *Confessions of a Candidate* (1925).

The Other Oxford, by C. Fenby (1970).

Viscount Grey, *Twenty Five Years*, 2 vols (New York, 1925).

*Sir Edward Grigg (L.G. Lib., Oldham, 1922), *Three Parties or Two: An Appeal to Liberals and Conservatives* (1931).

*Viscount Haldane, *Richard Burton Haldane: An Autobiography* (1929).

Haldane, by Major-General Sir Frederick Maurice (1937).

Haldane of Cloan, by D. Sommer (1960).

Lord Haldane: Scapegoat for Liberalism, by S. Koss (1969).

Sir Percy Harris (Asq. Lib., Bethnal Green South-west, 1922), *Forty Years in and out of Parliament* (1947).

Sir Gordon Hewart (L.G. Lib., Leicester East, 1918; peer, 1922), *The New Despotism* (1929).

——, *Not Without Prejudice* (n.d.) [?1937].

F. W. Hirst, *The Consequences of the War to Great Britain* (1934).

*Austin Hopkinson (L.G. Lib., then independent, Mossley, 1918 and 1922), *The Hope of the Workers* (1923).

*Leslie Hore-Belisha (Asq. Lib., Devonport, 1922). *The Private Papers of Hore-Belisha*, by R. J. Minney (1960).

Sir R. Hudson, *Sir Robert Hudson: A Memoir*, by J. A. Spender (1930).

Lord Inchcape. *Lord Inchcape*, by H. Bolitho (1936).

*J. M. Kenworthy (Asq. Lib., Rotherham, 1918; Central Hull, 1919 and 1922), *Will Civilisation Perish?* (1927).

——, *Sailors, Statesmen, and Others* (1933).

J. M. Keynes, *The Economic Consequences of the Peace* (1919).

——, *Mr. Lloyd George's General Election* (1920).

——, *Reconstruction in Europe*, 12 sections (1922–3).

J. M. Keynes, *A Revision of the Treaty: Being a Sequel to the Economic Consequences of the Peace* (1922).

——, *The Economic Consequences of Mr. Churchill.* Published in the U.S.A. as *The Economic Consequences of Sterling Parity* (1925).

——, and H. D. Henderson, *Can Lloyd George Do It? The Pledge Examined* (1929).

——, *The General Theory of Employment, Interest, and Money* (1936).

——, *Essays in Biography* (1951).

The Carthaginian Peace, or the Economic Consequences of Mr. Keynes, by E. Mantoux (1946).

The Life of Lord Keynes, by Sir Roy Harrod (1951).

Viscount Knutsford, *In Black and White* (1926).

O. F. Maclagan (Asq. Lib., then L.G. Lib., Rugby, 1918), *Coalition Government: A League of Parties as an Efficient Method of Government* (1922).

T. J. Macnamara (L.G. Lib., Camberwell North-west, 1918, 1920 and 1922), *Tariff Reform and the Working Man* (1910).

——, *Labour at the Crossroads* (1923).

C. F. G. Masterman (Asq. Lib., West Ham-Stratford, 1918; Clay Cross, 1922), *England after the War* (1923).

C. F. G. Masterman: A Biography, by L. Masterman (1939).

Reginald McKenna (Asq. Lib., Pontypool, 1918), *Postwar Banking Policy* (1928).

The Life of Reginald McKenna, 1868–1943: A Memoir, by S. McKenna (1948).

*Sir Alfred Mond (L.G. Lib., then prefixless Lib., Swansea East, 1918 and 1922), *Why Socialism Must Fail* (1923).

——, *Socialism: What it Really is* (1923).

——, *Liberalism and Modern Industrial Probems* (Llanelly, 1925).

——, *Industry and Politics* (1927).

——, *Imperial Economic Unity* (1930).

Alfred Mond: First Viscount Melchett, by H. Bolitho (1933).

*Sir Leo G. Chiozza Money, *Elements of the Fiscal Problem* (1903).

——, *Riches and Poverty* (1905).

——, *The Nation's Wealth* (n.d.).

——, *Things that Matter: Papers upon Subjects which are, or ought to be, under Discussion* (1912).

——, *The Triumph of Nationalisation* (1920).

——, *Can War be Averted?* (1931).

*Sir John Morris-Jones, *Doctor in the Whips' Room* (1955).

Ramsay Muir (Asq. Lib., Rochdale, 1922), *Liberalism and Industry* (1920).

——, *Government under the Three-Party System* (1929).

——, *How Britain is Governed* (1930).

——, *Trade Unionism and the Trade Union Bill* (n.d. [?1927].

——, *The Record of the National Government* (1936).

A. C. Murray (L.G. Lib., then prefixless Lib., Kincardine and West Aberdeen, 1918 and 1922), *Master and Brother: Murrays of Elibank* (1945).

——, *At Close Quarters* (1946).

*H. Nathan (ed.), *Liberal Points of View* (1927).
    Strong for Service: Lord Nathan of Churt, by H. M. Hyde (1968).

W. R. Nicholl, *William Robertson Nicholl: Life and Letters*, by T. H. Darlow (1925).

Marquess of Reading. *Rufus Isaacs, First Marquess of Reading*, by 2nd Marquess, 2 vols (1943 and 1945).

Sir J. Tudor Rees (Asq. Lib., then L.G. Lib., Barnstaple, 1918 and 1922), *Reserved Judgment* (1956).

Viscount Rhondda. *Life of Viscount Rhondda*, by J. V. Morgan (1918).

Lord Riddell, *Lord Riddell's War Diary* (1933).

——, *Lord Riddell's Intimate Diary of the Peace Conference and After* (1933).

——, *More Pages from my Diary, 1908–1914* (1934).

J. M. Robertson (Asq. Lib., Wallsend, 1918), *Trade and Tariffs* (1908).

——, *Fiscal Policy after the War* (1916).

——, *Liberalism and Labour* (1921).

——, *The Meaning of Liberalism* (rev. ed., 1923).

J. M. Robertson, *Political Economy of Free Trade* (1928).

B. S. Rowntree, *Poverty: A Study in Town Life* (1901).

——, *Land and Labour* (1911).

——, *How the Labourer Lives* (1913).

——, *Industrial Unrest: A Way Out* (1922).

——, *Poverty and Progress: A Second Social Survey of York* (1951).

——, *Poverty and the Welfare State: A Third Social Survey of York* (1951).

*Sir Walter Runciman (L.G. Lib., Dewsbury, 1918; Edinburgh North, 1920; Berwick, 1922), *Liberalism as I See it* (1927).

Sir Herbert Samuel (Asq. Lib., Cleveland, 1918), *Liberalism: An Attempt to State the Principles and Proposals of Liberalism in England* (1902).

——, *Memoirs* (1945).

 Viscount Samuel: A Biography, by J. Bowle (1957).

C. P. Scott. *C. P. Scott of the Manchester Guardian*, by J. L. Hammond (1934).

 C. P. Scott's Political Diaries, ed. T. Wilson (1970).

*Sir Geoffrey Shakespeare (prefixless Lib., Wellingborough, 1922), *Let Candles Be Brought In* (1949).

*Sir John Simon (Asq. Lib., Walthamstow East, 1918; Spen Valley 1919 and 1922), *Three Speeches on the General Strike* (1926).

——, *Comments and Criticisms* (1930).

——, *Retrospect* (1952).

Harold Spender (prefixless Lib., Bath, 1922), *The Fire of Life: A Book of Memories* (n.d.).

J. A. Spender, *Life, Journalism, and Politics*, 2 vols (1927).

 J. A. Spender, by Wilson Harris (1946).

Harold Storey, *The Liberal Handbook* (1923).

T. C. Taylor, *Taylor of Batley*, by G. A. Greenwood (1957).

A. S. Swann (Asq. Lib., Maryhill, 1922), *The Letters of Annie S. Swann*, ed. M. R. Nicholl (1945).

*C. P. Trevelyan (Ind. Radical, Elland, 1918; Labour, Newcastle Central, 1922), *From Liberalism to Labour* (1921).

John Ward (L.G. Lib., Stoke, 1918 and 1922), *With the Diehards in Siberia* (1920).

*Josiah Wedgwood (Ind. Radical, then Labour, Newcastle-under-Lyme, 1918 and 1922), *The Economics of Inheritance* (1929).
  The Last of the Radicals, by C. V. Wedgwood (1955).
*E. Hilton Young (L.G. Lib., Norwich, 1918 and 1922), *The System of National Finance* (2nd ed., 1924).

2 BOOKS ON LIBERALISM AND THE LIBERAL PARTY

P. F. Clarke, *Lancashire and the New Liberalism* (1971).
R. Douglas, *A History of the Liberal Party, 1895–1970* (1971).
L. T. Hobhouse, *Liberalism,* reprint (1919).
J. A. Hobson, *The Crisis of Liberalism* (1909).
C. S. Jones, *The Call to Liberalism* (1921).
Land and Nation League, *Towns and the Land* (n.d.) [?1926].
Land Enquiry Committee, *The Land* (1913).
H. Langshaw, *Socialism and the Historic Function of Liberalism* (1925).
Liberal Industrial Inquiry, *Britain's Industrial Future* (1928).
Liberal Land Committee, *The Land and the Nation* (1935).
R. B. McCallum (ed.), *The Radical Alternative* (1962).
——, *The Liberal Party from Earl Grey to Asquith* (1963).
National Association of Merchants and Manufacturers to Resist State Interference with Trade, *Pamphlets, 1920–1922.*
Jorgen Rasmussen, *The Liberal Party: A Study in Retrenchment and Revival* (1965).
Sir Henry Slesser, *A History of the Liberal Party* (1944).
R. Smith, *A Liberal Window on the World* (n.d.) [?1946].
J. Vincent, *The Formation of the Liberal Party* (1966).
A. Watkins, *The Liberal Dilemma* (1966).
T. Wilson, *The Downfall of the Liberal Party* (1966).

VI Books on the Labour Party

1 BOOKS ON OR BY LABOUR SUPPORTERS ACTIVE IN 1918–22

C. G. Ammon (Camberwell North, 1918 and 1922), *Labour's Dynamic* (1923).
Norman Angell (Rushcliffe, 1922), *The Great Illusion* (1909 and 1933).

Norman Angell, *The Economic Functions of the League* (1920)
——, *The Great Illusion—Now* (1938).
——, *The Steep Places* (1947).
——, *After All* (1951).
C. R. Attlee (Limehouse, 1922), *The Social Worker* (1920).
——, and W. A. Robson, *The Town Councillor* (1925).
——, *The Labour Party in Perspective* (1937).
——, *As it Happened* (1954).
——, *A Prime Minister Remembers* (1961).
W. H. Ayles (Bristol North, 1922), *What a Socialist Town Council Would Be* (1923).
Alfred Barnes (East Ham South, 1922), *Cooperative Aims in Politics* (1925).
George Barnes (Coalition Labour, Gorbals, 1918), *From Workshop to War Cabinet* (1924).
A. Barton (Sheffield-Park, 1918), *A World History for the Workers* (1922).
Margaret Bondfield (Northampton, 1920 and 1922), *A Life's Work* (n.d.) [?1949].
    Margaret Bondfield, by M. A. Hamilton (1924).
H. N. Brailsford (Montrose District, 1918), *The War of Steel and Gold* (1915).
——, *A League of Nations* (2nd ed., New York, 1917).
——, *Nailed to the Counter* (1923).
——, *Socialism for Today* (1925).
——, *Property or Peace?* (1934).
A. Fenner Brockway (Lancaster, 1922), *The Devil's Business.* Suppressed in 1914, reissued in 1926.
——, *Lloyd George and the Traffic in Honours* (1922).
——, *The Bloody Traffic* (1933).
——, *Death Pays a Dividend* (1944).
——, *Inside the Left* (1942).
——, *Outside the Right* (1963).
George Burgess (Maidstone, 1918), *Every Man's Wages* (1922).
C. R. Buxton (Accrington, 1918 and 1922), *Electioneering up to Date* (1906).
——, *The Secret Agreements* (1918).
——, *The World after the War* (1920).
——, *In a Russian Village* (1922).
——, *What is Socialism?* (n.d.) [?1925].

Noel E. Buxton (Asq. Lib., then Labour, Norfolk North, 1918 and 1922), *Balkan Problems and European Peace* (1918)

——, and T. P. Conwell-Evans, *Oppressed Peoples and the League of Nations* (1922).

J. R. Clynes (Platting, 1918 and 1922), *Memoirs*, 2 vols (1937).

G. D. H. Cole, *British Trade and Industry* (1932).

——, *A History of Socialist Thought*, 7 vols (1953–60).

——, *A History of the Labour Party Since 1914* (1948).

——, and E. Burns, *The Workers' Register of Labour and Capital* (1923).

——, and R. Postgate, *The Common People, 1716–1938* (1938).

W. Crooks (Woolwich East, 1918), *From Workhouse to Westminster: The Life Story of Will Crooks*, by G. Haw (1909).

E. Hugh J. N. Dalton (Cambridge 1922 by-election; Maidstone, 1922), *The Capital Levy Explained* (1922).

——, *Principles of Public Finance* (1923).

——, *Practical Socialism for Britain* (1935).

——, *Call Back Yesterday* (1953).

——, *The Fateful Years* (1957).

——, *High Tide and After* (1962).

G. L. Dickinson, *The European Anarchy* (1916).

——, *The Future of the Covenant* (1920).

    Goldsworthy Lowes Dickinson, by E. M. Forster (1934).

J. J. Dodd (prospective candidate, Hereford, 1922, but withdrew), *If Labour Wins* (1922).

Lord Elton, *Among Others* (n.d.).

J. Bruce Glasier, *The Meaning of Socialism. Manchester* (n.d.) [?1920].

M. A. Hamilton, *Uphill all the Way* (1953).

P. Hastings (Wallsend, 1922), *The Autobiography of Sir Patrick Hastings* (1948).

    Sir Patrick Hastings, by H. M. Hyde (1960).

Stephen Hobhouse, *Forty Years and an Epilogue* (1951).

J. A. Hobson (Combined English Universities, 1918), *Imperialism: A Study* (1902).

——, *Gold Prices and Wages* (1913).

J. Hodge (Gorton, 1918 and 1922), *Workman's Cottage to Windsor Castle* (n.d.).

Frank Hodges, *My Adventures as a Labour Leader* (n.d.) [?1924].

G. Isaacs (Southwark North, 1918; Gravesend, 1922), *George Isaacs: Printer, Trade Union Leader, Cabinet Minister*, by G. Eastwood (1952).

Thomas Johnston (West Stirling, 1918 and 1922), *Memories* (1952).

F. W. Jowett (Bradford East, 1918 and 1922), *Socialism over Sixty Years: The Life of Jowett of Bradford*, by A. F. Brockway (1946).

David Kirkwood (Dumbarton District, 1918 and 1922), *My Life of Revolt* (1935).

George Lansbury (Bow and Bromley, 1918 and 1922), *Your Part in Poverty* (1917).

——, *My Life* (1928).

——, *My England* (n.d.) [?1934].

——, *Looking Forwards—and Backwards* (1935).

——, *This Way to Peace* (1939).

My Father, by E. Lansbury (n.d.).

George Lansbury, by R. Postgate (New York, 1951).

Jack Lawson (Seaham, 1918; Chester-le-street, 1922), *A Man's Life* (1932).

J. Ramsay MacDonald (Leicester East, 1918; Woolwich East, 1921; Aberavon, 1922), *Socialism and Society* (1905).

——, *Socialism after the War* (Manchester, n.d.) [?1918].

——, *Parliament and Revolution* (Manchester, 1919).

——, *Socialism, Critical and Constructive* (1921).

——, *Wanderings and Excursions* (1925).

——, *The Socialist Movement* (n.d.).

The Life of James Ramsay MacDonald, by Lord Elton (1939).

MacDonald as Diplomatist, by G. Glasgow (1924).

James Ramsay MacDonald, by M. A. Hamilton (1929).

James Ramsay MacDonald, by H. Tiltman (1929).

From Doughty Street to Downing Street: The Rt Hon. J. Ramsay MacDonald, M.P., by H. Tracey (n.d.) [?1924].

The Tragedy of Ramsay MacDonald, by L. Weir (n.d.).

J. McGovern, *Neither Fear nor Favour* (1960).

Kingsley Martin, *Father Figures* (1966).

C. R. Morden (Hammersmith North, 1918; Finsbury, 1922, as independent), *League of Nations* (1921).

E. D. Morel (Dundee, 1922), *Red Rubber* (3rd ed., 1907).

——, *The Outbreak of the War: Being a Letter to the Executive of the Birkenhead Liberal Association* (Letchworth, n.d.) [?1914].

——, *Truth and the War* (1916).

——, *The Black Man's Burden* (1920).

——, *The Horror on the Rhine* (1921).

——, *The Poison that Destroys* (1922).

    E. D. Morel, by F. S. Cocks (1920).

Lord Parmoor, *Retrospect* (1936).

F. W. Pethick-Lawrence (Islington South, 1922), *The Capital Levy, or, how Labour would settle the War Debt* (1920).

——, *Fate has been Kind* (1943).

    Pethick-Lawrence, by V. Brittain (1963).

Dr Marion Phillips, *Women's Work in the Labour Party* (1923).

A. A. W. H. Ponsonby (Ind. Radical, Dunfermline District, 1918; Labour, Brightside, 1922), *Wars and Treaties, 1815–1914* (1918).

——, *The Camel and the Needle's Eye* (n.d.).

H. Roberts, *England: A National Policy for Labour* (1923).

F. H. Rose (Aberdeen North, 1918 and 1922), *Our Industrial Jungle* (1926).

Alfred Salter (Bermondsey West, 1918 and 1922). *Bermondsey Story*, by A. F. Brockway (1949).

J. Sexton (St Helen's, 1918 and 1922), *Sir James Sexton, Agitator* (1936).

Emmanuel Shinwell (Linlithgow, 1918 and 1922), *The Britain I Want* (1943).

——, *Conflict without Malice* (1955).

Sir Henry Slesser (Leeds Central, 1922), *Judgment Reserved* (n.d.).

Robert Smillie (Morpeth, 1918), *My Life for Labour* (1924).

H. Snell (Huddersfield, 1918; Woolwich East, 1922), *Men, Movements, and Myself* (1938).

Philip Snowden (Blackburn 1918; Colne Valley, 1922), *Socialism and the Drink Question* (1908).

Philip Snowden, *Socialism and Syndicalism* (n.d.).

——, *The Living Wage* (n.d.).

——, *Labour and National Finance* (1920).

——, *If Labour Rules* (1923).

——, *An Autobiography*, 2 vols (1934).

——, *Mr. Lloyd George's New Deal* (1935).

    Philip Snowden, by C. Cross (1966).

Mrs Philip Snowden, *Through Bolshevik Russia* (1920).

——, *A Political Pilgrimage in Europe* (1921).

Stephen Spender, *Forward from Liberalism* (1937).

——, *World within World* (1951).

J. H. Thomas (Derby, 1918 and 1922), *When Labour Rules* (1920).

    J. H. Thomas, by G. Blaxland (1964).

    The Life Story of the Rt Hon. J. H. Thomas, A Statesman of the People, by S. Paul (n.d.).

Will Thorne (Plaistow, 1918 and 1922), *My Life's Battles* (1924).

Ben Tillett (Salford North, 1918 and 1922), *Memories and Reflections* (1931).

Joe Toole (Everton, 1922), *Fighting through Life* (1935).

H. Tracey et al., *The Book of the Labour Party: Its History, Growth, Policy and Leaders*, 3 vols (1925).

L. Urquhart, *Labour's Russian Policy* (1922).

Beatrice Webb, *My Apprenticeship* (n.d.).

——, *Our Partnership* (1948).

——, *Diaries, 1912–1924*, ed. M. Cole (1952).

——, *Diaries, 1924–1932*, ed. M. Cole (1956).

Sidney Webb (London University, 1918; Seaham, 1922), *How to Pay for the War* (1916).

——, and B. Webb, *A Constitution for the Socialist Commonwealth of Great Britain* (1920).

——, and B. Webb, *A History of Trade Unionism, Extended to 1920* (New York, 1920).

H. G. Wells (London University, 1922), *The New Machiavelli* (1913).

——, *Experiment in Autobiography*, 2 vols (1934).

T. Williams (Don Valley, 1922), *Digging For Britain* (1965).

2 BOOKS ON THE LABOUR PARTY

R. Page Arnot, *The Scottish Miners* (1955).

——, *South Wales Miners, 1898–1914* (1967).

P. Bagwell, *The Railwaymen* (1963).

E. Barry, *Nationalisation and British Politics* (1965).

R. Bassett, *1931: Political Crisis* (1958).

F. Bealey and H. Pelling, *Labour and Politics, 1900–6:A History of the Labour Representation Committee* (1958).

M. Beer, *A History of British Socialism*, 2 vols (1921).

Emil Burns, *The General Strike, May 1926: Trades Councils in Action* (1926).

——, *Right Wing Labour: Its Theory and Practice* (1961).

L. Chester, S. Fay and H. Young, *The Zinoviev Letter* (1967).

H. Clegg, *General Union: The National Union of General and Municipal Workers* (Oxford, 1957).

——, A. Fox and A. F. Thompson, *A History of British Trade Unions Since 1889* (Oxford, 1964).

C. A. Cline, *Recruits to Labour: The British Labour Party, 1914–1931* (Syracuse, New York, 1963).

M. Cole, *Story of Fabian Socialism* (1961).

E. Davies, *The Case for Railway Nationalisation* (n.d.).

S. Desmond, *Labour: The Giant with Feet of Clay* (1921).

R. Fox, *The Class Struggle in Britain, 1912–1923* (1933).

M. A. Fitzsimons, *The Foreign Policy of the Labour Government, 1945–1951* (Notre Dame Ind., 1952).

S. Graubard, *British Labour and the Russian Revolution, 1917–1924* (1956).

M. A. Hamilton, *The Labour Party Today* (n.d.).

M. Harrison, *Trade Unions and the Labour Party Since 1945* (1960).

Q. Hogg, *The Left Was Never Right* (1945).

R. Hunter, *Violence and the Labour Movement* (n.d.).

E. Hyams, *The New Statesman* (1963).

E. Janosik, *Constituency Labour Parties in Britain* (1968).

R. W. Lyman, *The First Labour Government, 1924* (n.d.) [?1957].

Mrs Le Mesurier, *The Socialist Woman's Guide to Intelligence* (1929).

A. M. McBriar, *Fabian Socialism and English Politics, 1884–1918* (1966).

Sir Charles Macara, *Bolshevism: Conscription of Wealth* (Manchester, 1922).

Sir Lynden Macassey, *Labour Policy: False and True* (1922).

S. Maccoby, *English Radicalism*, 6 vols (1955 et seq.).

K. Middlemas, *The Clydesiders* (1965).

R. Miliband, *Parliamentary Socialism: A Study in the Politics of Labour* (1964).

F. Millar (ed.), *Socialism: Its Fallacies and Dangers* (5th ed., 1923).

P. P. Poirier, *The Advent of the Labour Party* (1958).

S. Pollard, *A History of Labour in Sheffield* (1962).

E. A. Pratt, *The Case against Railway Nationalisation* (n.d.).

D. N. Pritt, *The Labour Government, 1945–1951* (1963).

G. Radford, *Labour and the Moneyed Man* (n.d.).

J. Scanlon, *Cast off all Fooling* (n.d.).

A. Shadwell, *The Socialist Movement, 1824–1924* (1925).

——, *The Breakdown of Socialism* (1926).

——, *The Future of Socialism* (1929).

Sheffield Trades and Labour Council, *1858–1958* (Sheffield, 1958).

J. Symons, *The General Strike* (1959).

P. Thompson, *Socialists, Liberals, and Labour* (1967).

J. E. Williams, *The Derbyshire Miners* (1962).

E. Windrich, *British Labour's Foreign Policy* (Stanford, California, 1952).

VII Books on the Communist Party

T. Bell, *John Maclean: A Fighter for Freedom* (Glasgow, 1944).

Communist Party, *The Reds and the Labour Party* (1926 ed.).

F. Copeman, *Reason in Revolt* (1948).

William Gallacher (Dundee, 1922), *The Rolling of the Thunder* (1947).

——, *The Case for Communism* (1949).

——, *Revolt on the Clyde* (1949).

——, *Rise Like Lions* (1951).

——, *The Tyrant's Might is Passing* (1954).

Essays in honour of William Gallacher, ed. P. Kemp-Aschraf and J. Mitchell (East Berlin, 1966).

W. Hannington, *Behind Prison Bars* (1926).
——, *Industrial History in Wartime* (1940).
A. Horner, *Incorrigible Rebel* (1960).
J. T. W. Newbold (Motherwell, I.L.P. 1918, Communist 1922), *The Politics of Capitalism* (1918).
E. and C. Paul, *Creative Revolution: A Study in Communist Ergatocracy* (1920).
H. Pelling, *The British Communist Party* (1958).
Harry Pollitt, *Serving My Time* (1941).
——, *Looking Ahead* (1947).
D. N. Pritt, *Autobiography*, 3 vols (1965–6).

VIII Other works used in preparing this book

1 ON AND BY DIPLOMATS AND CIVIL SERVANTS

D. Crow, *A Man of Push and Go* [G. Booth] (1965).
Viscount d'Abernon, *An Ambassador of Peace* (3 vols (1939).
——, *Portraits and Appreciations* (n.d.) [?1931].
Sir Almeric Fitzroy, *Memories*, 2 vols (n.d.) [?1923].
Lord Hankey, *Government Control in War* (Cambridge, 1945).
——, *The Supreme Command, 1914–1918*, 2 vols (1961).
——, *The Supreme Control at the Paris Peace Conference* (1963).
Lord Hardinge, *Old Diplomacy* (1943).
Lord Howard, *Theatre of Life*, 2 vols (1935).
Lord Newton, *Retrospection* (1941).
Viscount Sandhurst, *From Day to Day*, 2 vols (1935).

2 ON AND BY MILITARY FIGURES

I. Colvin, *The Life of General Dyer* (1929).
Lord Fisher, *Memories* (1919).
Lord French, *1914* (New York and Boston, 1919).
Lord Haig, *The Private Papers of Douglas Haig*, ed. R. Blake (1952).
Sir Charles Harington, *Tim Harington Looks Back* (1940).
Sir Basil Liddell Hart, *The Real War* (1930).
——, *Memoirs*, 2 vols (1965).
——, *Strategy: The Indirect Approach* (rev. ed., New York, 1967).

Sir N. Macready, *Annals of an Active Life*, 2 vols (New York, 1925).
Sir Frederick Maurice, *The Last Four Months* (1919).
——, *British Strategy* (1929).
C. à C. Repington, *Vestigia* (1919).
——, *The First World War, 1914–1918* (1920).
——, *After the War: A Diary* (1922).
——, *Policy and Arms* (1924).
Sir William Robertson, *From Private to Field-Marshal* (1921).
——, *Soldiers and Statesmen, 1914–1918*, 2 vols (1926).

3   ON AND BY OTHER PERSONS

T. Clarke, *My Northcliffe Diary* (1931).
A. Edwards [Archbishop of Wales], *Memories* (1927).
G. Harmsworth and R. Pound, *Northcliffe* (1959).
Sir A. Mackintosh, *Echoes of Big Ben* (n.d.).
Sir Compton Mackenzie, *My Life and Times, 1915–1923* (1966).
Sir Harold Nicolson, *King George V: His Life and Times* (1952).
T. P. O'Connor, *Memoirs of an old Parliamentarian*, 2 vols (1929).
Lord Rothermere, *Solvency or Downfall: Squandermania and its Story* (1921).
J. W. R. Scott, *'WE' and Me* (1956).
N. Tiptaft (Independent candidate, Handsworth, 1918 and 1922), *The Individualist* (1954).
J. E. Wrench, *Geoffrey Dawson and our Times* (1955).

4   BOOKS ON ELECTIONS

An annotated bibliography of books, articles and theses on British elections since 1885 may be found in M. Kinnear, *The British Voter: An Atlas and Survey Since 1885* (1968).

5   BOOKS ON POLITICAL ORGANISATION AND REGIONAL STUDIES

F. Bealey, J. Blondel and W. McCann, *Constituency Politics: A Study of Newcastle-under-Lyme* (1965).
S. Beer, *Modern British Politics* (1965).
M. Benney, A. P. Gray and W. H. Pear, *How People Vote* (1956).

A. H. Birch, *Small Town Politics* (1959).

J. P. F. Blondel, *Voters, Parties, and Leaders* (1963).

I. Budge and D. W. Urwin, *Scottish Political Behaviour* (1966).

M. Duverger, *Political Parties: Their Organisation and Activity in the Modern State* (1954).

S. E. Finer, *Anonymous Empire* (1958).

H. F. Gosnell, *Why Europe Votes* (Chicago, Illinois, 1930).

G. W. Jones, *Borough Politics* (1969).

R. T. Mackenzie, *British Political Parties* (2nd ed., 1963).

H. S. Milne and H. C. Mackenzie, *Straight Fight* (1954).

K. O. Morgan, *Wales in British Politics, 1868–1922* (Cardiff, 1963).

M. Ostrogorski, *Democracy and the Organisation of Political Parties* (New York, 1970).

P. Paterson, *The Selectorate* (1967).

A. Ranney, *Pathways to Parliament* (1965).

R. Rose, *Politics in England* (1963).

J. F. S. Ross, *Parliamentary Representation* (2nd ed., 1948).

——, *Elections and Electors* (1955).

6   BOOKS ON ECONOMICS AND SOCIAL HISTORY

Lord Askwith, *Industrial Problems and Disputes* (1920).

J. J. Astor et al., *The Third Winter of Unemployment* (1922).

——, *Is Unemployment Inevitable?* (1924).

S. H. Beaver and L. D. Stamp, *The British Isles: A Geographic and Economic Survey* (1954).

A. M. Carr-Saunders and C. Jones, *A Survey of the Social Structure of England and Wales* (2nd ed., Oxford, 1937).

Sir John Clapham, *An Economic History of Modern Britain*, III (reprint 1963).

W. H. Dawson, *Afterwar Problems* (1918).

E. Dewsnap, *The Housing Problem in England* (Manchester, 1907).

J. R. Hicks, U. K. Hicks and L. Postan, *The Taxation of War Wealth* (1941, reprint 1942).

E. Howarth and M. Wilson, *West Ham: A Study in Social and Industrial Problems* (1907).

K. E. Hunt, *Changes in British Agriculture* (Oxford, 1952).

J. A. Jackson, *The Irish in Britain* (1963).

A. Kirkcaldy, *British Finance, 1914–1921* (1921).

R. Lawton and C. M. Cunningham, *Merseyside* (1970).

W. G. Lyddon, *British War Missions to the U.S.A., 1914–1918* (1938).

A. G. Marshal, *Anglo-Russian Trade and its Possibilities* (1923).

B. Mitchell and P. Deane, *Abstract of British Historical Statistics* (Cambridge, 1962).

F. Reiss, *Unemployment Relief in Great Britain* (1924).

R. Reiss, *The New Housing Handbook* (1924).

Sir H. Ll. Smith, *The New Survey of London Life and Labour* (1932).

A. Williams, *Copartnership and Profitsharing* (n.d.).

7   OTHER BOOKS

'Cato' [Michael Foot, Frank Owen and Peter Howard], *Guilty Men* (1940).

M. Cowling, *The Impact of Labour, 1920–24* (1971).

C. Cross, *The Fascists in Britain* (1961).

R. C. K. Ensor, *England, 1870–1914* (1938).

Sir James Fergusson, *The Curragh Incident* (1964).

J. A. L. Fraser, *India under Curzon and After* (1912).

R. Furneaux, *Massacre at Amritsar* (1963).

'Gracchus', *Your MP* (1944).

C. Hazlehurst, *Politicians at War* (1971).

J. Johnston, *A Hundred Commoners* (1931).

R. B. McCallum, *Public Opinion and the Last Peace* (1944).

D. McCarthy, *Portraits* (1931).

J. S. Mills, *The Genoa Conference* (1922).

C. L. Mowat, *Britain between the Wars* (1955).

A. P. Nicholson, *The Real Men in Public Life* (1928).

A. P. Ryan, *Mutiny at the Curragh* (1956).

A. J. P. Taylor, *English History, 1914–1945* (1965).

D. Walder, *The Chanak Affair* (1969).

T. W. Walding, *Who's Who in the New Parliament, 1922* (1922).

Index

parison with Joseph Chamberlain in Birmingham, 88, 175, 184; out of contact with southern Wales, 182; no Welsh lieutenant, 182; relations with Welsh Asquithians, 183, 190, 194

Relations with cabinet colleagues: elevates role of Prime Minister, 7; absences from House of Commons, 8, 22, 103; dismissals of Hayes Fisher, 9, Henderson, 9, Addison, 11, Montague, 109; quarrels with Churchill, 10, 17, 96

Relations with Conservatives: relies on associates to watch Conservative M.P.s, 8; on future of Conservative Party (1921), 95; speaks to Kent Conservatives (1921), 95; fails to punish Younger, 105; denies favouring an early election (1922), 105; Diehards oppose, 106; describes Younger as second-rate brewer, 107

Relations with Liberals: and J. M. Hogge, 8; actions of in 1918 election, 40–3; attitude to reunion in 1919, 43, 45; in 1920–2, 49; in 1923, 212

Foreign and Irish policy: changes in, 6, 14, 16, 17, 19; basic stability of, 16; Irish policy, 13–15; Russia, 17–18; Turkey, 19, 114, 121; Cannes and Genoa conferences, 20, 103, 111

Other references: relations with the press, 22–5; indispensability of after 1918, 75, 182; 'shaking hands with murderers', 80–1, 113; in 1922 election, 155–6.

Local party organisations: Liberal, 46–7, 189; Lloyd George Liberal, 48, 72, 85, 92, 95, 145, 184, 194; Conservative, 62; finances of, 65; powers of, 64–8

Local elections, Nov 1922, 159–61

Locker-Lampson, Oliver (C M.P., Huntingdonshire, then Hands-

worth; Austen Chamberlain's Parliamentary Private Secretary), 27, 125

London, 71, 85, 198

Lonsdale, 35n.

Lords Reform: Diehards on, 82; Younger on (Jan 1921), 95, (Jan 1922), 103; Lloyd George on (Nov 1921), 98; not an issue in 1922 election, 139

Lough, Thomas (AsqL cand, Islington W.), 42

Lowther, Col Claude (C M.P., Lonsdale), 94

Loyd, A. T. (C M.P., Abingdon), 149

McCurdy, Charles A. (LGL M.P., Northampton; LG's Chief Whip, 1921–3): on Lloyd George's options in early 1922, 48; favours early election in 1922, 101, 102, 105, 121; misunderstands Austen Chamberlain, 104; on Conservative M.P.s, 110; favours Liberal reunion (1923), 211

MacDonald, J. Ramsay (Lab cand, Leicester E. and Woolwich E.; M.P., Aberavon; leader of Labour Party), 137, 176; 'boneless wonder', 199; on Liberal-Labour relations, 200

McKenna, Reginald (AsqL cand, Pontypool), 44, 208

Mackenzie, R. T., 56, 70

Maclean, Sir Donald (AsqL, Peebles and S. Midlothian; AsqL House leader), 114

Macmillan, Harold (C M.P., Bromley, Prime Minister), 217

Macnamara, T. J. (LGL M.P., Camberwell N.W.; LG's Minister of Labour), 101, 104

McNeill, Ronald (Diehard M.P., Canterbury, later peer), 112

Majorities, small, table of (1918–70), 152

Manchester Guardian, 99, 103, 135, 166

Manchester Liberal Federation, 200

Manville, Edward (C M.P., Coventry), 131